1595
073

TOU(

MW00769234

TOUCHING LIBERTY

ABOLITION, FEMINISM, AND
THE POLITICS OF THE BODY

KAREN SÁNCHEZ-EPPLER

University of California Press
Berkeley · Los Angeles · London

University of California Press
Berkeley and Los Angeles, California

University of California Press, Ltd.
London, England

First paperback printing 1997

© 1993 by Karen Sánchez-Eppler

Library of Congress Cataloging-in-Publication Data

Sánchez-Eppler, Karen.
    Touching liberty : abolition, feminism, and the politics of the body /
Karen Sánchez-Eppler.
        p. cm.
    Includes bibliographical references and index.
    ISBN 0-520-21234-7 (pbk. : alk. paper)
    1. American literature—19th century—History and criticism. 2. Slav-
ery—United States—Anti-slavery movements—History—19th century.
3. Feminism and literature—United States—History—19th century 4. Politics and literature—United States—History—19th century. 5. Women and
literature—United States—History—19th century. 6. Jacobs, Harriet A.
(Harriet Ann), 1813–1897—Political and social views. 7. Dickinson, Emily,
1830–1886—Political and social views. 8. Whitman, Walt, 1819–1892—Political and social views. 9. Slavery and slaves in literature. 10. Body, Human,
in literature.
    I. Title.
PS217.S55S26 1993
810.9'003—dc20   92-20377
                                                                        CIP

Printed in the United States of America

9   8   7   6   5   4   3   2   1

The paper used in this publication meets the minimum requirements of
American National Standard for Information Sciences—Permanence of
Paper for Printed Library Materials, ANSI Z39.48-1984. ⊚

The author gratefully acknowledges permission to reprint two chapters of
this book that were previously published elsewhere. Chapter 1 appeared under its own title in *Representations* 24 (copyright 1988 by the Regents of the
University of California) and has been reprinted in *The New American Studies*,
edited by Philip Fisher (Berkeley: University of California Press, 1991), in *The
Culture of Sentiment: Race, Gender, and Sentimentality in Nineteenth-Century
America*, edited by Shirley Samuels (New York: Oxford University Press,
1992), and as "Vincoli corporei: le intersezioni retoriche di femminismo e
abolizionismo" in *Communità: revista di informazione culturale* 193/194 (March
1992). Chapter 2 appeared as " 'To Stand Between': A Political Perspective
on Whitman's Poetics of Merger and Embodiment" in *ELH* 56 (copyright
1989 by Johns Hopkins University Press).
    Emily Dickinson's poetry is reprinted by permission of the publishers
and Trustees of Amherst College from *The Poems of Emily Dickinson*, ed.
Thomas H. Johnston (Cambridge, Mass: The Belknap Press of Harvard University), copyright © 1951, 1955, 1979, 1983 by the President and Fellows of
Harvard College. Poetry copyright © 1929, 1935 by Martha Dickinson Bianchi; copyright © renewed 1957, 1963 by Mary L. Hampson is reprinted by
permission of Little, Brown and Company.

To Benigno

Contents

Acknowledgments   ix

Introduction: Representing the
Body Politic   1

1. Bodily Bonds: The Intersecting Rhetorics of
Feminism and Abolition   14

2. To Stand Between: Walt Whitman's Poetics of
Merger and Embodiment   50

3. Righting Slavery and Writing Sex:
The Erotics of Narration in
Harriet Jacobs's *Incidents*   83

4. At Home in the Body: The Internal Politics of
Emily Dickinson's Poetry   105

Coda: Topsy-Turvy   133

Notes   143

Select Bibliography   175

Index   189

Acknowledgments

The writing of this book has been buoyed and companioned by many people.

Marcie Frank, Alexandra Halasz, Elizabeth Hanson, and Joseph Harrison have read and argued with me since the earliest stages of this project. They have done more to shape the ways I think and write than I can ever thank them for.

In their own different ways Michèle Barale, Brenda Bright, Rhonda Cobham-Sanders, Francis Couvares, Thomas Dumm, P. Gabrielle Foreman, Judith Frank, Allen Guttmann, Carolyn Karcher, Barry O'Connell, Andrew Parker, Shirley Samuels, Martha Sandweiss, Valerie Smith, and Sasha Torres have clarified my thinking and enlivened these pages. Their friendship and their companionship in teaching and writing have given me courage and great pleasure.

This book grew out of my doctoral dissertation, and I am grateful to my advisors. Sharon Cameron's luminous insights and demands for precision have made my arguments far stronger than they would have been without her. I owe her thanks for not indulging my frequent wish that this be good enough, and for the faith in and commitment to my work that helped make it better. Larzer Ziff's unfailing good humor, intellectual generosity, and lucid prose have been a source of inspiration and support. The patience and skill of Doris Kretschmer and Erika Büky of the University of California Press have made the final transformations easy.

My parents, Klaus and Joyce Eppler, have nurtured me toward this project in all manner of ways. Their confidence and commitment make even the hardest things seem possible. My sister, Amy Eppler-Epstein, has shaped and shared my

x

vision of the world; my writing finds its ground in her work for social justice and social change.

Finally my thanks to Alma and Elias Sánchez-Eppler, whose births and growing have done much to slow this process, and more to make it happy. And to Benigno Sánchez-Eppler whose presence, intellectually and emotionally, suffuses this writing and my life.

Introduction
Representing the Body Politic

In antebellum America, as in all states and all times, the "body politic" was inhabited by an immense variety of distinct bodies, well-fed or hungry, smooth-skinned or callused, strong or exhausted, old, young, or middle-aged, male or female, dark-skinned or light or somewhere between. The relation of the social and political structures of the "body politic" to the fleshy specificity of embodied identities has generally been masked behind the constitutional language of abstracted and implicitly bodiless "persons," so that, for example, it did not seem absurd for the founding fathers to reckon slaves as "three-fifths of a person." To fraction an abstract "person" does not require amputations. Such abstractions have not, however, gone uncontested. This book investigates a crack in the hegemonic rhetoric of political disembodiment. I argue that from the early 1830s through the Civil War, these assumptions of a metaphorical and fleshless political identity were disrupted and unmasked through the convergence of two rhetorics of social protest: the abolitionist concern with claiming personhood for the racially distinct and physically owned slave body, and the feminist concern with claiming personhood for the sexually distinct and domestically circumscribed female body. Moreover, just as the notion of the universal, and so incorporeal, "person" has had cultural ramifications that far exceed its appearance in constitutional rhetoric, the development of a political discourse and a concept of personhood that attests to the centrality of the body erupts throughout antebellum culture. The extent to which the condition of the human body designates

identity is a question of American culture and consciousness
as well as politics, and so it is a question whose answers can
be sought not only in political speeches but also in a variety
of more ostensibly aesthetic forms, from sentimental fiction
and personal narratives to those conventionally most ahistorical of texts, lyric poems. In the chapters that follow I trace
the implications of a bodily definition of identity through the
polemical fictions of feminist-abolitionists, Harriet Jacobs's
slave narrative, and the poetry of Walt Whitman and Emily
Dickinson. The apparent heterogeneity of this cultural do-
main foregrounds the issues of difference—generic, social,
bodily—at stake in my study.

In an effort to justify political activism to "the Christian
Women of the South," Angelina Grimké resorts to a conventionally religious and yet shockingly lurid metaphor. She
compares the scandalously public work of antislavery women
to the pious and familial act of Martha pushing the stone
from her brother Lazarus's closed grave:

> *Our business* is to take away the stone which has covered up
> the dead body of our brother, to expose the putrid carcass, to
> show *how* that body has been bound with the grave-clothes of
> heathen ignorance, and his face with the napkin of prejudice,
> and having done all it was our duty to do, to stand by the ne-
> gro's grave in humble faith and holy hope, waiting to hear the
> life giving command of "Lazarus, come forth." This is just
> what Anti-Slavery Societies are doing; they are taking away
> the stone from the mouth of the tomb of slavery, where lies the
> putrid carcass of our brother.

Her insistence on "uncovering the loathsome body to popular sight" seems an excessive, necroscopic metaphor for abolitionist concern.[1] To describe the slave as a putrid carcass
evinces the very recoil of racial prejudice against which
Grimké writes. It registers, as well, a horror of embodiment,
since Grimké epitomizes the body in the loathsome fact of its
decay. By exemplifying the body in this way Grimké raises
the stakes of her rhetoric, but—testifying to her ambivalence—she also decomposes the body she claims to reveal. In
the pages that follow I explore the causes and ramifications of

this ambivalence. For now, I want to suggest that the hyperbolic insistence on embodiment in Grimké's rhetoric is not only essential for both abolitionist and feminist discourses but indeed functions more generally to reconfigure cultural conceptions of the corporeality of identity. By equating slavery with the lump of flesh and liberty with the act of animating that flesh, Grimké calls the lie on the incorporeal national ideal of a free and equal American citizenry. As she writes, the putrid corpse, the abused black body of the slave, and the abstract "body" of the state constantly replace each other until it becomes impossible to keep them apart. Forcing attention not on some vague conception of freedom but on the details of bodily corruption, the political point of this passage lies precisely in the demand that so excessive a metaphor be understood as literal.

The human body has always served as an emblem for conceptions of the body politic.[2] The bodily biases of the state are evident in the white male privilege that has pertained within American society. Feminist political theorists are reappraising the constitutional rhetoric of disembodied, naturally equal and interchangeable "persons" to reveal its complicity in maintaining just such privilege. Their arguments suggest not only that this juridical "person" has always implicitly occupied a white male body, but, more important, that success in masking this fact has secured and legitimized the power that accrues to that body.[3] Authority derives from simulating the impossible position of the universal and hence bodiless subject. All the "men" who, Thomas Jefferson declared, "are created equal" shed their gender and their race; in obtaining the right to freedom and equality they discard bodily specificity. The problem, as feminists and abolitionists surely suspected, was that women and blacks could never shed their bodies to become incorporeal "men".[4] The feminist and abolitionist interest in presenting "the loathsome body to public sight" thus engages a double agenda: it reveals the bodily basis of women's and blacks' exclusion from political power and uncovers the physical attributes of whiteness and maleness implicit in such power.

Although in terms of national history feminism and abolition may have served to unmask traditional abstract definitions of political identity, the organizational unity of the American Anti-Slavery Society was itself among the victims of this definitional flux. The society's 1833 charter, or "Declaration of Sentiments," followed constitutional norms in opening its membership to "persons." Because no women signed the charter, though a number were present and some even spoke at these founding meetings, it seems fair to assume that in 1833 the society understood "persons" to connote "men." By 1840, however, Abby Kelley was prepared to insist that the charter's reference to "persons" included female persons like herself and therefore sanctioned her election to the governing business committee. Kelley's election precipitated the fracturing of the American Anti-Slavery Society, although historians disagree on the ideological importance of feminism in this division. I am less concerned here with the causes and ramifications of this schism than with what it illustrates about the instability of political identity in this period, even among the ranks of the radical left.[5] The debates over Kelley's election reveal how volatile the concept of the juridical "person" had become in antebellum America, for the story of this election is in part the story of the contentious development of a newly physical understanding of political identity and so of a new sense of what different bodies such "persons" might have.

The eventual success of feminist-abolitionist rhetoric in redefining political identity to acknowledge bodily specificity is apparent in the language of the Fourteenth and Fifteenth Amendments to the United States Constitution. The Fourteenth Amendment protects the franchise of the nation's "male inhabitants." Because it was unclear that such language would necessarily include black men, the Fifteenth Amendment supplemented this rhetoric of sexual specificity with additional bodily criteria: "the right . . . to vote shall not be denied or abridged . . . on account of race, color, or previous condition of servitude." These amendments introduce the notion of a corporeal political identity and a racially and sexually distinct citizenry into constitutional language. The Constitution had previously contained no mention of race or sex and had not specifically barred black or female suffrage.[6]

This "success" contains multiple ironies. In acknowledging that political identity cannot be distinguished from an embodied identity, the amendments simultaneously include and ignore or exclude different bodies, so that in practice the constitutional turn to a terminology of embodied citizenry actually provides a defense against feminist incursions. The problems raised by the Fourteenth Amendment accentuated the split between feminist and abolitionist concerns, exacerbating divisions and asymmetries that had been inherent in the movements all along. The greater irony, however, lies in the way that this shift in constitutional rhetoric was matched by a shift in political demands. With the end of the Civil War, the campaigns for the rights of women and blacks turned from the question and symbol of the body to address not their corporeal oppression but their juridical exclusion. For postwar feminists and freemen the right to vote replaced the status of the human body as a sign of membership in the body politic. Thus this political and cultural concern with the corporeality of identity effectively increased the centrality of the demand for suffrage. The irony is that in focusing on suffrage, these movements of social protest came to reiterate the rhetoric of abstract personhood that had traditionally erased and silenced their distinct flesh.

This shift from embodiment to suffrage delimits my project. Though rhetorical and ideological trends can rarely be contained between precise dates, I locate this siege on the political abstraction of personhood between the rise of abolitionist politics in the early 1830s and the passage of the Fifteenth Amendment in 1870, and I confine my investigation to that period.[7] More significant, this shift serves to demarcate the theoretical impetus of my project, since the historical relation between embodiment and suffrage exemplifies what may be at stake in representation as both a political and a semiotic or literary system.[8] An elected representative government presumes that one's ideas, thoughts, needs, and desires can be adequately embodied by someone else. The representative's job is to mark the constituents' presence at the scene of power, negotiation, and debate. Political representation enacts the fiction of a bodiless body politic. Literary representation depends, of course, on a similar though not identical system of proxies: words stand in for an absent physical world.

An account focused on the representation of a corporeally based identity in nineteenth-century American writings inadequately describes the experiences of any actual bodies. My cover photograph, for example, records the structures of dominance that adhere not only to abolitionist altruism, but also to its depiction. The photograph portrays Harriet W. Murray, a Northern teacher at the Penn School on St. Helena island, reading to her recently freed pupils "Elsie and Puss." The pose itself is quite conventional: similar tableaus of a demurely dressed white woman seated in right profile and reading to a group of standing black children can be found among the collections of many early freedmen's schools. Such pictures are clearly designed as testaments to the efficacious but benign potential of these fledgling schools to civilize the black population of the South. Props for Northern fund-raising, these images promise that black literacy contains no threat, and that learning to read will only increase the childlike docility and affection thought characteristic of the African race. Mailing a similar photograph to her Northern family, Laura M. Towne, director of the Penn School, commented fondly, "I send the enclosed picture of me with three of my pets."[9]

Although the Penn school operated into this century, black interest in Northern-run schools waned, with many ex-slaves preferring to organize their own schools. Northern teachers complained of this ingratitude for "the charity which northern friends are so graciously bestowing," but they remained largely blind to the ease with which their humanitarian concern could produce patterns of authority and subordination, dominance and dependence not wholly dissimilar from those associated with the ministrations of the plantation mistress. Suggesting such proprietorship, Laura Towne explains, "We have got to calling them *our* people and loving them really—not so much individually as the collective whole—the people and *our* people."[10] Indeed, the very conventionality of this photograph betrays the subordination entailed in such beneficent poses. The woman's arm around one little girl's waist compels her participation as much as it embraces. While the scene intends to represent the girls as already enjoying the benefits of compliance with the civilizing generosity of her teachers, and her teachers' culture, the child behind the chair disrupts these nice arrangements. Staring straight at the camera, she challenges the naturalizing illusion of benevolence; her gaze makes us aware of how the act of photographing structures this scene. Her face expresses both fascination with and fear of the technology that would frame and preserve her, choreographed into the subject position of the slave Reconstructed—not the slave emancipated for self-determination.

Like this caught yet resistant little girl, the whipped, worked, auctioned, sexually violated, and sexually desiring bodies that figure in my discussions are both rhetorical and real. Michel Foucault's distinction between the "intelligible body" represented through discourse and the "docile-useful body" disciplined by social control best articulates the double relation between bodies and their representations at issue here. These are not Foucault's concerns, but the laboring body of the slave and the sexually productive body of the woman are among our culture's most obvious examples of such "useful" flesh. Foucault's assertion that what we take to be a "natural body" proves instead a socially constructed "political anatomy" suggests the limits to the liberal ideal of freeing the body through discourse.[11] I situate my efforts to describe this historically localized rhetoric of embodiment within recent debates over the relation between the human body and the discourses that name it.

Emily Martin has examined the differences in language and imagery used by the medical profession and a diverse group of interviewed women to describe the processes of female reproduction. Her findings demonstrate how attitudes toward the body are culturally ordered and offer a detailed example of the social and linguistic construction of the body. Elaine Scarry's work virtually inverts this argument, suggesting instead that the inexpressible and undeniable nature of bodily experience, especially pain, enables the construction of the social world. For her it is the body's desperate resistance to the enclosure of its experience that drives language. In analyzing how the bodies of women and slaves are figured in contemporaneous political and literary texts, my work draws upon the contradictions between these two ways of understanding the relation between bodies and rhetorics. It charts a circle in which the physical oppression and the juridical exclusion of black and female bodies give rise to a political movement and a literature that strive (as Scarry suggests) to speak the body, but that in so representing the body (as Martin suggests) exploit and limit it.[12]

To acknowledge the rhetorical limits of antislavery writing is not to discount these efforts to represent an embodied personhood. The language of the Constitution and of later suffrage campaigns evades the bodies of those they would enfranchise. The writers with whom I am concerned practice no such evasions, but the act of representing the body does not ensure the integrity of the thing represented. Angelina Grimké's depiction of slavery as a putrid corpse insists on the physical aspects of this political problem; but the stink and mold that emphasize the bodiliness of slavery also mark the gradual degeneration of that body. Such instability is in the simplest sense inevitable, since language can never *be* but can only inadequately represent the things it describes. In the texts I discuss, however, the effacement of the body must be understood in more explicitly political and violent terms. The bodies depicted in these texts reveal not only the limits of representation but also the threatening possibilities of radical difference. I am concerned precisely with the ways in which rhetoric effaces and contains the real, not only with the physical and juridical violence directed against women and slaves, but also with the violence of representation and the anxieties about difference inherent in the appropriation of their flesh for the purposes of political and literary discourse.[13]

Those purposes have traditionally been considered distinct. In calling attention to the double meaning of representation, I am suggesting that political and literary discourses share a homologous—though not identical—relation to the problem of embodiment. As I trace the implications of a corporeal identity through feminist and abolitionist writings, Jacobs's narrative, and Whitman's and Dickinson's poems, I do not, however, intend simply to collapse distinctions of meaning or genre. Rather I am concerned with the dynamics of intersecting rhetorics: how the figures generated by one discourse may be altered or subsumed through contact with another.[14] By *discourse* I mean any historically specific structure of assertions, vocabularies, categories, and beliefs; thus, though I rely predominantly on the linguistic manifestations of such structures, *discourse* can refer to a variety of institutional or social practices. For example, there exist both slavery (the fact of bondage) and the discourse of slavery (the pattern of statements, definitions, and beliefs that both enables the fact of bondage and mediates subsequent accounts of it). The term *intersection* is a purposely fluid one, and refers not only to intentionally forged connections (feminists drawing upon the imagery of slavery to depict "the bonds of womanhood," or Whitman conjoining lyric and narrative formal conventions) but also to thematic and imagistic coincidences that textual analysis reveals in contemporary writers like Jacobs and Dickinson, who could not have known about each other's work. These unintentional connections ultimately prove the most significant for my purposes, as they appear indicative not only of individual patterns of influence but of more pervasive cultural concerns. Although feminism, abolition, and the resulting emphasis on the corporeality of identity can be seen to permeate American consciousness and cultural expression, they do not necessarily produce a homogenous "spirit of the age." Indeed my focus on rhetorical intersections suggests how the problems of a corporeal identity change with the differently embodied perspective of each speaker.

In chapter 1 I explore the intersections of feminist and abolitionist rhetoric to expose the contradictions and asymmetries inherent in the identification of free woman with slave woman. My analysis uncovers the exploitation inherent in this also empowering political alliance. Chapter 1 focuses primarily on politically motivated sentimental fiction. Chapter 2 moves from Walt Whitman's foray into this reformist genre in his temperance novel *Franklin Evans* to the poetry of the 1855 *Leaves of Grass;* this trajectory raises questions about the interrelation of narrative and lyric modes. More directly relevant to my thesis, the discussion relates his poetics of merger and embodiment to contemporary political divisions over the body of the slave. Such a reading does not simply mark the union of politics and poetry, though it does attest to their connectedness; instead it assesses both the political and the poetic force generated by such an alliance and the concomitant dangers of literary appropriation. Whitman's project of poetic embodiment, which would permit his multiple migratory "I" to inhabit the body of the other in all its difference, and his project of poetic merger, which would encompass and negate all differences within his single swelling "I," contradict each other, yet both locate the possibility of social reconciliation within the speaking self.

What it means to absorb the issues of the social world into the person and flesh of the writer changes radically with the writer's position. The progression of these chapters is chronological, but it also traces a movement toward increasingly privatized utterance. Thus, while my discussion of Whitman describes his attempts to unite personal and social concerns, my discussion of *Incidents in the Life of a Slave Girl* in chapter 3 instances Harriet Jacobs's efforts to disentangle her autobiographical desire to write down the self from her political desire to write an abolitionist polemic. The very connections that Whitman celebrates become for her a source of pain. In particular, for Jacobs the act of writing often seems to recapit-

ulate the sexual violations at stake in the scenes she narrates.
Linda Brent escapes from slavery by hiding herself in distinctly domestic and confining spaces; that such spaces
should serve as a method of escape—however ambivalent—
provokes a reevaluation of the relation between the structures of domesticity and the structures of slavery described
in my first chapter.

The contradictory links among domesticity, embodiment,
and freedom also ground my discussion of Emily Dickinson's
poetry in chapter 4, where, however, the project of affirming
freedom and identity have been internalized and so appear
disjoined from any political or social program. In contrast to
Whitman's strategies of inclusion and Jacobs's failed attempts
at separation, Dickinson's writing locates within her own
identity, her own words, and her own flesh the divisions
these other texts have described as social. Yet this relocation
within the self ought not to be understood as a complete disjunction from antebellum political activism, since the most
radical and polemical of abolitionists would have been the
first to aver that ultimately all reform must take place "within
the human heart." In the earlier chapters I find that the identifications forged between women and slaves, between politics and poetry, between personal and social meanings, and
between a variety of generic forms, rather than equitably reconciling these different subjects and mediums of discourse,
frequently served to subordinate one discourse to another.
The questions raised by Dickinson's work corroborate this
pattern, but by inverting it, for her poems enforce not a
union but a splitting, not only of discourse but even of the
self that would say it.

The case of Dickinson is extreme. Her poetry flamboyantly
insists on its radical privacy, on its internalization of social
concerns. This sort of historical detachment has generally
been ascribed to lyric utterance; in this, as in so much else,
Dickinson's poetry presses lyric conventions to their limits.
Dickinson criticism has frequently analyzed the mechanisms
by which her poetry resists referentiality; I suggest that in this
resistance her poems not only make evident the fragmented

nature of lyric utterance but also lay bare the contradictory connections between embodiment and representation. Dickinson's poetry reveals how for the self, as much as for the state, the physical aspect of personhood simultaneously informs and inhibits all acts of representation—political as well as semiotic. Thus the shift to a focus on suffrage, that is, to representational politics, can never get rid of the challenges posed by bodily differences; it can only mask them within the formless and representative body of the state.

In the last few years critics have shown an increasing interest in the impact of slavery on the literary imagination of antebellum America.[15] My decision to trace feminist and abolitionist discourse through the lyric, rather than the novel, distinguishes mine from the majority of these efforts. But this decision is also strategic in more important ways, since claims have often been made for the depoliticized and atemporal status of lyric utterance. My purpose is not to deny the aesthetic value of lyric form, but rather to record some of the ways in which these aesthetic maneuvers interact with more explicitly social or political discourses. Ultimately, such a project demonstrates the ideological relevance and potency not just of the lyric but of all formal structures. In novels, where the task of depiction often envelops a great deal of the social world, and so makes issues like slavery or woman's rights thematically visible, the ideological impact of the novelistic structure itself is more easily discounted. Analyzing lyric poetry, and especially such referentially resistant lyrics as Dickinson's, disables an emphasis on thematic political content and instead reveals how aesthetic, stylistic, and formal mechanisms come to accrue ideological significance.

The variety of rhetorical intersections I have sketched above is not merely heuristic. Rather, these intersections exemplify and confront debates within contemporary literary and cultural studies—debates that themselves have more general social and political import. For example, the challenges that racial difference poses for feminism have been— belatedly and still inadequately—acknowledged within feminist discourses both inside and outside the academy. The asymmetries I have found in the feminist-abolitionist practices of nineteenth-century America remain only too relevant now. Similarly, the question of the relations between literature and history, between form and ideology, and between canonical and noncanonical texts underlies critical arguments over the political efficacy and critical validity of "New Historicism."[16] My own practice here rests on the double assumption that all expression is necessarily embedded in politics and that all politics is necessarily rhetorically structured. Furthermore, in any given instance the social and literary implications of these interweavings are never fully under authorial control and may well prove multiple or even contradictory. Thus I do not find rhetorical structures either inherently subversive or inevitably conservative: from the sentimental to the lyric they do cultural work, but the ideological valence of that work does not remain fixed.

In the end I come to the allegory of my own authorship. I began this project out of the desire to articulate connections between social action and literary expression and therefore to define my own critical work as, at least potentially, politically productive. I hoped that the structure of political alliance that linked feminists and abolitionists would provide an appropriate and empowering model for an alliance between poetry and politics. I had intended, that is, to tell a happier story about the insight and strength to be found in strategies of coalition, both political and rhetorical. Instead, as I worked, the relation between feminism and abolition increasingly seemed to be characterized by patterns of exploitation, appropriation, and displacement; similarly the potential for aesthetic erasures and absorptions marred any simply positive reading of the links between poetry and politics. This does not mean, however, that the chapters that follow merely trace a bleak story of disillusionment. Neither narratives of inevitable failure nor stories of easy cohesion or success, they are useful cautionary tales, important precisely because they articulate some of the obstacles to embracing and heeding difference.

1

Bodily Bonds
The Intersecting Rhetorics of Feminism and Abolition

As Lydia Maria Child tells it in 1836, the story of the woman and the story of the slave are the same story.

> I have been told of a young physician who went into the far Southern states to settle, and there became in love with a very handsome and modest girl who lived in service. He married her; and about a year after the event a gentleman called at the house and announced himself as Mr. J. of Mobile. He said to Dr. W., "Sir, I have a trifling affair of business to settle with you. You have married a slave of mine." The young physician resented the language; for he had not entertained the slightest suspicion that the girl had any other than white ancestors since the flood. But Mr. J. furnished proofs of his claim . . .

Convinced, and under the threat of having his wife sold at public auction, the doctor bought her for eight hundred dollars. When he informed her of the purchase, "the poor woman burst into tears and said, 'That as Mr. J. *was her own father,* she had hoped that when he heard she had found an honorable protector he would have left her in peace.' "[1] The horror of the story lies in the perversion of an almost fairytale courtship—complete with a suitor who has traveled far, a modest girl, and love—into an economic transaction, and the perversion of the bonds of paternity into the profits of bondage. It is the collapse of the assumed difference between family and slavery that makes this anecdote so disturbing: the institutions of marriage and slavery are not merely analogous, they are coextensive and indistinguishable. The passages of the woman from father to husband and of the slave from one

14

master to another are conflated. The new husband and the new master are one man, needing only one name, for bourgeois idealizations of marriage and Southern apologies for slavery both consider him an honorable protector.

This merger of slavery and marriage redefines love and protection as terms of ownership, thereby identifying the modest girl, object of this love and honorable protection, as an object of transaction. Significantly, Child places her story within a section of her *Anti-Slavery Catechism* that asserts the difficulty of distinguishing the bodies of slaves from the bodies of free people. Indeed the story concludes a catalogue of bodily features ("nose prominent," "tibia of the leg straight") that do not protect one from enslavement.[2] In this story the composite of bodily traits that identify a girl as marriageable proves misleading, putting into question the presumption that the body can provide reliable information about the institutional and racial status of the whole person. What matters about the girl for Child's purposes is that a doctor intimately acquainted with her flesh perceives no hint of blackness.[3] If the body is an inescapable sign of identity, it is also an insecure and often illegible sign.

In Child's story the conflation of woman and slave, and of marriage and bondage, results from difficulties in interpreting the human body. The problems of having, representing, or interpreting a body structure both feminist and abolitionist discourses; indeed the rhetorics of the two reforms meet upon the recognition that for both women and blacks their physical difference from the cultural norms of white masculinity obstructs their claim to personhood. Thus the social and political goals of feminism and abolition depend upon an act of representation, the inscription of black and female bodies into the discourse of personhood. Despite this similarity of aims, the alliance attempted by feminist-abolitionist texts is never particularly easy or equitable. Although the identifications of woman and slave, marriage and slavery that characterize these texts may occasionally prove mutually empowering, such pairings generally tend toward asymmetry and exploitation. This chapter interrogates the intersection of antebellum feminist and abolitionist discourses by examining the attitudes toward black and female bodies revealed there, how these two types of bodies are equated, and the inevitable costs of such equations. The composite term that names this intersection, *feminist-abolitionist*, has come into currency with the writings of twentieth-century historians. Women involved in the abolitionist and woman's rights movements also tended to advocate temperance, to oppose prostitution, and to reform schools, prisons, and diets; they referred to themselves as "universal reformers." My use of the term *feminist-abolitionist* is thus an anachronistic convenience: the hyphen neatly articulates the very connections and distinctions that I intend to explore. In this chapter I focus on writings in which the rhetorical crossings of women and slaves predominate: the political speeches and pamphlets that equate the figure of the woman and the figure of the slave; the sentimental novels and giftbook stories in which antislavery women attempt to represent the slave and more obliquely depict their own fears and desires, so that the racial and the sexual come to displace one another; and the more conservative Sunday-school primers that, in trying to domesticate slavery, recast its oppressions in familial terms, demonstrating the complicity of the two institutions and hence the degree to which domestic and sentimental antislavery writings are implicated in the very oppressions they seek to reform.

The intersection of antebellum feminist and abolitionist projects, organizations, and rhetoric has been frequently interrogated, though the historical implications of the connections remain controversial.[4] In particular, accounts of the beginnings of American feminism have debated the nature of this intersection, arguing over the extent to which the male abolitionist tradition can be credited for the development of feminist political activism and ideology. Did women's consciousness of their own oppression derive from the analogies between the position of women and that of slaves revealed by abolitionist analysis?[5] Or did the "protofeminist" sensibilities of those female benevolence and reform organizations that predate the radical activities of abolitionist women provide a sufficient source for a feminist ideology?[6] Did the abolitionist movement simply offer an education in political strategies and analysis to women who were already well aware of their inferior status?[7] Or did the antagonism that met and attempted to silence female antislavery agents prove the final outrage, catalyzing the feminist movement?[8] Identifying origins and tracing influences, the questions raised by historians have treated the overlapping concerns of feminists and abolitionists merely as signs and symptoms of these causal relations. The questions I ask in this chapter focus not on the causal links between these two movements, but on the nature of their coincidence, since it is within the space where feminism and abolition overlap that they most directly confront the bodily grounds of the period's disparate threats to personhood. This space is not, of course, simply a scene of concord. In replacing a causal inquiry with a study of conceptual and rhetorical intersections, I demonstrate that the issues of appropriation (who owes what to whom) at stake in the historians' debates were first manifested in the feminist-abolitionists' often conflicting attitudes toward black and female bodies.

Feminists and abolitionists were acutely aware of the dependence of personhood on the condition of the human body, since the political and legal subordination of both women and slaves was predicated upon biology. Medical treatises of the period consistently assert that a woman's psyche and intellect are determined by her reproductive organs.[9] Indeed, to the political satirist, the leaders of the woman's rights movement are nothing but wombs in constant danger of parturition:

> How funny it would sound in the newspapers, that Lucy Stone, pleading a cause, took suddenly ill in the pains of parturition, and perhaps gave birth to a fine bouncing boy in court; or that Rev. Antonia Brown was arrested in the middle of her sermon in the pulpit from the same cause, and presented a "pledge" to her husband and the congregation. . . . A similar event might happen on the floor of Congress, in a

storm at sea, or in the raging tempest of battle, and then what
is to become of the woman legislator?[10]

In this lampoon the reproductive function interrupts and replaces women's attempts to speak; their public delivery of arguments, sermons, and service is superseded by the delivery
of children. The joke betrays male fear of female fertility
while fashioning the woman's womb and its relentless fecun-
dity into a silencing gag.

The body of the black was similarly thought to define his
or her role as servant and laborer. Subservience, one Southern doctor explained, was built into the very structure of African bones. The black was made "submissive knee-bender"
by the decree of the Almighty, for "in the anatomical confor-
mation of his knees, we see 'genu flexit' written in his physical structure, being more flexed or bent than any other kind
of man."[11] As God writes "subservience" upon the body of
the black, in Latin, of course, the doctor reads it; or, more
crudely, as the master inscribes his name with hot irons ("he
is *branded on the forehead* with the letters A.M. and *on each cheek*
with the letters J.G."), or the fact of slavery with scars ("his
back shows *lasting impressions of the whip,* and leaves no doubt
of his being a *slave*"), the body of the slave attains the status
of a text.[12] Thus the bodies of women and slaves were read
against them, so that for both the human body functions as
the foundation not only of a general subjection but also of a
specific exclusion from political discourse. For women and
slaves the ability to speak was predicated upon the reinterpretation of their flesh. They share a strategy of liberation: to
invert patriarchal readings and so reclaim the body. Transformed from a silent site of oppression into a symbol of that
oppression, the body becomes within feminist-abolitionist
discourse a means of gaining rhetorical force.

Though the female body, and particularly female sexual
desires, are at least covertly inscribed within feminist-
abolitionist texts, the paradigmatic body reclaimed in these
writings is that of the slave. The slave, so explicitly an object
to be sold, provides feminism, as well as abolition, with its
most graphic example of the extent to which the human body

may designate identity. "The denial of our duty to act [against slavery] is a denial of our right to act," wrote Angelina Grimké in 1837, "and if we have no right to act then may *we* well be termed the 'white slaves of the North' for like our brethren in bonds, we must seal our lips in silence and despair."[13] As I have already suggested, the alliance between black bodies and female bodies achieved by the rhetorical crossing of feminist-abolitionist texts was not necessarily equitable. Grimké grounds her right to act and speak on her identification with the muteness of the slave. Yet in so claiming this right she differentiates herself from her "brethren" in bonds. The bound and silent figure of the slave represents the woman's oppression and so grants the white woman access to political discourse denied the slave, exemplifying the way in which slave labor produces—both literally and metaphorically—even the most basic of freedom's privileges.[14]

In feminist writings the metaphoric linking of women and slaves proves ubiquitous: marriage and property laws, the conventional adoption of a husband's name, or even the length of fashionable skirts are explained and decried by reference to women's "slavery."[15] This strategy emphasizes the restrictions of woman's sphere, and, despite luxuries and social civilities, classes the bourgeois woman among the oppressed. Sarah Grimké, beginning her survey of the condition of women with ancient history, notes that "the cupidity of man soon led him to regard woman as property, and hence we find them sold to those who wished to marry them," while within marriage, as defined by nineteenth-century laws of coverture, "the very being of a woman, like that of a slave, is absorbed in her master."[16] "A woman," Elizabeth Cady Stanton explains to the Woman's Rights Convention of 1856, "has no name! She is Mrs. John or James, Peter or Paul, just as she changes masters; like the Southern slave, she takes the name of her owner."[17]

The image of the slave evoked not simply the loss of "liberty," but the loss of all claims to self-possession, including the possession of one's body. At stake in the feminists' likening of women to slaves is the recognition that personhood

can be annihilated and a person owned, absorbed, and unnamed. The irony inherent in such comparisons is that the
enlightening and empowering motions of identification that
connect feminism and abolition come inextricably bound to a
process of absorption not unlike the one that they expose.
Though the metaphoric linking of women and slaves uses
their shared position as bodies to be bought, owned, and
designated as a grounds of resistance, it nevertheless obliter-
ates the particularity of black and female experience, making
their distinct exploitations appear identical. The difficulty of
preventing moments of identification from becoming acts of
appropriation constitutes the essential dilemma of feminist-
abolitionist rhetoric.

The body of the woman and the body of the slave need
not, of course, merge only through metaphor, and it is hardly
surprising that the figure of the female slave features prom-
inently in both discourses. Yet even in the case of the literally
enslaved woman, the combining of feminist and abolitionist
concerns supports both reciprocal and appropriative strategies. The difference between the stereotypic cultural conceptions of black and female bodies was such that, in the crossing of feminist and abolitionist rhetoric, the status of the slave
and the status of the woman could each be improved by an
alliance with the body of the other. Their two sorts of bodies
were prisons in different ways, and for each the prison of the
other was liberating. So for the female slave, the frail body of
the bourgeois lady promised not weakness but the modesty
and virtue of a delicacy supposed at once physical and moral.
Concern for the roughness and impropriety with which slave
women were treated redefined their suffering as feminine
and hence endowed with all the moral value generally attributed to nineteenth-century American womanhood.[18] Conversely for the nineteenth-century free woman there were
certain assets to be claimed from the body of the slave.
"Those who think the physical circumstances of women
would make a part in the affairs of national government un-
suitable," Margaret Fuller argues, "are by no means those
who think it impossible for Negresses to endure field work

even during pregnancy."[19] The strength to plant, and hoe, and pick, and endure is available to the urban middle class woman insofar as she can be equated with the laboring slave woman, and that equation suggests the possibility of reshaping physical circumstances. Fuller's words provide a perfect example of the chiasmic alignment of abolition and woman's rights, for, though embedded within a discussion devoted to feminist concerns, this passage achieves a double efficacy, simultaneously declaring the physical strength of the woman and implying the need to protect the exploited slave.[20]

Just as the figure of the female slave served feminist rhetorical purposes, she also proved useful in abolitionist campaigns and was frequently employed to attract women to abolitionist work. William Lloyd Garrison, for example, headed the "Ladies Department" of *The Liberator* with the picture of a black woman on her knees and in chains; beneath it ran the plea, "Am I not a woman and a sister?"[21] Such tactics did not attempt to identify woman's status with that of the slave but relied upon the ties of sisterly sympathy, presuming that one woman would be particularly sensitive to the sufferings of another. Indeed such a strategy emphasized the difference between the free woman's condition and the bondage of the slave, since it was this difference that enabled the free woman to work for her sister's emancipation.

The particular horror and appeal of the slave woman lay in the magnitude of her sexual vulnerability, and the Ladies Department admonished its female readers to work for the immediate emancipation of their one million enslaved sisters "exposed to all the violence of lust and passion—and treated with more indelicacy and cruelty than cattle."[22] The sexual exploitation of female slaves served abolitionists as a proof that slave owners laid claim not merely to the slave's time, labor, and obedience—assets purchased, after all, with the wages paid by the Northern industrialist—but to their flesh. The abolitionist comparison of slave and cattle, like the feminist analogy between woman and slave, marks the slip from person to chattel.[23] More startling than the comparison of the slave to a cow, however, is the Ladies Department's equation

of indelicacy with cruelty, for set beside the menace of brand-
ings, whippings, beatings, and starvation, rudeness seems
an insignificant care. This concern with indelicacy becomes
explicable, however, in terms of the overlap of feminist and
abolitionist discourse. To the male abolitionist the application
of those notions of modesty and purity that governed the
world of nineteenth-century ladies to the extremely different
situation of the slave must have seemed a useful strategy
for gaining female support on an economic, political, and
hence unfeminine issue. Viewed from this perspective the
language of feminine modesty simply reinforces traditional
female roles. Even here, however, the emphasis on sexual
exploitation suggests that the abolitionist's easy differentiation between the free woman and the enslaved one may
conceal grounds of identification. For in stressing the aspect
of slavery that would seem most familiar to a female readership, the abolitionist press implicitly suggests that the Ladies
Department's readers may be bound like the slaves they are
urged to free.

As the Grimkés and Stanton demonstrate, feminist-
abolitionists emphasize the similarities in the condition of
women and slaves; nevertheless, their treatment of the figure
of the sexually exploited female slave betrays an opposing desire to deny any share in this vulnerability. The same metaphoric structure that enables the identification of women and
slaves can also preclude such identification. Thus in the writings of antislavery women the frequent emphasis on the specifically feminine trial of sexual abuse projects the white
woman's sexual anxieties onto the sexualized body of the female slave. Concern over the slave woman's sexual victimization displaces the free woman's fear of confronting the sexual
elements of her own bodily experience, either as a positive
force or as a mechanism of oppression. The prevalence of
such fear is illustrated by the caution with which even the
most radical feminist thinkers avoid public discussion of
"woman's rights in marriage"; only in their private correspondence do the leaders of the woman's rights movement
allude to sexual rights. "It seems to me that we are not

ready" to bring this issue before the 1856 convention, Lucy Stone writes to Susan B. Anthony:

> No two of us think alike about it, and yet it is clear to me that question underlies the whole movement, and all our little skirmishing for better laws and the right to vote, will yet be swallowed up in the real question viz.: Has woman a right to herself? It is very little to me to have the right to vote, to own property, etc., if I may not keep my body, and its uses, in my absolute right. Not one wife in a thousand can do that now.[24]

The figure of the slave woman, whose inability to keep her body and its uses under her own control is widely and openly recognized, becomes a perfect conduit for the largely unarticulated and unacknowledged failure of the free woman to own her own body in marriage. In one sense, then, it is the very indelicacy of the slave woman's position that makes her a useful proxy in such indelicate matters.

Garrison's Ladies Department attests to the importance of women to the antislavery movement. In 1833 the Boston Female Anti-Slavery Society was founded as an "auxiliary" to the all-male New England Anti-Slavery Society. By 1838 there were forty-one female auxiliary societies in Massachusetts alone.[25] The function of these auxiliaries was to provide support—mostly in the form of fund-raising—for the work of the male organizations. Thus the auxiliaries behaved much like other female philanthropic or benevolence societies, and most of the women who worked in them gave no public speeches, wrote no political pamphlets, and did not see their antislavery activities as challenging the traditions of male authority and female domesticity. Nevertheless, in their work against slavery these female societies transformed conventional womanly activities into tools of political persuasion, "presenting," as Angelina Grimké explained, the slave's "kneeling image constantly before the public eye." Toward this end they stitched the pathetic figure of the manacled slave onto bags, pincushions, and pen-wipers ("Even the children of the north are inscribing on their handiwork, 'May the points of our needles prick the slaveholders' conscience' "), and wrote virtually all of the sentimental tales that describe the slaves' sufferings.[26]

In many ways, then, the antislavery stories that abolitionist women wrote for Sunday school primers, juvenile miscellanies, antislavery newspapers, and giftbooks need to be assessed as a variety of female handiwork, refashioned for political, didactic, and pecuniary purposes. The genre is fundamentally feminine: not only were these stories—like virtually all the domestic and sentimental fiction of the period—penned primarily by women, but women also largely controlled their production, editing the giftbooks and miscellanies that contained them and publishing many of these volumes under the auspices of Female Anti-Slavery Societies.[27] The most substantial and longest-lived abolitionist publishing endeavor of this type, the *Liberty Bell* giftbook produced by the Boston Female Anti-Slavery Society, provides the most obvious illustration of these practices and one that subsequent antislavery collections sought to imitate.[28] In their efforts to raise funds, the Boston auxiliary organized an Anti-Slavery Fair, and it was for the sixth fair, as a further educational and fund-raising gesture, that the *Liberty Bell* was published. Under Maria Weston Chapman's skillful editorial direction it appeared at virtually every Fair from 1839 to 1858, to be sold alongside the quilts and jams.[29] The minutes of the committee for the tenth Anti-Slavery Fair claimed that the *Liberty Bell* "always doubles the money invested in it." Since the cost of producing the volume was three to four hundred dollars (covered by donations drawn largely from among the contributors), the committee's claim would assess the *Liberty Bell* at slightly less than a fifth of the fair's average proceeds of four thousand dollars a year.[30]

One important feature of the tales published in the *Liberty Bell* was that they were considered salable. The depiction of the slave was thought to have its own market value. The reasons the volumes sold, moreover, appear paradoxically at odds both with each other and with abolitionist beliefs. On the one hand, the horrific events narrated in these tales attract precisely to the extent that the buyers of these representations of slavery are fascinated by the abuses they ostensibly oppose. For, despite their clear abolitionist stance, such stories are fueled by the allure of bondage, an appeal that suggests that the valuation of depictions of slavery may rest upon the same psychic ground as slaveholding itself. On the other hand, the acceptability of these tales depends upon their adherence to a feminine and domestic demeanor that softens the cruelty they describe and makes their political goals more palatable to a less politicized readership. Explaining the success of the *Liberty Bell,* Chapman admits as much, suggestively presenting her giftbook as a mother who treats the public "like children, to whom a medicine is made as pleasant as its nature permits. A childish mind receives a small measure of truth in gilt edges where it would reject it in 'whity-brown.' "[31] Though it was plain by giftbook standards, the embossed leather and gilded edges of the *Liberty Bell* permitted it to fit without apparent incongruity into any household library. Despite their subject matter, the antislavery stories it contained attempt a similar and uneasy compliance with the conventions that governed nineteenth-century domestic fiction. The contradictory nature of antislavery fiction's appeal thus raises more general questions about what it means to depict slavery and hence about the politics and power of representation.

Critics have frequently argued that sentimental fiction is an inappropriate vehicle for educating the public to slavery's real terrors.[32] This criticism, however, simply echoes the authors' own anxieties about the realism of the stories they tell. Almost every antislavery story begins by citing its source: a meeting with the hero or heroine, an account of the events in the newspaper, or most often and simply, just having been told.[33] "The truth of incidents" claimed in Harriet Beecher Stowe's preface to *Uncle Tom's Cabin* is documented by her subsequently published *Key* to the novel—the genre's most sustained and impressive attempt to demonstrate its veracity.

But her very effort to prove that her novel is "a collection and arrangement of real incidents . . . a mosaic of facts," propounds the difference between her narrative and her key to it, since "slavery, in some of its workings, is too dreadful for the purposes of art. A work which should represent it strictly as it is, would be a work which could not be read."[34] The reading of these stories, and therefore both their marketability and their political efficacy, depends upon their success in rearranging the real. The decision to rearrange it into sentimental tales is highly appropriate, not only because of the dominance of the form during the period, nor simply because of its popular appeal and consequent market value, but also because sentimental fiction constitutes an intensely bodily genre. The concern with the human body as site and symbol of the self that links the struggles of feminists and abolitionists also informs the genre in which nineteenth-century women wrote their antislavery stories.

The tears of the reader are pledged in these sentimental stories as a means of rescuing the bodies of slaves. Emblematic of this process, Child's story "Mary French and Susan Easton" relates how the white Mary, kidnapped, stained black, and sold into slavery, is quite literally freed by weeping; her true identity is revealed because "where the tears had run down her cheeks, there was a streak whiter than the rest of her face."[35] Her weeping seems to dissolve racial barriers and make Mary recognizably white. Mary's tears idealize the power of sentiment to change the condition of the human body, or at least, read symbolically, to alter how that condition is perceived.

The ability of sentimental fiction to liberate the bodies of slaves is, moreover, intimately connected to the bodily nature of the genre itself. Sentiment and feeling refer at once to emotion and to physical sensation, and in sentimental fiction these two versions of *sentire* blend as the eyes of readers take in the printed word and blur it with tears. Reading sentimental fiction is thus a bodily act, and the success of a story is gauged, in part, by its ability to translate words into heartbeats and sobs. This physicality of the reading experience radically contracts the distance between narrated events and the moment of their reading, as the feelings in the story are made tangibly present in the flesh of the reader. In particular, tears designate a border realm between the story and its reading, since the tears shed by characters initiate an answering moistness in the reader's eye.[36] The assurance in this fiction that emotion can be attested and measured by physical response makes this conflation possible; the palpability of the character's emotional experience is precisely what allows it to be shared. In sentimental fiction bodily signs are adamantly and repeatedly presented as the preferred and most potent mechanisms both for communicating meaning and for marking the fact of its transmission.[37]

Sentimental narrative functions through stereotypes, so that upon first encountering a character there is no difficulty in ascertaining his or her moral worth. In sentimental writing the self is externally displayed, and the body provides a reliable sign of who one is. Nina Gordon, the heroine of *Dred* (Stowe's other antislavery novel), develops an instinctive goodness more potent than her lover Edward Clayton's principled virtue. In her instantaneous and unproblematic discrimination of good from evil, Nina provides a paradigm for reading the novel that contains her.

> Looking back almost fiercely, a moment, she turned and said to Clayton:
> "I hate that man!"
> "Who is it?" said Clayton.
> "I don't know!" said Nina. "I never saw him before. But I hate him! He is a bad man! I'd as soon have a serpent come near me as that man!"
> "Well, the poor fellow's face isn't prepossessing," said Clayton. "But I should not be prepared for such an anathema. . . . How can you be so positive about a person you've only seen once!" . . .
> "Oh," said Nina, resuming her usual gay tones, "don't you know that girls and dogs, and other inferior creatures, have the gift of seeing what's in people? It doesn't belong to highly cultivated folks like you, but to us poor creatures, who have to trust to our instincts. So, beware!"[38]

Skill in reading the body of the stranger does not belong to the highly cultivated man who talks of what is prepossessing and what an anathema but to girls who hate and will call a man bad. To Nina Mr. Jekyl's face is "very repulsive," and in feeling herself repelled, pushed away by his visage, she weighs the evidence of his character in the reaction of her body to his body. Jokingly shared with dogs, the girl's capacity to read signs by instinct is as physical as the traits it correctly interprets. The succeeding chapters prove the accuracy of Nina's reaction to Mr. Jekyl, and so endorse her and the sentimental novel's mechanisms of assessment.[39]

Nina Gordon is the ideal reader of all sentimental fiction, not simply of antislavery tales, but her ability to read bodies correctly is more important for antislavery fiction, in which the physical vocabulary has been suddenly enlarged to include very different-looking bodies that make the interpretive task more difficult. The problem, for the antislavery writer, lies in depicting a black body that can be instantly recognized not only as a loyal or a rebellious servant, but also as a hero or a heroine. Stowe introduces Dred:

> He was a tall black man, of magnificent stature and proportions. His skin was intensely black, and polished like marble. A loose shirt of red flannel, which opened very wide at the breast, gave a display of a neck and chest of herculean strength. The sleeves of the shirt, rolled up nearly to the shoulders, showed the muscles of a gladiator. The head, which rose with an imperial air from the broad shoulders, was large and massive, and developed with equal force both in the reflective and perceptive department. The perceptive organs jutted like dark ridges over the eyes, while that part of the head which phrenologists attribute to moral and intellectual sentiments rose like an ample dome above them.[40]

A magnificent, herculean, and imperial gladiator—with these words Stowe arrays Dred in the vocabulary of classical heroism. That gladiators were often slaves only strengthens the claims Stowe desires to make for this slave. The density of such terms, however, equally evinces her sense of the difficulty of granting and sustaining Dred's heroic status. She therefore supplements her attempt to fashion Dred into a polished black marble icon of classical heroism with the pseudo-scientific language of phrenology. The phrenologist, like the reader of sentimental fiction, reads internal characteristics from the external signs offered by the body. By enlisting the phrenologist in her descriptive task, Stowe garners the authority of study for what she has previously presented as instinctual knowledge. Her need for these multiple buttresses attests to the frailty of this structure. The precariousness of Dred's heroic stature is all the more telling because in Stowe's description the heroic and the phrenological have combined to present him less as a man than as a monument. A structure of magnificent proportions crowned by an ample dome, this massive figure of polished marble achieves a truly architectural splendor. Stowe has not so much described Dred as built his body.

Stowe's difficulty in creating a slave-hero is best demonstrated, however, not by the body she constructs him in but by the features she silently omits. For though Stowe describes Dred as having eyes of that "unfathomable blackness and darkness which is often a striking characteristic of the African eye," she avoids detailing the rest of his visage. In "The Slave-Wife" Frances Green, less sensitive to the racism that underlies this dilemma, gives her hero, Laco Ray, a face that exemplifies Stowe's problem:

> Tall, muscular, and every way well-proportioned, he had the large expansion of chest and shoulders that are seen in the best representations of Hercules. He was quite black, the skin soft and glossy; but the features had none of the revolting characteristics which are supposed by some to be inseparable from the African visage. On the contrary they were remarkably fine—the nose aquiline—the mouth even handsome—the forehead singularly high and broad.[41]

Green's Laco Ray inhabits in 1845 virtually the same body Stowe gives to Dred in 1856, confirming the genre's reliance on stereotypes: every hero, even a black one, is simply another in a familiar series of "best representations of Hercules." In making her black Hercules, however, Green registers her need to reject "the revolting characteristics" of nose, mouth, and brow that she criticizes others for supposing "inseparable from the African visage." Her desire to separate them is, obviously, as suspect as the assumption of their inseparability. Her own insecurity about attaining such a separation betrays itself in adverbs as she constantly modifies her description to emphasize its unexpectedness: *remarkably* fine, *even* handsome, *singularly* high and broad; what she finds most exceptional about Laco Ray's features is that they belong to him. Making a black hero involves not only dyeing the traditional figure of the hero to a darker hue, but also separating blackness from the configuration of traits that in the bodily grammar of sentimental fiction signals revulsion. In replacing or omitting revolting features, both Green and Stowe remake the black body to mold the slave into a hero. These features revolt, moreover, not only because they fail to conform to white criteria for beauty but, more interestingly, because they threaten to overturn sentimental fiction's stable matrix of bodily signs.

The project of depicting the body of the sympathetic black thus becomes a project of racial amalgamation. Child's story of Mary French's transition, from white to black and back to white again, begins with an idyllic scene in which Mary and her free-black playmate Susan frolic with a white and black spotted rabbit. In its alternating patches of color, the rabbit presents an ideal of amalgamation that would not blur racial distinctions into mulatto indifferentiation but rather preserve the clarity of difference without the hierarchies of valuation imposed by prejudice. The problem in Child's story, as in those of Stowe and Green, is that this sort of equality in difference becomes impossible to maintain. Susan, kidnapped with Mary, cannot prove her right to freedom by her bodily traits; her father (afraid of being kidnapped himself) cannot search for her; and Mary's father does nothing to pursue this search once he has redeemed his own daughter. Thus the tears produced by sentimental fiction offer a merely self-reflexive liberation: white tears may free Mary's white body, but they can do nothing for Susan's black one.

The racial prejudice implicit in Child's only half-happy ending is obviously one of her points. Nevertheless her concluding remarks instance just such racial hierarchy. "The only difference between Mary French and Susan Easton is," she explains, "that the black color could be rubbed off from Mary's skin, while from Susan's it could not."[42] Despite her clear desire for a different answer, the only solution to racial prejudice Child's story can offer is rubbing off blackness, and, though she does not say this, it is impossible to imagine what one could produce by such a purging except whiteness.[43] If Mary's liberating tears offer, as I have argued, a perfect emblem for sentimental fiction's power to emancipate, that emblem includes the recognition that the freedom it offers depends upon the black being washed white.[44] The problem of antislavery fiction is that the very effort to depict goodness in black involves the obliteration of blackness.[45]

Child's story challenges the prevalent bodily vocabulary that interprets dark skin as an unvarying sign of slavery: for Susan, being black and being a slave are not the same thing. Yet whatever Susan's "right to be free," even under antebellum law, the blackness of her body is itself described as a form of enslavement, and one that no act of emancipation can rub off. The painful longing for such an emancipation from one's own skin is explored in Eliza Lee Follen's story "A Melancholy Boy." Throughout most of this story Follen relates a series of anecdotes about the good but inexplicably unhappy Harry, without in any way describing his physical appearance, though the publication of this piece in the *Liberty Bell* would prompt readers to expect that some abolitionist issue is at stake. In the last paragraph of her tale, Follen "discover[s] the cause of Harry's melancholy":

> I was returning from a walk, and saw him at a little brook that ran behind my house, washing his face and hands vehemently, and rubbing them very hard. I then remembered that I had often seen him there doing the same thing. "It seems to me, Harry," I said, "that your face and hands are clean now; and why do you rub your face so violently?" "I am trying," he said, "to wash away this color; I can never be happy till I get rid of this color. . . ."[46]

Harry does not name his color, though he does distinguish himself from the other boys: "they are all white." Follen too refrains from naming "this color," so that the story centers upon the absence of the word *black*. Both Harry and Follen attempt to escape his blackness, not only by violent scrubbings but also by suppressing the word that names it. In Harry's hopeless efforts to attain personhood through the denial of his body, antislavery fiction locates the problems of representation established by the encounter between sentimental narration and abolitionist ideals within the psyche of the very entity it wishes to represent.

With its reliance on the body as the privileged structure for communicating meaning, sentimental fiction thus constantly reinscribes the troubling relation between personhood and corporeality that underlies the projects of both abolition and feminism. The issues I have been exploring are not peripheral to feminist concerns, for by responding to the representational problems posed by the black body with a rhetoric of racial amalgamation, the women who wrote these antislavery stories encode the racial problematic within a sexual one. The "rubbing off" of blackness that characterizes antislavery fiction emulates the whitening produced by miscegenation. Moreover, miscegenation provides an essential motif of virtually all antislavery fiction, for even in those stories in which escape, slave rebellion, or the separation of families dominate the plot, its multiple challenges suffuse the text. My identification of the human body as the site at which feminist and abolitionist discourses intersect can be further particularized in the images of the black woman's rape by the white man; or their unsanctioned, unprotected, and unequal love; or the always suppressed possibility of the white woman's desire for the black man; or the black man's never sufficiently castrated attraction to the white woman; or, most of all, in the ubiquitous light-skinned slave whose body attests to the sexual mingling of black and white. Though it marks the intersection of abolitionist and feminist discourses, the body of the light-skinned slave means differently for each of them: the less easily race can be read from this flesh, the more clearly the white man's repeated penetrations of the black body are imprinted there. The quadroon's one-fourth blackness represents two generations of miscegenating intercourse, the octoroon's three—their numerical names attesting to society's desire to keep track of an ever less visible black ancestry even at the cost of counting the generations of institutionalized sexual exploitation.

Critical discussions of the mulattoes, quadroons, and octoroons who figure in these texts have dealt almost exclusively with the obvious racist allegiances that make a light-skinned hero or heroine more attractive to a white audience, and that presume that the feelings of identification so essential for sentimental fiction cannot cross race lines.[47] I am not interested in defending either authors or audiences from this charge. My discussion of the rhetoric of amalgamation already suggests that the light-skinned body is valued in this fiction precisely because of its ability to mask the alien African blackness that the fictional mulatto is nevertheless purported to represent. I would contend, however, that an acknowledgment of this racism ought to inaugurate, not foreclose, discussion of antislavery fiction's fascination with miscegenation. For at stake in this obsession with the fictionalized figure of the mulatto is the essential dilemma of both feminist and abolitionist projects: that the recognition of ownership of one's own body as essential to claiming personhood is matched by the fear of being imprisoned, silenced, deprived of personhood by that same body. The fictional mulatto combines this problematics of corporeality and identity for both discourses because miscegenation and the children it produces stand as a bodily challenge to the conventions of reading the body, thus simultaneously insisting that the body is a sign of identity and undermining the assurance with which that sign can be read. Moreover, stories of miscegenation inevitably link the racial and the sexual, demonstrating the asymmetry of abolitionist and feminist concerns—and the now familiar ways in which, by identifying with her enslaved sister, the free woman comes to betray her.

In the American South miscegenation usually took the form of the rape and concubinage of slave women by their white masters. Caroline Healey Dall's "Amy," published in the *Liberty Bell* of 1849, tells this story, and records in its telling the interlocking structure of patriarchy's dual systems of racial oppression and sexual exploitation. The story begins with a marriage: "In Southern fashion, Edith was not quite 16 when she was wooed and won, and borne, a willing captive, to a patriarchal dwelling." Edith's ambiguous role as a willing captive within the patriarchal systems of marriage and slaveholding becomes more sinister and more evident as the story progresses and she eventually proves willing to prostitute her slave and half sister Amy. "The offspring of a lawless and unrequited affection," Amy, Dall explains, "had, nevertheless, unconsciously dedicated her whole being to vestal chastity. But nothing availed." The problem of Amy's ancestry is not, despite prevailing cultural expectations, that as the child of lawless sexuality she has inherited lascivious desires but rather that as the child of sexual exploitation she has inherited the role of being exploited. Her body displays not only a history of past miscegenation but also a promise of future mixings.

A friend of Edith's new husband sees Amy, reads both her desirability and her vulnerability on her "graceful form," and reenacts a parodic version (or is it?) of the wooing and winning with which the story begins. The woman Charles Hartley must woo in order to win Amy is, however, not Amy but her mistress, Edith. In this transaction Amy is prostituted as much by the white woman's reluctance to discuss sex as by the white man's desire to indulge in it. For as Charles keeps pressing Edith to procure Amy for him, Edith comes to see her slave's sexual modesty as a threat to her own delicacy:

> Not only did the whole subject distress her, but to be so besought on such a subject, by one until lately a stranger, was a perpetual wound to her delicacy. She felt herself losing ground in her own self-respect. Her husband regarded it as a

desecration, and repeatedly asked whether her own life was to be worn out in defense of Amy.

In the end, concurring with her husband's insistence on the sanctity of her delicacy, Edith signs the "deed of transfer." In Dall's story the pairing of feminist and abolitionist concerns proves double-edged: for if Edith's inability to prevent male desire, or refute male conceptions of feminine purity, allies her to her powerless slaves and names her a captive of patriarchy, she nevertheless complies fully in Amy's sexual victimization. The role of feminine delicacy which she accepts is paid for not just by her own loss of efficacy but by Amy's destruction. Dall's critique of female delicacy identifies it as an essential prop both for the subordination and demoralization of women and for the exploitation of slaves. The narrative voice in which Dall tells this story, however, conforms to the requirements of the delicacy it condemns. In describing Amy as "dedicated . . . to a vestal chastity," it is the narrator, not Edith's husband, who first equates female purity with the sacred, while in calling the lust that fathered Amy "affection" Dall mitigates the very evil her story was intended to expose. The problem is that traditional notions of female purity attach both to the body—in its vulnerability to rape or enforced concubinage—and to language. The conventions of chastity count speech as a sexual assault; hence Edith can describe Charles's propositions as a "perpetual wound." Dall fears that to name explicitly the obscene events that comprise her plot would be experienced by her readers as the infliction of wounds. The cultural critique that she voices is leveled at her own prose, for in respecting the sensibilities of her readers she adheres to the dictates of a linguistic delicacy that, she has demonstrated, simultaneously protects against and inflicts physical indecencies.[48]

The sacrifice of Amy's chastity serves not only to defend Edith's delicacy but also, paradoxically, to provide her with a variety of safely mediated sexual experiences. After all, it is to Edith that Charles brings his suit for sexual favors, and—after the requisite protestations of lost self-respect—it is Edith who yields. That she can yield Amy's body rather than her own demonstrates the usefulness of the slave woman as a surrogate for the white woman's sexuality, and particularly the usefulness of the mulatta, who in being part white and part black (and in Amy's case, being more explicitly half sibling and half not) simultaneously embodies self and other. Thus, through the prostitution of Amy, Edith gains a degree of sexual license forbidden the proper bourgeois woman.

Edith's husband and her husband's friend, however, fill virtually interchangeable roles in this narrative, both equally involved in demanding Edith's compliance. Her husband's anger over her desecration is directed at her initial defense of Amy's chastity, not at Charles's presumption in bringing the matter up. Consequently, even Edith's passive and unconscious circumvention of sexual prohibitions ultimately demonstrates that the white woman, like her slave, remains a sexual possession of the white man. In these terms fictional depictions of the slave woman's sexual vulnerability may themselves constitute an act of betrayal not unlike Edith's own, for in such stories antislavery rhetoric disguises, and so permits, the white woman's unacknowledgeable feelings of sexual victimization and desire. The insights and emotions granted to the white woman by such conflations of the racial and the sexual remain divorced from her body. If, as Lucy Stone insisted, the ability to control the "uses" of one's own body constitutes the most basic condition of freedom, then for the white woman the strongest proof that she is not owned by the white man lies in the inadmissible possibility of using her body elsewhere—a possibility only granted her, within antislavery fiction, through a vicarious reading of the body of the slave.[49]

In antislavery fiction the story of the white woman's desire for the black man is not told, and his desire for her is constantly reduced to the safer dimensions of a loyal slave's nominally asexual adoration of his good and kind mistress.[50] Child comes closest to voicing these desires not in her fiction but in her first abolitionist tract, *An Appeal in Favor of that Class of Americans Called Africans.* While this book established her as an abolitionist leader, it cost her both her popular readership (so many subscriptions to the *Juvenile Miscellany* were canceled by horrified parents that the series was forced to fold), and, with her expulsion from the Athenaeum, her position in Boston literary society.

Perhaps chief among the *Appeal*'s many challenges to societal norms was Child's call for the repeal of antimiscegenation laws.[51] Although her attack on these discriminatory statutes explicitly distinguishes between society's refusal to sanction interracial marriage and its willingness to condone such liaisons out of wedlock, she implies that what is at stake in these contradictory attitudes is not miscegenation per se but rather the patriarchal melding of sexual and racial oppression that assures the supremacy of the white man, granting only to him the freedom to choose his sexual partners.

> An unjust law exists in this Commonwealth, by which marriages between persons of different color is pronounced illegal. I am perfectly aware of the gross ridicule to which I may subject myself by alluding to this particular; but I have lived too long, and observed too much, to be disturbed by the world's mockery. . . . Under existing circumstances, none but those whose condition in life is too low to be much affected by public opinion, will form such alliances; and they, when they choose to do so, *will* make such marriages in spite of the law. I know two or three instances where women of the laboring class have been united to reputable, industrious colored men. These husbands regularly bring home their wages, and are kind to their families. If by some odd chances, which not unfrequently occur in the world, their wives should become heirs to any property, the children may be wronged out of it, because the law pronounces them illegitimate. And while this injustice exists with regard to *honest*, industrious individuals, who are merely guilty of differing from us in a matter of taste, neither the legislation nor customs of slaveholding States exert their influence against *immoral* connexions.

In the next paragraph she discusses the "temporary connexions" made by "White gentlemen of the first-rank" and New Orleans quadroons.[52] Her examples of illegal miscegenating marriages pointedly make the woman white and the man black, while the case of the quadroon concubine pairs race and sex differently. Child's care in this passage to discriminate her own desires from those she discusses indicates the strength of the taboo against which she writes. For even as she disclaims any concern for the "world's mockery," Child admits the impossibility, at least under the prevailing social conditions, of any but the very low so utterly discounting public opinion as to enter into such a union. Child risks a defense of this most subversive version of miscegenation only when she has placed the sturdy barrier of class between herself and the women who enact it. By asserting that the female laborers who choose black mates are "merely guilty of differing from us in a matter of taste," Child insists on the disstinction between tastes and morals, and on the comparative insignificance of the former. But by using this moment to forge an identification with her readers based on a shared set of tastes, she backs away from her argument, suggesting the power of social sanctions to delimit desires. Thus even here, in perhaps the most daring argument in her most daring text, Child refrains from denouncing society's distaste for a form of miscegenation that would threaten and exclude the white man. Instead, as she names herself part of the social "us," her persuasive strategy of identification collapses into a defensive one.

In light of Child's caveats it is hardly surprising that, at least so far as I am aware, no antislavery fiction admits to the possibility of a white woman loving or wedding a black man.[53] Yet I suggest that this forbidden desire constitutes a repressed but never completely obliterated narrative within even the most conventional of these stories. Recalling Stowe's and Green's portraits of their black heroes, it is now evident that one of the tasks implicit in the amalgamating strategies that constructed these Herculeses is the creation of a black man who can be easily assimilated to the white woman's sexual tastes. Once again it is the figure of the mulatta who permits this desire to be inscribed. The light skin of the mulatta names her white, yet her black ancestry keeps her union with the black hero from being labeled miscegenation. Through this figure the love of a white-skinned woman and a black-skinned man can be designated, and even endorsed, without being scandalous. The polysemous body of the fictional mulatta simultaneously expresses the white woman's desires and protects her from them by marking them safely alien.

Clearly not intended to articulate a feminist position, Frances Green's "The Slave-Wife" tells the familiar abolitionist story of a slave woman's sexual exploitation by her master, despite her—legally null—marriage. But because of her complexion this story encloses another narrative, the tale of a white woman's preference for a black lover. Even hidden under the mask of the mulatta, this story of the inadmissible union of a white woman and a black man is so threatening that it must be dismantled at the very moment it is made, so that the story becomes a sequence of alternating disavowals and contradictions.

Laco Ray's description of his wife proffers a double reading of her race: "She was white. At least no one would suspect that she had any African blood in her veins." The modifications that follow cannot erase the clarity of that first adamant assertion of her whiteness. Laco's wife is named Clusy; it is a slave name, unfit for a free-born woman, so that Clusy's name and her body sustain the tension already noted between her African blood and white flesh. Just as Clusy's flesh, ancestry, and name offer conflicting signs to her identity, the story's plot consists of a series of displacements in which Laco Ray and his master alternately claim the trophy that is Clusy. Their competition, like Clusy's ambiguous race, serves to contain the white woman's scandalous desire for the black man; for as master and husband each attempt to claim exclusive sexual rights, the question of the woman's choice and desire is made moot. Laco Ray's narration of this rivalry makes it clear that he sees the price of loss as the distinctly patriarchal threat of castration:

> She was beautiful. She was in her master's power. She was in the power of every white man that chose to possess her, she was no longer mine. She was not my wife.

The question of "The Slave-Wife" is whether or not a black man can possess a woman—particularly a white woman—and from its very title, which simultaneously makes Clusy a wife and yet fetters that role with the apparently contradictory one of slave, the answer remains ambiguous.

Despite Laco's sense of dispossession, the white man's power never quite controls Clusy. Finally, as Laco reports it, Clusy, continuing to reject the master's "wishes," "was bound to the stake; and while cruel and vulgar men mocked her agony, THERE *our babe was born!*" The torture that attempts to make Clusy the white man's sexual property only succeeds in eliciting proof of her sexual intimacy with a black man. Yet once again the message is double, for the child who marks Laco's potency in the face of the master's power is stillborn. Weak from childbirth and beatings, Clusy escapes with Laco Ray only to die before reaching Canada. The story ends here with a stalemate. The inconclusiveness of both Laco's and his master's attempts to claim Clusy reflects Green's own incapacity to give the white woman to the black man, even as it attests to her desire to do so.

Laco's final request that his auditor "publish it abroad" recasts the story not as one of male possession, whether white or black, but as one of female desires and female virtue:

> for if any woman can hear [this story] without a wish, a determination to labor with all her might to abolish THE SLAVERY OF WOMAN, I impeach her virtue—she is *not* TRUE—she is NOT PURE.[54]

The passage asserts that sexual virtue consists not of a delicacy that eschews sexual topics but of a purity that opposes sexual exploitation. This definition of sexual virtue makes abolition a question of woman's rights. Laco's phrase "the slavery of woman" carries two meanings, and Clusy's story illustrates the impossibility of separating them.

What interests me about this merger of feminist and abolitionist arguments is that unlike many of the instances discussed above, Green's narrative appears to be oblivious to the connections it nonetheless makes. The rhetoric of "The

Slave-Wife" stresses the contradictions inherent in Clusy's double role as chattel and spouse; it disregards the ways in which the two terms might be identical and Green's title a tautology. Thus the story defines slavery as a woman's issue at the same time that it writes woman's desire out of woman's rights, denying and hiding the sexual body of the white woman. Yet by depicting Laco Ray and his master as rival claimants for the possession of Clusy, her positions as wife and slave are implicitly made analogous: in both cases she is male property, and in neither case are her desires, including her subversive preference for her black husband, permitted autonomous expression. From a feminist perspective these implications discredit Laco Ray's desire to have Clusy as his own, and hence to own her, and they therefore undermine his sympathetic position in Green's abolitionist argument. That the links between sexual and racial oppression strategically forged by feminist-abolitionists hold, even within narratives whose logic is jeopardized by this coupling, suggests that these links have become so normative as to be unavoidable. Thus the antislavery stories written by women who appear to have no intention of questioning marital or familial relations constantly employ rhetoric or depict scenarios that jar against their benign assumptions about woman's proper domestic place.

Antislavery fiction's focus on miscegenation evades the difficulties of representing blackness by casting the racial problematics of slavery into the terms of sexual oppression. In defining the question of ownership of one's body as a sexual question, the ideal of liberty and the commercial concept of ownership attain not only an intimately corporeal but also an explicitly marital or domestic dimension. This presentation of slavery as sexual, marital, and domestic abuse thematizes the structure of the genre as a whole, since antislavery stories attempt to describe slave experience within the feminine forms of domestic fiction. Sentimental antislavery stories are constructed on the foundation of a presumed alliance between abolitionist goals and domestic values, an alliance fraught with asymmetries and contradictions. The domestic realm of women and children occupies, after all, a paradoxical place in feminist and abolitionist arguments. For feminists, it constitutes not only the source of woman's power, but also, antithetically, the sphere in which she finds herself incarcerated. For abolitionists, the domestic values that ostensibly offer a positive alternative to the mores of plantation society simultaneously mask slavery's exploitations behind domesticity's gentle features.

Situated outside the specifically abolitionist forums provided by antislavery societies, even further detached from the woman's rights movement, and aimed at the most sentimental figure of the domestic scene—the good child—the antislavery stories written for Sunday school primers baldly exemplify the narrative disjunctions inherent in attempts to domesticate slavery. Julia Coleman and Matilda Thompson's collection of such stories, *The Child's Anti-Slavery Book*, first published by the evangelical American Tract Society in 1859 and then twice reprinted in the "Books for Sunday School" series of a New York publisher, provides a characteristic and fairly popular sample of the genre. The collection constantly inscribes its own domesticity.

The introduction, "A Few Words about American Slave Children," begins by describing the loving, happy homes of the American free children who constitute its readership. Such homes are then replicated within the stories themselves. Thus "Aunt Judy's Story" narrates the life of this elderly ex-slave through a frame in which Mrs. Ford tells her children the tale of their impoverished neighbor, with daughter Cornelia "leaning her little curly head against her mother's knee," while they discuss the likelihood of Judy's children having been torn away from her maternal knee. The virtue of the Ford home marks every exchange. If Cornelia is "getting a little impatient," the narrator turns to remind the child reader, who might mistakenly see this moment as condoning such behavior, that it was "only a little, for Cornelia was remarkable for her sweet and placid disposition." Bountiful meals are consumed in every chapter, and neither parent ever passes up an opportunity for a moral lesson; nor does Mrs. Ford ever fail to revel in "every act of kindness to the poor and needy performed by her children." In these Sunday-school stories, lessons in patience and generosity—the everyday virtues of domestic life—inextricably mingle with the teaching of antislavery. The Fords treat Aunt Judy as a site for the moral education of their children, while the promised story of her life serves as a didactic and desirable form of entertainment: "Dear papa, tells us a story with a poor slave in it, won't you?" Cornelia implores.[55]

The subordination of the poor slave to the family who tells her story bespeaks the dominance inherent in the act of representation: the Ford children "profit" from Aunt Judy in a manner more moralistic than, but not sufficiently distinct from, the material profits reaped by the slaveowners her story teaches them to condemn. On the other hand, the family these children inhabit, and the lessons of patience and selflessness they are taught, reproduce under the benign guise of domesticity a hierarchy structurally quite similar to that of slavery itself.[56] The sentimental and domestic values engaged in the critique of slavery are compromised by the connection and implicated in the very patterns they are employed to expose. The values of the loving family embodied in the doting mother and the dutiful child look, despite all disclaimers, and despite all differences, much like the values of the plantation. But because the domesticity of women and children is glorified in these stories, the fact of subjugation and the disavowal of freedom implicit in domestic values remain masked.

Coleman and Thompson's defensive insistence on the differences between slavery and family suggests that even the most emphatically domestic writers were aware of the danger that their stories might collapse the very distinctions they were designed to uphold. For example, when in "A Few Words about American Slave Children" they attempt to differentiate between the experiences of slave and free children, the similarities between the two haunt their arguments.

> Though born beneath the same sun and on the same soil, with the same natural right to freedom as yourselves, they are nevertheless SLAVES. Alas for them! Their parents cannot train them as they will, for they too have MASTERS.

"They too have masters," the passage explains, and, whatever is learned about the powerlessness of slave parents, the notion that all children have masters is equally clear—for who, except the child, stands on the other side of that "too"? This conception of all children as unfree slips between the emphatic insistence (so emphatic because so precarious?) that "Children, you are free and happy. . . . *You are free children!*" Yet the very description of this freedom reveals it to be, at best, deferred.

> When you become men and women you will have full liberty to earn your living, to go, to come, to seek pleasure or profit in any way that you may choose, so long as you do not meddle with the rights of other people.[57]

In short, the liberty described is projected into the future, not attainable for the child within the family structure. The male bias of even this deferred freedom is made obvious by a nearly identical passage from another antislavery book for children from the period. *The Child's Book on Slavery, or Slavery Made Plain* was published as part of a series "for Sabbath Schools" in Cincinnati.

> When the Child grows to be a man or woman he can go and do for himself, is his own ruler, and can act just as he pleases, if he only does right. He can go and come, he can buy and sell; if he has a wife and children, they cannot be taken away, and he is all his life *free.*[58]

The absurdity of the child grown to be a woman ever having a wife makes it clear that the passage's slide into the singular masculine pronoun, and everything logically attributable to *him*, is not only idiomatically conventional but poignantly symptomatic. Indeed, the ability to have "a wife and children," like the ability to "go and come" or "buy and sell" defines freedom, so that the juxtaposition of these pairs categorizes women and children not as potential free persons, but rather as the signs and conditions of another's freedom. The freedom so defined in these antislavery books is available to neither child nor woman. The domestic ideology that informs the genre can no more accommodate an actual, corporeal, and present freedom than can the slave ideology itself.

The homological ideologies of the family and of slave society need not imply, antislavery writers insist, that both structures support the same meanings: thus the patriarchal pattern that would signal exploitation and power in the case of a plantation society could mean benevolent protection and love within a familial setting. "The relation between the child and the parent is first and chiefly for the child's good, but the relation between the slave and his master is for the master's pleasure," the anonymous author of *The Child's Book on Slavery* explains. In both cases the less powerful "must obey" the more powerful, but, the author asserts, the good garnered by such obedience accrues differently.[59] Leveled against proslavery assurances that bondage is beneficial to the weaker African race, this logic also defends against the specter of parental pleasure in the subservience of the child, and by extension, of patriarchal pleasure in the conventions of domestic hierarchy. The difference between slavery and domestic order is cast as a conflict between selfish hedonism and benevolence; in this Sunday-school primer, the critique of pecuniary motives is displaced by a discussion of moral considerations.[60] By situating antislavery discourse within an idealized domestic setting, these stories purport to offer moral and emotional standards by which to measure, and through which to correct, the evils of slavery. The problem is that these standards are implicated in the values and structures of authority and profit they seek to criticize. The contradictions inherent in the alliance of abolitionist thought and domestic ideals can be identified, in part, as the conflict between a structural or material and an emotional or moral conception of social reality. Failing to discover tangible and stable grounds on which to distinguish idealized domestic values from the abhorred system of slavery, antislavery writers retreat to the realm of the intangible; once they do so their arguments for the difference between slavery and domesticity reconstruct this opposition in terms of the tension between physical and spiritual ontologies and epistemologies.

Feminist-abolitionist awareness of the need to recognize the links between one's identity and one's body, and of all the difficulties inherent in such a recognition, informs, as I have argued, the problems of representation that characterize antislavery fiction. The domestic and sentimental conventions of this fiction, however, also subscribe to a moral, emotional, and fundamentally spiritual code that devalues bodily constraints to focus on the soul. As employed in the service of patriarchal authority, the distinction between body and soul traditionally functioned to increase, not decrease, social control over the body. Historically this distinction had buttressed Christian apologies for slavery as it enabled the pious simultaneously to exploit bodies and save souls.[61] Similarly, an emphasis on the special and discrete nature of the spiritual realm permitted women's souls a power denied their bodies. It has been frequently demonstrated that in losing economic and political power with the rise of bourgeois society, the American woman increased her value as the moral and spiritual guardian of the nation; her gain in moral status bolstered her exclusion from the political and commercial arenas.[62]

The writers of antislavery fiction seem well aware of the oppressive consequences of locating personhood in the soul. The hypocritical minister who defends slavery as a means of converting the heathens of Africa, and levies docility with the threat of hellfire for those who do not follow the Biblical injunction "Servants obey your masters," serves as a stock villain of this fiction. Equally familiar is the ineffectual kind mistress, who, like Stowe's Mrs. Shelby, is prevented by her husband from participating in economic decisions but is expected to provide piety and benevolence for the whole family.[63] Despite these depictions of how evocations of a spiritual reality can be used as a placebo for women's and slaves' lack of social power, antislavery fiction nevertheless endorses the belief in an alternate spiritual realm where power and efficacy are distributed differently. From this perspective the powerlessness of women and slaves does not matter, because, whatever the condition of their bodies, their souls remain blessed and free.

The most famous instance of such recourse to the refuge provided by a separate spiritual reality is, of course, the victory of Tom's spiritual power over Simon Legree's physical brutality.

> "Did n't I pay down twelve hundred dollars, cash, for all there is inside yer old cussed black shell? An't yer mine, now, body and soul?" he said, giving Tom a violent kick with his heavy boot; "tell me!"
>
> In the very depth of physical suffering, bowed by brutal oppression, this question shot a gleam of joy and triumph through Tom's soul. . . .
>
> "No! no! no! my soul an't yours, Mas'r! You have n't bought it,—ye can't buy it! It's been bought and paid for, by one that is able to keep it."[64]

In this passage Stowe insists on the oppressiveness of physical reality: the constraints of Tom's position can be weighed and measured; the boot is heavy. The triumph of Tom's soul is thus emphatically presented as rebutting material conceptions of personhood. In response to Legree's threats and abuses, Tom insists on the irrelevance of the condition of his body in identifying him as a man.[65] The primacy granted Tom's soul in constituting his identity is the culmination of a process evident throughout the novel. Although Stowe describes Tom's body explicitly and frequently in the same Herculean terms she later uses in her portrait of Dred, her emphasis on the childlike and feminine character of his soul supplants these physical descriptions so that in most readers' minds, and in George Cruikshank's 1852 illustrations, Tom appears effeminate and weak. Thus her celebration of Tom's soul serves to erase his flesh. Equally telling is Stowe's failure to imagine an America in which blacks could be recognized as persons. Perhaps the most disturbing insight of her novel is that the utopian freedom she constructs is predicated upon the absence of black bodies: Tom's "victory" wins him the freedom of heaven; George, Eliza, and the rest find theirs only in Liberia.

The Christian and sentimental vision of noncorporeal freedom and personhood obfuscates the conception of the corporeality of the self with which I credit feminist-abolitionist discourse. Yet I would argue that antislavery fiction's recourse to the obliteration of black bodies as the only solution to the problem of slavery actually confirms the ways in which feminist-abolitionist projects of liberation forced a recognition of the bodiliness of personhood. Antislavery writers' tendency to do away with bodies stands as a testimony to their terrified sense that the body is inescapable. Thus, graphically extending the ways in which the freedom praised by domestic fiction excludes women and children, the freedom offered by antislavery fiction regularly depends upon killing off black bodies, defining death as a glorious emancipation from plantation slavery. "A Thought upon Emancipation" in the *Liberty Chimes* offers this vision of immediate abolition:

> Even, now, the slave himself need no longer be a slave. Has he the heroism to prefer death to slavery and the system is at an end.
>
> Let the terrible determination go forth through all Slavedom, that the slave *will not* work—*will not* eat—*will not* rise up or lie down at the bidding of an owner and will be free or *die*, and it is done. Tomorrow's sun beholds a notion of freedom indeed.[66]

What is done, terminated, in this fantasy is not only slavery but all slaves. The apocalyptic tone of the piece does provide the radical reinterpretation of freedom it promises. Antislavery writing responds to slavery's annihilation of personhood with its own act of annihilation.

The obliteration of the body thus stands as the pain-filled consequence of recognizing the extent to which the body designates identity. Indeed this glorification of death is but a more extreme example of processes already evident in the domestic, amalgamating, and appropriative strategies that characterize the various attempts by feminist-abolitionist discourse to transform the body from a site of oppression into the grounds of resisting that oppression. The discovery that these efforts to liberate the body result in its repression and annihilation attests to the difficulties and resistance inherent in acknowledging the corporeality of personhood. The bodies feminists and abolitionists wish reclaimed, and the bodies they exploit, deny, or obliterate in the attempted rescue are the same.

2

To Stand Between
Walt Whitman's Poetics of Merger and Embodiment

The contradictory desires evident in feminist and abolitionist attempts to negate the very bodies they had pledged to liberate are not confined to the impassioned realm of oppositional politics. Rather, such contradictions bespeak the pressures slavery had placed far more generally on the culture's ability to define personhood. In this chapter I argue that this ambivalent desire for identity to prove at once embodied and disembodied provides both the basis for Walt Whitman's vision of national reconciliation and the formal structure of his poetics. In turning from feminist-abolitionist rhetorics to canonized poetry I hope to demonstrate that questions of national union, poetic style, and individual identity may be mutually constitutive.

At that moment in his early notebook jottings when Whitman first assumes his new voice and verse form, he defines what it means to be a poet, and specifically to be the poet of the body, in terms provided by American slavery. Claiming to reconcile racially distinct bodies, Whitman locates the poet in the sexually charged middle space between masters and slaves:

> I am the poet of slaves and of the masters of slaves
> I am the poet of the body
> And I am
> I am the poet of the body
> And I am the poet of the soul
> I go with the slaves of the earth equally with the masters

And I will stand between the masters and the slaves
Entering into both so that both shall understand me alike.[1]

Only two of these lines are actually preserved in *Leaves of Grass:* "I am the poet of the body, / And I am the poet of the soul" introduces the twenty-first section of the poem Whitman ultimately called "Song of Myself," offering a self-defining summation that has informed most subsequent readings of Whitman's poetics.[2] Slavery is not mentioned in any published version of section 21; it has disappeared, leaving the pairing of body and soul as its only trace. A sense of the political import of Whitman's poetics of embodiment is similarly absent from most critical assessments of his work.[3] Yet in these notebook lines Whitman depicts his strategy of singing the body as a practice derived from the dynamics of American slavery. My discussion of Whitman's poetics reassesses the political sources and implications of his corporeal poetry, demonstrating that his celebration of the body not only reinterprets the body but also uses that reinterpretation to redefine the political. Even Whitman's effacement of the political origins of his poetics, as in his deletion of master and slave from these lines, ultimately serves not to dismiss the political in favor of the personal and bodily, but rather to absorb each into the other, to demonstrate that the same issues that inform political practice also designate individual identity.

In locating the poet between master and slave, and between body and soul, Whitman attempts to claim for his poetry the power to mediate oppositions. Able to speak for both sides, the poet alone seems capable of overcoming both the difference between slave and master that divides American society and the division between body and soul that makes the identity of each individual problematic. Moreover, in locating the poet between these two concerns, Whitman proposes to equate political questions with the question of the body, and hence to relate the structure of social practices to the structure of personal identity. What I call Whitman's poetics of merger and embodiment refers, then, both to his poetic goal of healing radical divisions, social and personal, and to the poetic strategies by which he attempts to effect that goal.

Merger and embodiment are linked strategies in this poetics: merger, the perfect melding of opposites into a complete undifferentiated oneness, is best exemplified for Whitman in the physical imagery of the sexual embrace. What Whitman seeks in his poetry is simultaneously to express the particularity of bodily experience—he frequently compares his poetry to the human body—and to promote the healing sameness of merger. The practice of miscegenation or racial amalgamation associated with plantation slavery thus provides within Whitman's writings an historically resonant vocabulary with which to examine his poetics: in the scene of miscegenation racially distinct bodies merge. Presenting the poet as standing between master and slave, body and soul, the political and the personal, the ideals of merger and of bodily specificity, Whitman asserts the power of poetry, but such a presentation also inadvertently reveals the limitations of that power, the ways in which such poetry must remain contingent upon the very divisions it claims to heal.

Whitman's first notebook poetry records his developing sense of what it means to call himself "poet." The lines begin with a feat of autogenesis: "I am the poet," he writes, in a triumph of essentialism, a gesture of autonomous identity and agency. No sooner is this self-assured assertion of being made, however, than it is undermined. The "of" that relates the poet to his topic also appears as the tie between master and slave. Here Whitman recognizes that to assume the name of poet is to assume mastery and possession, but, as he further demonstrates, the line also weakens all claims to autonomy, for the slave comes first, identifying and so delimiting what it means to be master: after all, to be the "master of slaves" is a lesser, more circumscribed. claim than that of being "master." The relation signaled by "of" remains simultaneously possessive and partitive: does the topic belong to the poet or is the poet part of his topic?

In identifying himself as the poet of the body in the subsequent line, Whitman might appear to evade these problems, since the topic of the body seems to replace the dynamics of possession and mastery with one of identity. I would argue, however, that these lines ought to be read as apposites, and that in defining himself as both the poet of slavery and the poet of the body Whitman points to the interdependence of these two concerns. The question of mastery and the question of identity are ultimately the same question. As I have demonstrated in the previous chapter, the practices of American slavery call attention to the ways in which the condition and status of one's body designate identity. Whitman shared this insight, asserting in "Crossing Brooklyn Ferry" that "I too have received identity by my body" (l.63); thus Whitman's focus on the body repeats rather than escapes the failure of autonomy and the strictures of mastery with which these lines began. Whitman gives up here, breaking off the next line, inscribing only a beginning that trails away into blankness; in its incompleteness, "And I am" pathetically echoes Jehovah's own self-identifying tautology: I am what I am.

Whitman drew a slash across this verse, left a few lines of blank space on the page, and began again. The second version reverses the sequence so that now the pairing of body and soul introduces that of slave and master: the very ease of the reversal emphasizes Whitman's sense of these pairs as fundamentally the same. The third line originally read "Thus the slaves are mine and the masters are equally mine," making explicit the identification of poetry with mastery and the reliance of both on a notion of ownership. In the canceled line the poet stands as ultimate master, claiming ownership of all that the masters have, and beyond that, of the masters themselves. Here the equality of master and slave lies in their being "equally" possessed. Whitman's revision displaces the identification of poet with master, providing in its stead a concept of the poet as companion "go[ing] . . . equally with" slave and master. In making this change Whitman redefines the role of the poet: he replaces an essentialist conception of

the self-created poet with the anti-essentialist insight that poetic power results from occupying a specific relational position. The "I" who "will stand between" gains the ability to
be "understood," and so takes the name of poet, by occupying the place of linkage between the opposing but interde-
pendent roles of master and slave. That the desire to be under*stood* punningly recapitulates the hierarchic standing of
master and slave suggests the precariousness, if not the impossibility, of Whitman's poetic goal.

Whitman's first notebook poetry thus charts the development of his conception of the poet from an autonomous, self-
made being to a site of mediation. In this latter view the poet
is simply what stands between. If the poet articulates body
and soul, master and slave, these terms and relations similarly constitute the place and role of the poet. In these early
lines Whitman does more than merely stake out a topic.
Rather, by identifying the poet as mediator, he traces the
ways in which the oppositional nature of his subject matter
defines his poetic voice.[4] So later, in *Leaves of Grass*, Whitman
identifies miscegenation—the erotic merger of racially distinct bodies—as a model for poetic power, even as this new
voice makes the uttering of such topics possible.

"I Sing the Body Electric" comprises Whitman's most insistent demonstration of his ideal of poetic embodiment, that
the supple, flexing body of the "wellmade man," "conveys as
much as the best poem . . . perhaps more" (l. 11). His claim
that the wellmade body and the best poem are equally ex-
pressive suggests that flesh and words can serve as substitutes for each other. The programmatic aim of this poem is to
collapse the two meanings of *convey:* to present what is car-
ried by the body and what can be communicated by words as
the same. Significantly, Whitman fashions this "Poem of the
Body," as it was perhaps more appropriately entitled in 1856,
out of the least celebratory, most exploitative of discourses on
the body: the chant of the auctioneer hawking slaves.

A slave at auction!
I help the auctioneer. . . . the sloven does not half know his
    business.

Gentlemen look on this curious creature,
Whatever the bids of the bidders they cannot be high
    enough for him,
For him the globe lay preparing quintillions of years
    without one animal or plant,
For him the revolving cycles truly and steadily rolled.
                              (ll. 83–87)

Like the poet, the auctioneer stands between slave and master, product and buyer; the business of both is to sing the value of the thing at hand and to extract the assent of purchase from their audience. In usurping the place of the auctioneer, Whitman is, of course, criticizing his office, demonstrating that even the hyperbole of the auctioneer's pitch grossly understates the value of the item on the block: the human body, he opines, is hardly paid for by all time and the entire world. But he is also inadvertently demonstrating the uneasy parallels between his poetics and the practices of American slavery, the ways in which the act of celebrating a body resembles the act of selling one so that his task as poet corresponds to that of the auctioneer. The parallels prove even closer, for Whitman's concept of embodiment is delimited by the body of the slave.

On the auction block, regardless of any other claims to identity a slave might express, he or she is nothing but body, flesh for sale. The slave at auction provides the quintessential instance of what it means for one's identity to be entirely dependent upon one's body. Though many other human bodies are celebrated in this poem, and throughout Whitman's poetry, to a significant degree Whitman's fundamental image of the body remains that of the slave: one central example of the completely corporeal person. The description of the negro driver in "Song of Myself" suggestively matches in the details of dress and posture the drawing of Whitman that replaces his name on the title page of the 1855 *Leaves of Grass*.

The negro that drives the huge dray of the stoneyard. . . .
    steady and tall he stands poised on one leg on the
    stringpiece,

His blue shirt exposes his ample neck and breast and
      loosens over his hipband,
His glance is calm and commanding. . . . he tosses the
      slouch of his hat away from his forehead,
The sun falls on his crispy hair and moustache. . . . falls on
      the black of his polish'd and perfect limbs.
                                                    (ll. 220–23)

Whitman's placement of the drawing, as has often been argued, privileges flesh, or at least the image of flesh, over
name or word as a pointer to identity. It is the first instance of
the book's complex and self-conscious strategies of self-
incarnation: "Whoever touches this book touches a man."
The substitution of a portrait for his name, and the similarities between that portrait and his description of a black man
indicate comparable efforts on Whitman's part to assert the
corporeality of his own identity.

To argue that in Whitman's poems the challenge of bodiliness gains its absoluteness and urgency from even an indi-
rect comparison of the black salable body of the slave and his
own is, however, to tell only half the story. Whitman proposes to unify a discordant America by creating a poetry that
would reconcile bodily differences. The intense bodiliness of
the slave at auction thus simultaneously initiates Whitman's
poetic project and poses the major obstacle to its achievement. The auction block initiates Whitman's poetic project by
staging his attempt to negotiate the space between master
and slave. It poses the major obstacle to the achievement of
this project of poetic reconciliation because, though Whitman insists on the materiality of all being, and particularly of
our sense of otherness, he can find no way to heal these divisions that does not dissolve the bodies out of which his poetry is made. Despite his exuberant rhetoric of celebration,
despite his insistence that in singing the body this poem
overcomes all bodily differences, the costs and contradictions
inherent in his double goals of merger and embodiment remain visible. So, as auctioneer in "I Sing the Body Electric,"
Whitman gradually strips away the slave's skin, dismember-
ing the body in the act of celebrating it, until all that is left is
eternal and ubiquitous blood.

Examine these limbs, red black or white. . . . they are very
    cunning in tendon and nerve;
They shall be stript that you may see them.
Exquisite senses, lifelit eyes, pluck, volition,
Flakes of breastmuscle, pliant backbone and neck, flesh not
    flabby, goodsized arms and legs,
And wonders within there yet.
Within there runs his blood. . . . the same old blood. .
    the same red running blood;

(ll. 91–96)

Here Whitman evokes blood as a physical equalizer: something of the body that is, nevertheless, not implicated in the
bodily differences of skin "red, black or white." In asking us
to imagine this blood as distinct from the bodies that contained it, Whitman nevertheless insists that it serve as a
metonym for those bodies, recalling them even as it would
replace them. The refrain of blood promises to function as refrains usually do, to promote the comfort of repetitive, nos-
talgic sameness. Yet Whitman's reliance on blood in his effort
to merge the body of the slave into a generalized humanity is,
to say the least, disturbing. From the auction block an appeal
to blood too easily recalls the bloody backs of whipped
slaves. In the lore of plantation slavery, as in all racist discourses, blood is precisely where race dwells, and the gene-
alogy and value of light-skinned slaves is traditionally measured in drops of black and white blood.[5] Whitman's poetics
of merger and his poetics of embodiment both initiate and
contradict each other. For just as Whitman's celebration of the
body results in pulling apart the slave's flesh to facilitate the
merger of the slave's notoriously different body into a vision
of human sameness, Whitman's chorus of merger and inclusion repeats the bloody, physical differentiations of plantation life.

Long before Whitman developed his new poetics of
merger and embodiment, his depictions of slavery anticipated the dynamics of the later poetry. As early as 1842 and

the publication of his "temperance novel" *Franklin Evans,*
Whitman had begun to explore what it might mean to "enter
into both" slaves and masters. Franklin Evans, in his simul-
taneous sexual allegiances to the slave Margaret and the free
Mrs. Conway, occupies a middle position that prefigures, in
gothic style, the mediating role Whitman later advocated in
his notebook poetry, and so suggests some of the dangers
and limitations of that role.

The Virginia chapters of *Franklin Evans,* making up nearly
one-third of the novel, "intrude" as Leslie Fiedler observes,
"so inappropriately upon Whitman's temperance novel"[6]
that their prominence attests to something other than an interest in the ills of drink. Whitman's attempts to connect the
story of Margaret and Mrs. Conway to his ostensible temperance theme actually serve less to explain the horrific events,
or even to identify them as a punishment for drunkenness,
than to represent intoxication itself as an issue of color.
Evans, who during the preceding chapters has left his inno-
cent rural childhood to pass through a recurring series of in-
ebriate depravities and improbable rescues, arrives in Virginia at the plantation of Mr. Bourne, where, during an
evening of wine-filled revels, he marries Bourne's slave.
Evans's marriage to the creole Margaret results, as it were,
from the darkness of drink. "In persons who use wine,"
Whitman writes,

> The mind becomes, to use an expressive word, *obfusticated,*
> and loses the power of judging quickly and with correctness.
> It seems, too, that the unhappy victim of intemperance cannot
> tell when he commits even the most egregious violations of
> right; so muddied are his perceptions, and so darkened are all
> his powers of penetration. And the worst of it is, that even in
> his sober moments, the same dark influence hangs around
> him to a great degree, and leads him into a thousand follies
> and miseries.[7]

This is, I believe, the only time in *Franklin Evans* that Whitman calls attention to his choice of words, and even as he
transforms obfuscated into a new word of his own, his de-
light in its expressiveness spills out into other words: percep-

tions are "muddied," powers of penetration "darkened" until "the same dark influence hangs" over the entire passage. By finding the word that links intoxication and miscegenation, Whitman imbues Evans with blackness. With the coining of this new word, moreover, Whitman evokes not only blackness, but also the corporeal nature of plantation authority, since the elided middle term between *obfuscate* and *obfusticate* seems to be *fustigate*.[8] The suppressed centrality of *fustigate*, a word that evokes the punitive beatings of slavery, is particularly suggestive in view of Whitman's identification of the middle place with the role of the poet. As with the blood of the auctioned slave, the mergers offered by Whitman's poems frequently depend upon a variety of batterings. Thus, even before Evans's marriage and the arrival of blue-eyed Mrs. Conway place him between dark and fair-skinned lovers, alcohol has already fashioned him into the cipher of a violent, muddied, and *obfusticated* whiteness.

In miscegenation Whitman finds an extremely potent instance of mediation, a blatant demonstration that otherness can be reconciled, that the opposites of black and white can meet and blend. For Franklin Evans, hero and narrator of this novel, to become the locus of racial mergers, he must displace the tale's most obvious figure of miscegenation, the creole Margaret. Following sentimental conventions, Evans first describes Margaret as an amalgam, "luscious and fascinating": her complexion "just sufficiently removed from clear white, to make the spectator doubtful whether he is gazing on a brunette, or one who has indeed some hue of African blood in her veins" (204). With each description, however, Margaret's skin appears darker and the claims of her African ancestry grow less doubtful; in short, Evans's narration transforms her from an emblem of undecidability into a repository of African otherness. In this way Evans simultaneously evacuates the space where black and white meet (so that he may occupy it himself) and erects the poles of difference that make this mediation meaningful. Responding to Margaret's questions about the "northern beauty," Evans identifies the two women as perfect and absolute opposites:

" 'You have been told the truth,' said I; 'she is wonderfully fair, not dark and swarthy, which I detest!' and I turned away, sure of the effect of the sharp arrow I had winged" (209). The fair versus the dark, the adored versus the detested; by asserting difference Evans initiates discord, and consequently can position himself—the "I" who describes, loves, and hates—in the space between. The occupation of this space, the passage makes clear, requires the absolute otherness of binary opposition; and in the Virginia chapters Whitman depicts Evans at work manufacturing the discord that attests to his desirability.[9]

This middle place is not, however, simply the locus of desire, for merger ultimately requires the effacement of the mediator. In *Franklin Evans*, the self-destructive implications of mediation are figured not by Evans, but by the mulatto slave boy Louis. Like Evans, Louis stands between Margaret and Mrs. Conway. As Margaret's brother and Mrs. Conway's "page," he belongs to both women. Mrs. Conway had exacted Louis's services as a gift from the infatuated Evans; her insistence on taking Louis as her slave represents a mediated attack on Margaret, demonstrating that she, not the creole, controls Evans and his property. In claiming possession of Louis, Mrs. Conway wounds Margaret. Thus there is proper symmetry in Margaret's use of Louis as the weapon with which she first wounds Mrs. Conway: following his sister's instructions, Louis leads his new mistress to an infected cottage and so exposes her to some unnamed southern plague. Mrs. Conway does not, however, die of that disease, though, signaling the dangers of mediation, Louis ultimately does.

Louis's death provides an acute example of a process inherent in all acts of mediation: the role of linking opposites entails self-effacement. At the moment of merger the mediator disappears, becoming no more than the space in which diverse figures can meet and combine. For Evans such invisibility proves a sign of his power; it later does the same for the figure of the poet in *Leaves of Grass*, whose capacity to link all things often seems to depend upon his ability to pass secretly and invisibly between them. In displacing the self-destructive potential of mediation onto Louis, Whitman acknowledges the possibility that the most potent instances of authorial self-effacement may ultimately point to death. The plot of *Franklin Evans* emphasizes the sexual nature of Evans's mediation. Throughout most of the story, the bodies of Margaret and Mrs. Conway converge in their shared contact with his. As I have already suggested, the erotic notion of mediation made explicit in Evans's Virginia exploits is not confined to Whitman's novel. The poetic task Whitman identifies in the notebook fragment, for example, may suggest an erotic penetration: "entering into both so that both shall understand me alike." In this line Whitman claims that such penetration will not only permit contact with and comprehension of a suddenly passive "me," but beyond that, their common receptivity to the entering poet will somehow make master and slave "alike." When Evans incites Margaret's jealousy and anger by referring to her "dark and swarthy" skin, he characterizes his taunt in specifically penetrative terms: his words are " a sharp arrow." Not surprisingly, as the story progresses, Margaret's hatred of Mrs. Conway takes on an eroticized tenor. Indeed by far the most erotic scene in the novel concerns neither Evans's relations with Margaret, nor his flirtatious encounters with Mrs. Conway, but rather the scene in which, once Mrs. Conway's fever breaks, Margaret strangles her rival in her sickbed.[10]

> "Thank God!" sounded in a low murmur from her tongue; "thank God! I shall not die!"
> The sounds came faintly; but faint as they were, they sank into ears besides those of the speaker. They sank and pierced, with a dagger's sharpness, the soul of Margaret the creole: for she it was, whose eyes had been during those long three hours almost winkless at the room window. And was her rival, then, to get well once more? . . .
> Horrid purposes lighted up the creole's eyes as she softly put aside the curtains, and stepped into the room. With a stealthy pace she drew near to the sick woman's bed. . . .
> Still nearer and nearer came the wretched female: and now she stands by the very bedside. Unconscious yet, the lady is quiet and composed—fearing nothing and suspecting nothing. An instant more, and her throat is clutched by a pair

of tight-working hands. Startled with terror, she would
shriek, but cannot. What torture fills her heart! She turns,
and struggles and writhes; but those deadly fingers loosen
not their grasp.

The murderess presses upon her. Poor lady! Her soul feels
very sick, as in one little minute whole troops of remem-
brances, and thoughts, and dreads come over her. She grows
fainter and fainter. Her struggles become less energetic, and
her convulsive writhings cease. Still those terrible hands release not.

(225–26)

A third presence does, however, suffuse their dyadic combat.
Evans sleeps, undisturbed, in a nearby chair. The passivity
of his sleep both enables and contains their erotic meeting.
The two writhing women on the bed, are they not his dream?
It is, after all, his voice that tells their struggle and their
passion.

The victim in this sickroom struggle appears, invariably,
as a soul: first "the soul of Margaret" "pierced, with a dagger's sharpness"; and then the very sick soul of the poor lady
"clutched by a pair of tight-working hands." While the victims of violence are represented as souls, the attackers are
not simply bodies, but, with striking consistency, fragments
of bodies. The sounds that pierce Margaret's soul issue not
from Mrs. Conway, but from "her tongue"; and Mrs. Conway is strangled not by Margaret, but by "those deadly fingers," "those terrible hands." The combat that Evans incites
and describes thus presents in the gothic guise of rape and
murder the lovemaking that joins body and soul in the awe-
some embraces of "Song of Myself." Significantly, however,
in "Song of Myself" Whitman reverses the relation of body
and soul so that it is the soul that "plunged your tongue to
my barestript heart, / And reached till you felt my beard, and
reached till you held my feet" while the body is penetrated
and held (ll. 80–81). Prefacing this plunge of tongue and
reach of hands, Whitman writes:

> I believe in you my soul. . . . the other I am must not abase
>   itself to you,
> And you must not be abased to the other.

(ll. 73–74)

The mutual relinquishing of abasement he prescribes in these lines uncannily revises the mutual abasement figured in *Franklin Evans,* where Margaret and Mrs. Conway are each victim and each (however passively) aggressor in their struggle. Moreover, in the novel the cruelty and violence of sexuality belong alike to male and female, to penetrating tongue and to encircling hands. The mutuality of abasement forms a perfect circuit in the narrative. As she dies Mrs. Conway "grows fainter and fainter," echoing the "faintly but faint" sounds with which she unwittingly wounds Margaret.[11]

Evans's narration of Mrs. Conway's murder is not only erotic; it is also, strangely, voyeuristically, in the present tense. A familiar ploy of the suspense story, the shift into the present tense in mid-sentence—when, having drawn near, nearer and nearer, Margaret finally reaches her victim's bed—suggests that the act of merger does not occur once and elsewhere but perpetually now and here. The violence and eroticism of the meeting with otherness thus belongs not to the past and distant frame of narrative but to the immediate and present lineaments characteristic of lyric utterance. The fantasy produced within the conventional idiom of the horror story's suspenseful and proximate threats shockingly displays the merger of apparently opposed bodies that, as my discussion of the 1855 *Leaves of Grass* demonstrates, comes to define Whitman's poems.

> The diverse shall be no less diverse, but they shall flow and unite. . . . they unite now.
>
> ("The Sleepers," l. 178)

In offering the problematics of miscegenation and, more specifically, the story of Mrs. Conway's murder as a paradigm of Whitman's poetic practice, I am also raising questions about genre distinctions. I wish to demonstrate not only that the same politically grounded conception of miscegenation informs both *Franklin Evans* and the 1855 *Leaves of Grass* but also that Whitman's effort to mediate between the differences he sees and the idealized merger he desires exploits his effort to articulate the relationship between narrative and lyric modes. Whitman's thematic concern with merger and difference, and the social and political implications such a concern entails, is enacted by his treatment of poetic form. In particular, the interaction of lyric and narrative modes within his poems participates in the more general project of reconciling social divisions, and provides a formal manifestation of the contradictions inherent in this project.

Whitman's proposal, so disturbingly enacted by the shifting tenses with which he describes Mrs. Conway's murder, is that difference relies upon the temporal sequence of narrative, while merger depends upon the arresting of narrative and its replacement with the atemporality of the lyric. Merger always occurs for Whitman in the now of lyric pronouncement. It may be described in an oneiric future tense, but it can only be achieved in the performative present of the poet's saying. One reason for this is that temporality implies motion and change and therefore threatens to fracture whatever unity may be achieved in the stillness of any framed and frozen moment. For merger to reconcile difference requires the stopping of time: "now" ends the sentence.[12] As is evident in my reading of the Virginia section of *Franklin Evans*, however, the mediator's claim to reconcile differences depends upon the prior existence of those differences. The mergers Whitman seeks in his lyrics first require the recognition of discord. The stable opposition between lyric mergers and narrative difference cannot be so easily maintained. Within *Leaves of Grass* the determinate relations between moments of merger and moments of difference, and between lyric and narrative modes that Whitman seems to propose, do not hold. Instead these concepts and the relations between them constantly require renegotiation. My reading of "The Sleepers" elaborates the terms of these negotiations, exploring the significance of the problematic relation between merger and difference both for Whitman's political project of reconciling difference and for the hybrid generic form of his poems.

"The Sleepers" begins with the familiar figure of the poet in the midst.

> I wander all night in my vision,
> Stepping with light feet. . . . swiftly and noiselessly
>   stepping and stopping,
> Bending with open eyes over the shut eyes of sleepers;
> Wandering and confused. . . . lost to myself. . . .
>   ill-assorted. . . . contradictory,
> Pausing and gazing and bending and stopping.
>
> (ll. 1–5)

Wandering within a night vision, the "I" both passes among the sleepers, distinguished from them by his open eyes, and is one of them, dreaming his wanderings out of his own sleep. Confused, lost, ill-assorted, contradictory, the diversity Whitman attempts to unite through his mediating "I" is already present within that "I": the figure relied upon to reconcile diversity is itself diverse.[13] Within the night vision time proves similarly contradictory. "Pausing and gazing and bending and stopping," the actions that would connect the poet to the sleepers, are acts of attention that require a cessation of motion. Yet in these lines the figure of the poet remains enmeshed in a string of gerunds that casts each act of attention as but one in an endless series. Here every pause anticipates renewed motion: constantly stopping, the wanderer cannot stop.

Night's darkness and dreams proffer a model of atemporal nonsequential experience where the "I" is both container and contained, where time is simultaneously experienced as motion and as stillness, where boundaries are not fixed, and hence where differences can be dissolved. Omnipotent yet absent, like Evans asleep in his chair, the night demonstrates the power of authorial self-effacement. The night of "The Sleepers" exemplifies Whitman's lyric task, providing the poet with an example of mediation's power and therefore with a means of accomplishing the desired union. So while the poet's "I" still wanders among the sleepers, observing but not touching them, "the night pervades them and enfolds them" (l. 10) in a caress at once masculine and feminine. As we have seen, Whitman's understanding of all merger as erotic does not simply present sexual union as the most powerful image of union, but also, as here, strives to reconceive sexual intercourse as well, redefining it in reciprocal, bisexual terms. Pervading and enfolding the sleepers, the night is equally enfolded and pervaded by them. Bisexuality, like miscegenation, offers the body not as an irreducible and irreconcilable sign of absolute difference—male versus female, white versus black—but instead as the site where difference meets. The night teaches that the confusions and contradictions that appear to plague the poet in the poem's opening lines are, if rightly understood, the source of his strength; it is the ambiguity of the middle position that makes mediation possible. By encompassing the others' dreams and by entering into each one, the poet locates and transgresses boundaries in an act of fusion that imitates night's mediation.

> I dream in my dream all the dreams of the other dreamers,
> And I become the other dreamers.
>
> (ll. 29–30)

Whitman's claim to become the other dreamers climaxes in a tryst whose polymorphic eroticism forges identifications across gender and into darkness.

> I am she who adorned herself and folded her hair
>   expectantly,
> My truant lover has come and it is dark.
> Double yourself and receive me darkness,
> Receive me and my lover too. . . . he will not let me go
>   without him.
> I roll myself upon you as upon a bed. . . . I resign myself to
>   the dusk.
> He whom I call answers me and takes the place of my lover,
> He rises with me silently from the bed.
> Darkness you are gentler than my lover. . . . his flesh was
>   sweaty and panting,
> I feel the hot moisture yet that he left me.
>
> (ll. 46–54)

The "I" of this passage appears simultaneously male and female, identified with the poet even as it speaks for the adorned and expectant woman. Similarly, mirroring the woman's coy fondling of her hair, the darkness folds itself in two and becomes both the night and the lover embraced in nighttime fantasies. Thus the night not only provides the setting for tryst or dream, but also becomes a body in these encounters, "and takes the place of my lover." Displacing the lover's sweaty flesh, the gentle embrace of darkness erases the lover's body at the very moment that it makes that body black. Thus Whitman's fullest depiction in this poem of an erotic coupling that engages racial and sexual difference relies upon an image of the night which in its elusive intangibility diffuses all differences, masking both the physicality and the racial nature of the scene described. Indeed this passage recalls the "dark but comely" lover of *The Song of Solomon*; if there is a black body behind the night, it comes not from the plantation but from Biblical poetry.

The encounter between the woman and her lover is three times mediated, first by this act of intertextuality, then by the poet whose voice lays claim to the woman's body and reveals her desires, and last by the night in whose darkness the scene is quite literally embedded. Moreover, the night occupies the place of all otherness: it is the "you" that responds to the double "I" of woman and poet. This is the first "you" in the entire poem, and, though initially addressed to the darkness, it tends, as this pronoun so often does for Whitman, to point outward from the printed page, naming and implicating the reader.

> My hands are spread forth . . I pass them in all directions,
> I would sound up the shadowy shore to which you are
>   journeying.
>
> (ll. 55–56)

The pleasure of the woman stroking her lover, the night, her own body, is also the pleasure of the poet whose hands spread forth these lines, and who offers the sound of words to sound up the journey of our readings.

> Be careful darkness. . . . already, what was it touched me?
> I thought my lover had gone. . . . else darkness and he
>   are one,
> I hear the heart-beat. . . . I follow . . I fade away.
>   (ll. 57–59)

It is impossible to identify the source of this touch. Of course her own hands touch her, as do the poet's, as do the composite of lover and darkness, as do all the even more invisibly present readers. The touch marks the complete absorption of these multiple selves into darkness and indifferentiation that nevertheless persists in claiming a bodily and tactile presence until, like the orgasmic "I," all difference has faded away. The problems of bodily difference, and the strategy of resolving such dilemmas in a rhetoric of amalgamation, finally come to define Whitman's poetic task, not as theme or topic, but as the basic structure of poetic production. With its intense erotic charge, Whitman's poetics of merger here offers a powerfully positive and seductive apotheosis. It is important to recognize, however, that this passage, for all its erotic appeal, entails the same process of absorbing and decontextualizing bodily difference as that employed in "I Sing the Body Electric" when the auctioneer-poet strips off the flesh of the slave.

It is not, moreover, accurate to describe "The Sleepers" as a dream fantasia in which night's ambiguities enable the suspension of time and support the defiance of all difference, for despite these visions of merger, the swiftly fluctuating scenery of dreams is punctuated by narratives. So Whitman includes a description of Washington leaving his troops. So he tells the story—"My mother told me today as we sat at dinner together" (l. 110)—of an Indian woman who had stopped at the house selling rushes for weaving chairs and had spent the day beside the fire. These passages are not presented as part of the rhetoric of dreams, and instead of mergers they tell of separations. Washington "kisses lightly the wet cheeks one after another. . . . he shakes hands and bids goodbye to the army" (l. 109). Though Whitman's mother gave her "remembrance and fondness," the Indian woman "never came nor was heard of there again" (ll. 121, 126). In short these are stories of the loss that even fondness and manly kisses cannot overcome. What interests me about these losses is that Whitman does not simply oppose the union offered in dreams and wrought by his words to the external divisions and separations that painfully characterize so much of living; rather he reveals the instability of such oppositions, and the ways in which merger and difference, lyric and narrative are implicated in each other.

Like many of the dream images of merger, the first of these extended narratives begins with Whitman seeing some bit of external world: "I see a beautiful gigantic swimmer swimming naked through the eddies of the sea" (l. 81). In earlier passages such sight initiates moments of identification, mediation, and union.

> A shroud I see—and I am the shroud. . . . I wrap a body
>   and lie in the coffin;
> It is dark here underground. . . . it is not evil or pain
>   here. . . . it is blank here, for reasons.
>
> (ll. 76–77)

Seeing prompts becoming, and, in what by now should be a familiar pattern, the poet/shroud *wraps* a body and *lies in* the coffin, and from that middle place mediates between death's threat of blankness and the distinctions of reason. Though the scene may represent the ecstasy of sexual absorption as the equally dark obliteration that is death, it nevertheless remains within Whitman's structure of mediation, and as the poet speaks out of the grave his identification with the shroud promises to bridge even the radical otherness of death.

Similarly the relation between a naked swimmer and the sea appears at first to offer simply another permutation of the relation between a body and "the dark grave" (l. 79); at stake in both images is a sexualized encompassing that is also a lethal absorption. Unlike other acts of seeing in this poem, however, Whitman's vision of the swimmer does not succeed in reconciling differences. Instead it betrays the complicity of

Whitman's vision and descriptive powers in the divisions he
seeks to merge.

> I see a beautiful gigantic swimmer swimming naked
>   through the eddies of the sea,
> His brown hair lies close and even to his head. . . . he
>   strikes out with courageous arms. . . . he urges himself
>   with his legs.
> I see his white body. . . . I see his undaunted eyes;
> I hate the swift-running eddies that would dash him
>   headforemost on the rocks.
> What are you doing you ruffianly red-trickled waves?
> Will you kill the courageous giant? Will you kill him in the
>   prime of his middle age?
>
>   (ll. 81–86)

In decrying the death of the swimmer, Whitman acknowledges the gratuitous violence of a senselessly divided and an-
tagonistic world. His questions attest to his inability to heal
these divisions, despite all his claims and desires. Yet to read
these lines simply as assertions of Whitman's desire to heal
all wounds and resolve all differences, or as signs of his re-
pugnance at the violence and divisions that baffle his project
of poetic merger, is to ignore the disturbing logic of their syn-
tax. For Whitman is not just a helpless and appalled observer
of a violence distinct from his narration of it. The poet's initial report depicts concord, not violence: as the swimmer
swims "naked through the eddies of the sea," the water appears to caress him. But in describing them the poet renames
the eddies as something to be hated; his words anticipate
their violence and so create it. In asking the waves, "Will you
kill?" Whitman presents himself as willing the death the subsequent lines describe. Indeed, the entire description of the
drowning occurs in the anticipatory formulations of the poet's questions. Thus at the moment of questioning violence,
Whitman demonstrates the ways in which his poetry requires and is complicitous in the act of wounding. Moreover,
the erotic energy of this battering, as the water strikes the
swimmer's beautiful naked body, fuses destruction with sex-

ual pleasure. In so doing it neutralizes the interdependence of merger and division, cure and violence, enacted within the poem, recasting this troubling aspect of Whitman's poetic practice as a site of erotic release.[14]

That the same questions can be seen both as initiating discord and as demonstrating the horror of such divisions suggests that a simple opposition between moments of difference and moments of merger, and hence between lyric and narrative modes, is inadequate to explain Whitman's poetic project. Instead it becomes clear that Whitman's poetics of merger is equally a poetics of difference, since it is always differences and divisions that initiate his poems, making mediation not only possible but necessary. The historically grounded narratives of loss and separation that follow—the shipwreck of the *Mexico*,[15] Washington's farewell, the mother's story, the slave family split by sales—arise as responses to acts of violence inscribed by the poet. The stories suggest the poet's investment in violence and division; in turn, the lyric dream of universal reconciliation that ends the poem depends upon these narratives of separation. The generic instability of "The Sleepers," its fluctuation between lyrical evocations of a dream world and narrative reports of historical events, can thus be understood as a formal manifestation of a single attempt, poetic and political, to grapple with difference. The generic issues are not simply formal or mechanical; rather, as the following example illustrates, they carry urgently political implications.

Whitman deleted the last of the stories of separation from the 1881 edition of *Leaves of Grass:* in this expunged passage he assigns his "I" to the slave.

> Now Lucifer was not dead. . . . or if he was I am his
>   sorrowful terrible heir;
> I have been wronged. . . . I am oppressed. . . . I hate him
>   that oppresses me,
> I will either destroy him, or he shall release me.
>
> Damn him! how he does defile me,
> How he informs against my brother and sister and takes pay
>   for their blood,

> How he laughs when I look down the bend after the
> steamboat that carries away my woman.
>
>   (ll. 127–32)

The slave may call himself the heir of Lucifer, but the hated
"him that oppresses me" deserves that appellation as much
as the slave does, since it is the white man who imposes the
hell that produces the slave's hellish anger. White and black
meet, then, in their joint claim to the name of Lucifer. The
slave may occupy the position of speaker, but Lucifer mediates this union. Indeed his name is the only name either op-
ponent has. We only know that they are a black man and a
white from the blood money paid for brothers and sisters,
and from "the steamboat that carries away my woman."[16]
The cycle of oppression, hatred, and vengeance that links
these figures precedes the contextualizing markers that name
them free and slave, white and black. And even those markers provide contradictory evidence: though the speaker is
clearly a slave, in some lines the oppressor appears to be the
owner who does not release him, while in other lines he appears to be a slave-catcher and trader. The fluctuating identifications of the oppressor present the slave as the victim of
an undifferentiated white aggression. Thus the slave's curse
indicts not any particular oppressor but the entire system of
slavery and society's abusive response to racial difference.

By describing the motions of antagonism, and the climac-
tic resolution of that antagonism in destruction or release, before identifying these relations with the institution of slavery,
Whitman abstracts the historical particularities of slavery into
an apparently ahistorical poetic pattern of division and
merger. So even before Whitman removes this passage from
the poem, the passage itself can already be seen to thematize
its own erasure.[17] The section of this poem of mergers that
most explicitly addresses the political divisions of American
slavery also works to suppress that social content, enacting
the transformation of a specific historical narrative into a lyric
evocation of universal conditions. At stake in these frequent
shifts between lyric and narrative modes is the relation between Whitman's political concerns and his poetic ones. The

hybrid genre of "The Sleepers" demonstrates the dependence of Whitman's poetics of merger on the presence of social divisions. If Whitman's project of poetic merger relies upon, indeed proves complicitous with, an oppositional conception of society, it simultaneously strives to hide its contingent nature and to deny any such reliance. Thus the poet's outrage at the death of the swimmer and his complicity in the drowning can be located in the same lines; thus a single passage demonstrates the ways in which the hatred between master and slave informs the patterns of destruction and release characteristic of Whitman's poetics and dramatizes the suppression of that relation. The contingent relation between merger and difference cannot be straightforwardly acknowledged, for, once it is, the healing claims of a poetics of merger become moot.

It is, therefore, hardly surprising that "The Sleepers" ends in an emphatic reassertion of the poet's healing powers. "Elements merge in the night," Whitman exclaims (l. 141), and in the rhapsody that follows, all the figures that have appeared separately in earlier sections are recalled and included: "I swear they are averaged now. . . . one is no better than the other, / The night and sleep have likened them and restored them" (l. 161). The power to average difference that Whitman claims for night and for sleep is the power to halt time, always necessary for the achievement and perpetuation of mergers; it is the power Whitman seeks in lyric utterance. But though dreams may occur within a time or timelessness of their own, night does not exist outside time; indeed it measures time, marking the limit of each day.

> I too pass from the night;
> I stay awhile away O night, but I return to you again and
>   love you;
> Why should I be afraid to trust myself to you?
> I am not afraid. . . . I have been well brought forward
>   by you;
> I love the rich running day, but I do not desert her in whom
>   I lay so long:
> I know not how I came of you, and I know not where I go
>   with you. . . . but I know I came well and shall go well.

I will stop only a time with the night. . . . and rise betimes.
I will duly pass the day O my mother and duly return
    to you;
Not you will yield forth the dawn again more surely than
    you will yield forth me again,
Not the womb yields the babe in its time more surely than I
    shall be yielded from you in my time.

                                                    (ll. 195–204)

The cyclical pattern of night and day seems to offer a way
to overcome the movement and change inherent in temporality by containing this division within a larger structure of
sameness. But when at the poem's end the poet attempts to
adjudicate between night and day, pretending with frail bravado that the choice is his to make, it becomes evident that
time cannot be so easily held. "My time" is a vain boast. The
halting of time implicit in Whitman's notions of merger resists the narrative of history, and in doing so imposes an erasure on precisely those historically bound oppositions (slavery among them) that, at the same time, are recognized as
the source of his need to reconcile otherness. In order to
claim and maintain the unitive and healing power of night's
atemporal mergers, Whitman must erase and forget the
knowledge that his poems of merger originate in difference:
"I know not how I came of you, and I know not where I go
with you. . . . but I know I came well and shall go well."

In describing Whitman's vision of the mediating poet in
terms of interacting lyric and narrative modes, I am suggesting that the choice and manipulation of poetic style can exert
political force. Thus Whitman's conception of the poet as mediator itself establishes connections between literary and
social practices.[18] Such connections function not only to ex-
pand the notion of poetic efficacy but also to redefine what
constitutes political action. What I have been calling Whitman's poetics of embodiment amounts to the aspect of his

poetic style most deeply implicated in this process. For Whitman, the human body serves as the site where the issues of representation and the questions of political power intersect, and so it is in his treatment of the human body that Whitman most explicitly establishes links between poetry and politics and most radically revises the assumptions and practices of both.

In "I Sing the Body Electric" Whitman presents the body of the slave as an exemplary instance of embodiment: the salable flesh of the slave attests to the role of the human body in designating identity. It is not surprising, therefore, that Whitman's depictions of the slave serve to ground the poetics and politics of embodiment developed in "Song of Myself." Though other black bodies—most notably the negro driver and his team of horses—appear in the 1855 version of this long poem, and more are added in the new catalogues of the 1856 edition, the figure of the fugitive, of the black body in transition between slavery and freedom, predominates. Just as the slave on the auction block, a piece of merchandise, appears to encapsulate the materiality of being, the transitional status of the fugitive seems to denote the fluidity of identity.

Yet as we have seen, Whitman's celebration of corporeality in "I Sing the Body Electric" strips away the flesh it claims to sing, while here the slave's attempt to change his condition, to disentangle blackness from slavery, is represented through brutal marks upon his body. Moreover, the two scenes in "Song of Myself" in which Whitman depicts an escape from slavery to freedom also involve a transformation of the relation between the poet and his subject, a gradual elimination of the initial distance between the "I" that speaks and the body of the fleeing slave. In short, the transition of the fugitive from slave to freeman manifests the structure and implications of Whitman's poetics of embodiment from a variety of perspectives: individual, aesthetic, and political. The relation between identity and the human body, the relation between the poet and his subject matter, and the relation between poetry and political practice all cohere in Whitman's representation of the fugitive.

The figure of the runaway slave first appears in a series of verse paragraphs that pose varying personae for the poet: he is the solitary hunter, the ecstatic sailor on a Yankee Clipper, the playful companion of boatmen and clamdiggers, the witness of a marriage between a trapper and a squaw, and finally the host of a fugitive slave. As such a list makes clear, by the time the story of the slave is told, the flexibility of the poet's identity, the ease with which his "I" can be transferred from one subject to the next, has already been well established. Such metamorphoses are so characteristic of Whitman's verse that readers generally take them for granted.[19] In the depictions of the fugitive slave in "Song of Myself," however, Whitman carefully details this usually instantaneous transformation, laying bare some of the contradictions it entails. Anticipated by the fugitive "I" of Whitman's poem, the figure of the fugitive slave makes evident the predicament of that "I."

> The runaway slave came to my house and stopped outside,
> I heard his motions crackling the twigs of the woodpile,
> Through the swung half-door of the kitchen I saw him
>   limpsey and weak,
> And went where he sat on a log, and led him in and
>   assured him,
> And brought water and filled a tub for his sweated body
>   and bruised feet,
> And gave him a room that entered from my own, and gave
>   him some coarse clean clothes,
> And remember perfectly well his revolving eyes and his
>   awkwardness,
> And remember putting plasters on the galls of his neck and
>   ankles;
> He staid with me a week before he was recuperated and
>   passed north,
> I had him sit next me at table. . . . my firelock leaned in the
>   corner.
>
> (ll. 183–92)

While the fugitive remains outside of the house, the speaker retains the fixed integrity of an observing "I" clearly distinct from what it observes: "I heard his motions," "I saw him"; but once the speaker begins to tend the slave, he relinquishes this self-defining pronoun. In washing and clothing and giv- ing and remembering, the unique identity of the server is gradually absorbed by the body being served as each "and" further separates the act that follows from the "I" that desig- nates the actor. Only after the fugitive leaves for the north, becoming, for the first time since entering the house, an actor rather than a body being acted upon, does the speaker again assert his "I." Whitman's deployment of pronouns presents physical contact as capable of holding the differentiations of identity in abeyance.

Whitman claims in this passage that the slave's body not only represents but is the locus of social divisions, so that healing the galls caused by the physical iron fetters of slavery actually sutures the divisions between the enslaved and the free, black and white. The healing of the slave's body enables him to claim a free identity and become a grammatical sub- ject. In this passage physical contact merges the identities of host and slave, but the successful outcome of this merger, the slave's transformation into a freeman, requires that the bar- rier of pronominal difference be reerected. If the assertion of a separate "he" and "I" is necessary for the achievement of freedom, it nevertheless reinscribes the divisions emancipa- tion hoped to remove. The "firelock leaned in the corner" offers a sad reminder of the violence those divisions pro- duced within antebellum society. Indeed the question of the host's relation to the fugitive gains urgency from the pres- ence of the gun: how secure is their merger, how wary is their difference? A pious abolitionist sentiment would simply interpret the firelock as a promise of protection against exter- nal enemies, but within the house, self and other, enemy and friend, merger and difference are not so easily and perfectly identified. The waiting gun could equally well indicate the host's trust in the stranger beside him or his vigilant lack of trust. In the previous scene a gun has already suggested the precariousness and explosiveness of interracial contact. Whitman describes the trapper bridegroom: "One hand rested on his rifle. . . . the other hand held firmly the wrist of the red girl" (l. 189).

Over six hundred lines later, the figure of the fugitive re-appears, and this time Whitman attempts a more radical union, as if to demonstrate the limitations of his earlier strategy.

> The hounded slave that flags in the race and leans by the
>   fence, blowing and covered with sweat,
> The twinges that sting like needles his legs and neck,
> The murderous buckshot and bullets,
> All these I feel or am.
>
> I am the hounded slave. . . . I wince at the bite of the dogs,
> Hell and despair are upon me. . . . crack and again crack
>   the marksmen,
> I clutch the rails of the fence. . . . my gore dribs thinned
>   with the ooze of my skin,
> I fall on the weeds and stones,
> The riders spur their unwilling horses and haul close,
> They taunt my dizzy ears. . . . they beat me violently over
>   the head with their whip-stocks.
>
> (ll. 830–39)

The transference of the poet's "I" to the figure of the hounded slave, and the consequent merger of these two identities, is marked by the drib and ooze of wounded flesh. Here Whitman employs a manifestly corporeal vocabulary to articulate the union of poet and fugitive, demonstrating how his poetics of merger depends upon the notion of embodi-ment. There is a Doubting Thomas quality to this passage, as if probing the fugitive's wounds would assure the veracity of Whitman's poetic miracle: he would become the other, and so otherness would be eliminated. The fugitive's attempt to change his status and the poet's attempt to write this poem share, for Whitman, the same assumptions about the corpo-reality of identity: for the slave, escaping to freedom or re-turning to captivity entails a harrowing of his flesh; for the poet, telling this story involves representing that flesh as his own. Whitman's equation of poetry with bodily experience strives to defy any distinction between the written and the physical world.

Whitman's poetics of embodiment always, however, re-mains a poetics. Indeed what is so searing about his exorbitant claims to inhabit another's body is that the more fervently he asserts them, the more extravagant and impossible they appear.[20] The pathos of this inevitably failed poetic ideal is inscribed within the poem itself. Indeed Whitman's most adamant assertions of his poetics of embodiment consistently work to undermine their own authority. So Whitman's insistence that he does not describe the slave's experience, but rather embodies that experience, contains its own caveat: "All these I feel or am," he writes, suggesting that the tangible claims of embodiment may amount to nothing more than an imaginative projection of feeling. Moreover, the alternatives of feeling or being relate to the scene described with a remarkable lack of specificity. It is not just that the triumph of embodiment (I feel the bullets, I am the hounded slave) so easily collapses into the far lesser claim of sympathetic feeling, but that the assertion of embodiment expands to permeate the entire scene so that Whitman's "I" belongs to it "all," not only to the fugitive but to the fence that supports him and the buckshot and bullets that wound him. Normal distinctions between the animate and the inanimate are denied. The bullets gain a murderous intentionality; twinges of pain become the agents that inflict pain. Thus the embodiment claimed in these lines relies on a sense of identity that remains distinct from any specific corporeal manifestation and instead moves between them. Identity appears infinitely flexible and transferable at the very moment when Whitman attempts to locate it in the human body.

In asserting his poetics of embodiment Whitman thus raises questions about the validity of this ideal from two seemingly opposite perspectives: either poetic embodiment is impossible, bodies are discrete objects, and no amount of will or desire can eradicate their otherness, so that a poetics of embodiment can offer only the representations of a sympathetic but nevertheless alien imagination; or embodiment is possible, and the body is not a barrier to identification (since identity appears fluid, transferable, and only incidentally associated with any individual corporeal form), so that a poetics of embodiment can offer only the disintegration of all links between the body and identity. If the body defines identity, then a poetics of embodiment remains a potent fantasy; if, on the other hand, identity can be transferred from one body to another, then a poetics of embodiment might be achievable, but it would also be meaningless. As a defense against these undesirable positions Whitman redefines his poetics of embodiment so that it simultaneously insists that identity inheres in the flesh and that it is a matter of representation, infinitely mobile and ultimately indeterminate.

> Agonies are one of my changes of garments;
> I do not ask the wounded person how he feels. . . . I myself
>   become the wounded person,
> My hurt turns livid upon me as I lean on a cane and
>   observe.
>
> (ll. 840–42)

These lines provide a frequently quoted synopsis of Whitman's poetics of embodiment. What is finally most significant about them, however, is not the exorbitant claim to become the other, to put on another's body with the ease of changing clothes, but the odd doubleness with which Whitman retains the distance and difference of the observer. As he leans on a cane and observes, Whitman simultaneously presents himself as object and as subject, embodied and disembodied, the wounded person and the voice which describes that livid flesh.

The case of the fugitive slave provides Whitman with an extreme and definitive instance of the problematics of embodiment characteristic of his poetry as a whole. Whitman's focus on the body has a political as well as a poetic meaning. He proposes in *Leaves of Grass* that the divisions in the social fabric, the nature of identity, and the relation of the poet's word to the external world are not simply analogous, but finally identical questions. For in trying to reconcile an embodied and a disembodied conception of identity, Whitman makes clear that the divisions between self and other (white and black, master and slave) that inform the political delineations of personhood can be located with equal force within each person and within every act of utterance. I have suggested as much already in arguing that Whitman's first notebook poetry presents the relation between slave and master as an alternative means of articulating the relation between body and soul and in showing that Whitman's most powerful image for the comingling of body and soul reiterates the scene of miscegenation. The import of bodily difference manifested by American slavery challenges not only national unity but also any unitive conception of identity. By literalizing this challenge Whitman dismantles traditional distinctions between what is a personal and what a political issue: each stands equally well as an emblem for the other. Moreover, Whitman finds that poetry is constituted out of the same divide between the disembodied and the embodied, the intangible words that demand to be felt as a palpable world. What the miscegenating embrace of body and soul produces in "Song of Myself" is poetry:

> Loafe with me on the grass. . . . loose the stop from your
>   throat,
> Not words, not music or rhyme I want. . . . not custom or
>   lecture, not even the best,
> Only the lull I like, the hum of your valved voice.
> I mind how we lay in June, such a transparent summer
>   morning;
> You settled your head athwart my hips and gently turned
>   over upon me,
> And parted the shirt from my bosom-bone, and plunged
>   your tongue to my barestript heart,
> And reached till you felt my beard, and reached till you
>   held my feet.
>   (ll. 75–81)

Not only does the pair of body and soul indicate the divided nature of identity, but viewed separately body and soul each display the same split between the embodied and the disembodied. The soul has a corporeal form (a throat, a head), while the body lacks the impermeability, the strict boundaries, normally associated with flesh, so that a bosom-bone may be parted as easily as a shirt. This passage establishes not one mode for poetic production, but two: the regulated but undifferentiated lull that the body requests from the soul, and the fleshy communication of a plunging tongue. The dual conception of identity as simultaneously corporeal and incorporeal with which Whitman responds to the challenge of bodily difference results in a similarly dualistic notion of poetry.

In reading the relation Whitman traces between body and soul, or between hum and tongue, as reinscribing the problematics of a corporeal identity characteristic of American slavery, I am, therefore, also examining the erasure of such historical markers: Whitman's consistent decontextualizing of his imagery. "Song of Myself," for example, forges a conception of self and of song that is notorious for its claims of expansive universality. If I have presented miscegenation as an historically grounded model of Whitman's poetic practice, it nevertheless remains clear that Whitman's depiction of the sexual union of radically different kinds as the embrace of body and soul entails a dramatic relocation of social divisions, and hence the absorption of the political realm into the person of the poet. Whitman concluded his preface to the 1855 edition by setting up a criterion by which to judge the poems that follow: "The proof of a poet is that his country absorbs him as affectionately as he has absorbed it" (24). The claim of affection acknowledges the erotic nature of this standard. Whitman's ideal of absorption is fulfilled. For if Whitman's poetry does absorb the social divisions of antebellum America, and particularly the crisis over slavery, it is also absorbed by it. Thus the poet, the person whom Whitman imagined as capable of mediating between the social divisions exemplified by American slavery, finally comes to incarnate those divisions. Ironically, as the next chapter will argue, for an actual slave woman the ways in which her body incarnates social divisions does not prove a source of authorial power. Instead, for Harriet Jacobs the identity between flesh, world, and word that Whitman seeks serves only to fashion the act of writing into another site of oppression.

3

Righting Slavery and Writing Sex
The Erotics of Narration in Harriet Jacobs's Incidents

In her letters, Harriet Jacobs repeatedly voices the wish that her story conform better to prevailing feminine mores. The task of writing *Incidents in the Life of a Slave Girl,* Jacobs explains to the abolitionist Amy Post, would be less daunting "dear Amy if it was the life of a Heroine with no degradation associated with it," but it is not, and she finds it difficult to depict the degradations that a heroine would have no occasion to speak: "There are somethings I might have made plainer I know—Woman can whisper—her cruel wrongs into the ear of a very dear friend—much easier than she can record them for the world to read."[1] As she describes her reluctance to write about her life, and particularly as her stress on degradations and cruel wrongs suggests, to write about her sexual experiences, Jacobs substitutes the general figures of "Woman" and "Heroine" for her individual "I." The moment when she alludes to incidents so private that they ought to be whispered in the intimacy of friendship, rather than recorded for a reading world, is the moment when the intimate confessions of her letters give way to a generalized claim about feminine discourse.

Jacobs's book is not an intimate utterance but a highly public document; she explicitly enlists her words in antislavery reform. In particular, the sexual experiences on which her narrative centers fulfill an abolitionist agenda of displaying the horror and corruption of slavery. Thus, as all her readers have noted, the story Jacobs has to tell may well be unique among slave narratives in that it describes slavery primarily in terms of sexual experience. The pseudonymous Linda Brent, harassed by the sexual attentions of her master, Dr. Flint, evades his designs by becoming the concubine of a neighboring white gentleman to whom she bears two children. After hiding for seven years in her grandmother's attic, and after Mr. Sands—her white lover—buys their children from a deceived and enraged Dr. Flint, Linda escapes to the North, where she can again see her children but cannot provide them with a home. As such a plot summary makes clear, sexual harassment, sexual intercourse, and childbirth are not tangential to a narrative of enslavement, escape, and emancipation; they are that narrative.

In Jacobs's *Incidents in the Life of a Slave Girl* the insights into the corporeality of identity that feminist-abolitionists discovered in describing the physical otherness of the slave come to occupy the more threatening space of the writer's own body. The merger of the personal and the political, the writer and the social world, that I have shown to be characteristic of Walt Whitman's poetic project are literally enacted by Jacobs's narrative, as her personal and bodily experiences stand as evidence of the oppressions of slavery. Thus the ways in which the body of the slave grounds antebellum discourses of identity has another, and more ominous, meaning for the slave author. In Jacobs's narrative the constraints of her body and the constraints of her writing replicate each other. The loss entailed in producing a slave narrative derives from the idea, as Henry Louis Gates puts it, "that any human being would be demanded to write him or herself into the human community," and beyond this, from the recognition that such an act of self-writing assumes the same possessive and negating attitudes toward the body and bodily experience as slavery itself.[2] As Jacobs's distress at recording her personal experience in a public and political document demonstrates, many of the characteristics of slavery (degradation, exposure, exploitation) are implicated in the act of writing down those experiences. For Jacobs the act of writing is affiliated alternately with both self-mastery and enslavement.

Jacobs had not originally intended to tell her story herself. She had hoped that Harriet Beecher Stowe would write it for her. Indeed she offered Stowe not only her own history as a possible subject for the novelist's pen, but also the services of her daughter Louisa during Stowe's intended voyage to England. As Jacobs explained to Amy Post, "I thought Louisa would be a very good representative of a Southern Slave   she has improved much in her studies and I think she has energy enough to do something for the cause."[3] Stowe rejected both offers: she desired only to include Jacobs's story among the substantiating anecdotes compiled in her *Key to Uncle Tom's Cabin*, and "she was afraid," Jacobs wrote, angrily summarizing Stowe's objections, that such a journey "would subject [Louisa] to much petting and patronizing which would be more pleasing to a young Girl than useful and the English very apt to do it and [Mrs. Stowe] was very much opposed to it with this class of people."[4] Ironically, in treating both her life and her daughter as "representative" of Southern slavery, Jacobs anticipates the terms of Stowe's insult. In using this vocabulary, Jacobs reveals her desire to change how slavery is represented and the slave understood. Jacobs sees her own and Louisa's intelligence and energy as suiting them for the role of representative: she recognizes herself and her daughter as articulate, individualized advocates for the slave, rather than simply as sample slaves. To be representative, as Jacobs understood it, meant being presentable.[5]

In seeing the mother as an apt illustration for her *Key* and the daughter as a member of a preconceived "class," Stowe reads this representativeness differently. It is because she claims the role of representative slave that Jacobs's experiences can be alienated from her person and recast into the exemplary facts of Stowe's *Key*. Racist assumptions about the representative character of the slave permit Stowe confidently to predict Louisa's foibles. Moreover, the symmetry of Stowe's response to the double offer of daughter and tale reveals the symmetrical situations of servitude and narrative.

In Stowe's response both the representative slave girl and the representation of a slave girl are denied the integrity of individuation.

Only after Stowe had refused to write Jacobs's story as "a history of my life entirely by itself" did Jacobs begin her work on *Incidents*.[6] It could be argued that she set about recounting her life as an antidote to Stowe's denigrating response. In writing the story herself, however, Jacobs cannot completely avoid the problems posed by her claim to presentable representativeness. Although Jacobs's "conversation and manners inspire . . . confidence," although she "has so deported herself as to be highly esteemed," although, in short, she was an eminently presentable black woman, the sexual story she wished to tell rendered her not presentable at all.[7]

Analogies between representation and slavery, the story and the slave woman, pervade Jacobs's writings, so it is hardly surprising that the tactics by which she ultimately escaped from slavery come to inform her treatment of her new narrative confines. "I had no motive for secrecy on my own account," Jacobs insists in her "Preface" as she defends the fact that she has "concealed the names of places, and given persons fictitious names" (1). Lydia Maria Child, who edited and introduced the anonymous *Incidents*, advised such concealments "out of delicacy to Mrs. Willis," Jacobs's employer and the woman who had procured her freedom.[8] That Jacobs's identity had to be occluded to protect the name of a mistress, however generous and beloved, illustrates the easy expendability of black identities. Yet clearly Jacobs's use of the pseudonym "Linda Brent," which provides a mechanism of escape highly valued by any fugitive, is not without advantages. She had, after all, admitted to finding the secrecy of whispers easier than public utterance. Jacobs signed the name "Linda" to an antislavery letter she wrote to the *Liberator*; one she sent to the *New York Tribune* is simply signed "a fugitive," and her own strategy for escaping from slavery bears a marked similarity to her mode of pseudonymous authorship. Jacobs hid for seven years in the attic of her grandmother's house, watching the master from whom she fled through a hole bored in the wall of her hiding place. Like her grandmother's attic, the figure of Linda Brent places Jacobs in close proximity to those who are seeking her and yet leaves her carefully concealed.[9] And like this attic—"a very small garret . . . only nine feet long and seven feet wide. The highest part was three feet high, and sloped down abruptly to the loose board floor" (114)—the refuge Jacobs finds in *Incidents* proves a confining one.

The analogy between how Jacobs manages to escape from slavery and how she comes to represent it emphasizes not only the equation for the slave author of the position of the slave and that of the literary subject, but also the literary ramifications of such an equation. Jacobs's narrative provides a particularly appropriate site for my inquiry both because her attention to the sexual aspects of slavery necessarily insists on its bodily implications and because this sexual concern has resulted in a certain generic instability. The anomalous product of a slave woman, Jacobs's text juxtaposes the traditionally male adventures of the slave narrative with the white middle-class femininity of the domestic novel.[10] As Jacobs writes her story, Linda Brent acts out the problems inherent in this hybridization of slave and domestic narrative forms.

Unlike the heroes of slave narratives, Linda escapes not by fighting or running but by burrowing into domestic spaces. Besides the "loophole of retreat," as Jacobs calls the secret garret, Linda hides beneath the kitchen floorboards and atop the spare featherbeds in the home of a sympathetic, but slave-owning, white woman. She locates freedom in feminized spaces; but while she haunts these houses, she cannot occupy them. She never comes to inhabit the domestic; rather, as a slave and particularly as a female slave she *is* the domestic. In her effort to escape, her body literally lines the floors and ceilings of houses, just as in servitude her body and its labor sustains the Southern home.[11] Significantly, the peephole she bores in the wall of her grandmother's attic does not provide her with a view of the house's interior. She cannot watch her grandmother care for her children; instead she watches the street where, powerless to intervene, she sees her son attacked by a dog or threatened by her master.[12]

The domestic scene she cannot see from her attic remains just as elusive in the freedom of her final page:

> Reader, my story ends with freedom; not in the usual way, with marriage. I and my children are now free! We are as free from the power of slaveholders as are the white people of the north; and though that, according to my ideas, is not saying a great deal, it is a vast improvement in *my* condition. The dream of my life is not yet realized. I do not sit with my children in a home of my own. I still long for a hearthstone of my own, however humble. I wish it for my children's sake far more than for my own. (201)

Fairy tales traditionally grant three wishes, and Jacobs repeats hers three times, but ultimately "children," "home," and the thrice reiterated "my own" prove a single, continuously denied dream. As Jacobs sees it, only in claiming possession, only by inhabiting rather than making the domestic, can she assure that she and her children are not property. Apologizing for the inadequacies of her style, Jacobs explains in her preface that she was "compelled . . . to write these pages at irregular intervals, whenever I could snatch an hour from household duties" (1). Although the domestic constitutes the conditions under which she writes, the feminine travails that order her plot, and the locus and the goal of the story she tells, Jacobs's narrative is nevertheless a document of exclusion from the domestic. Melding the slave narrative and the domestic novel, Jacobs reveals the social and political paradox behind her problem of genre: slavery can create the private, domestic realm precisely because the slave has no privacy and no claim on domestic space or domestic utterance. Might Jacobs conceive of feminine discourse as whispers because she cannot properly occupy domestic space or speak out loud there? In the harsh confines of her grandmother's attic Linda felt "a very painful sensation of coldness in my head; even my face and tongue stiffened, and I lost the power of speech" (122).

Desiring a home for her "children's sake far more than for [her] own," and concluding her narrative with the solace that "all the gloomy recollections" of slavery required by the task of writing are accompanied by "tender memories of my good old grandmother," Jacobs postulates maternity as a rejoinder to slavery (201). Maternity is, of course, an alternative means of locating the domestic: children replace houses as signs of a title to domesticity and an ability to engage in feminine discourse or to claim the status of a virtuous and valuable woman. In Jacobs's book, however, motherhood, like home, provides only the most paradoxical of refuges. Describing her own childhood, Jacobs explains:

> When I was six years old, my mother died; and then, for the first time, I learned, by the talk around me, that I was a slave. My mother's mistress was the daughter of my grandmother's mistress. She was the foster sister of my mother; they were both nourished at my grandmother's breast. In fact, my mother had been weaned at three months old, that the babe of the mistress might obtain sufficient food. They played together as children; and, when they became women, my mother was a most faithful servant to her whiter foster sister. On her death-bed her mistress promised that her children should never suffer for any thing; and during her lifetime she kept her word. They all spoke kindly of my dead mother, who had been a slave merely in name, but in nature was noble and womanly. I grieved for her, and my young mind was troubled with the thought who would now take care of me and my little brother. I was told that my home was now to be with her mistress; and I found it a happy one.
>
> . . . .
>
> When I was nearly twelve years old, my kind mistress sickened and died. As I saw the cheek grow paler, and the eye more glassy, how earnestly I prayed in my heart that she might live! I loved her; for she had been almost like a mother to me. (6–7)

The roles of mother, sister, slave, and mistress tangle in this report. The assumption that infants who suckle at the same breast become sisters, or that the woman who "take[s] care of me" and provides "my home" is "almost" a mother, derives from a familial conception of social relations, a desired fusion of slavery and maternal domesticity. But if the young Linda suggests the naivete of one just learning her social place, the irony of her confusion is, nevertheless, perfectly clear. In her will the mistress who is "almost like a mother" bequeaths Linda to her five-year-old niece. Her mistress had taught her the scriptural precept to "love thy neighbor as thyself," but, Jacobs concludes, "I was her slave, and I suppose she did not recognize me as her neighbor" (8).[13] The asymmetry of social place that allows the mistress to appear almost as a mother while the slave is not recognizable as a neighbor instantly disentangles familial and plantation relations, revealing the difference and distance hidden in the word "almost." In fact it is with the death of this mistress, rather than that of her mother, that Linda can be said to learn that she is a slave; and it is with the death of this mistress that the first chapter, "Childhood," ends.

This rupture of the felt similitude between mother and mistress reiterates a division already discernible in their suckling. To call mother and mistress "foster-sisters" is to suggest that a certain parity and relatedness adhere to sharing the same breast. But the story Jacobs tells reveals that rather than produce social equality, sharing the same breast becomes itself a means of imposing the hierarchies of slavery.[14] Weaning the slave in order to provide more milk for the mistress denies both sisterhood and the presumed primacy of familial or maternal ties; it subjugates the claims of biological and emotional relations to the economic relations of the plantation.

In Jacobs's narrative the act of breast-feeding proves emblematic of plantation society, demonstrating how slavery denies the possibility of separating the personal from the political, since the body itself, and all that makes and maintains it, remains constantly liable to commodification. The slave nurse is not simply a completely corporeal person; she is, beyond that, comestible, literally consumed by her owners and their offspring. The ability to nurse, like the ability to bear children and to provide sexual gratification, manifests the particular utility of the female slave, a utility resulting not simply from the labor performed by her body but rather from her body itself. That this grandmother, whose body nourished the bodies of both of Linda's mistresses, also provided "for all [Linda's] comforts, spiritual or temporal," reveals, however, that the commodification of her capacity for generation and nurturance does not destroy its potential for empowerment (11).[15] The meals and clothes the grandmother makes for Linda, coming as they do despite plantation prohibitions, grant Linda a source of sustenance external to the domestic economy of the plantation.[16] Although obviously tenuous and limited, these acts of nurturance nevertheless provide a degree of autonomy sufficient to affirm for Linda that her body and her identity are not completely subsumed into her position as slave. In revealing the maternal to be simultaneously a means of subverting the plantation economy and a commodity within that economy, Jacobs discovers the limits of her own proposal for a domestic liberty.

The connections Jacobs draws between public records and intimate whispers, liberty and domesticity, derive from the dual nature of her narrative task: to depict the intersection of slavery and sexual exploitation. Jacobs's conflation of the two creates an explicitly textual dilemma, one that functions both thematically and structurally. The narration of this "life of a slave girl," and particularly of the events that comprise Linda's harassment by Dr. Flint and resultant sexual relation with Mr. Sands, is interspersed with incidents and even whole chapters at best peripheral to Linda's personal story. For example, within a single chapter, the story of Linda's first sexual confrontation with Dr. Flint intertwines with the stories of her uncle Benjamin's much thwarted but ultimately successful escape to the North and of her brother William's resistance to the taunts and cuffings instigated by his young master.[17] On a larger scale, between a chapter devoted to Dr. Flint's angry refusal to allow Linda to wed a free-born black man and the chapter in which, in an effort to protect herself from and to spite Dr. Flint, she decides to become Mr. Sands's lover, Jacobs places a chapter entitled "What Slaves Are Taught to Think of the North" and another called "Sketches of Neighboring Slaveholders." Similarly, between the two chapters which recount the births of Linda's two children, fathered by Mr. Sands, Jacobs inserts a chapter-length discussion of Southern responses to Nat Turner's rebellion (an addition that Child had suggested might be of interest to a Northern audience), and a chapter on "The Church and Slavery."[18] The content of these digressive chapters largely conforms to the descriptions of slavery regularly published in abolitionist pamphlets.

Like the strategy of displacement employed in her letter to Post, Jacobs's narrative digressions disperse and so conceal issues of sexuality within the more general political context of slavery. But, considering that accounts of all the lies, violence, surveillance, and religious justification that buttress the institution of slavery constitute the essential and ubiquitous abolitionist narrative, it is equally valid to read the story of Linda's sexual experiences as a series of digressions within this more general abolitionist text. In juxtaposing these generic exposés of the horrors of slavery with the individual and more personal account of Linda's sexual experiences, Jacobs's text raises questions about the adequacy of abolitionist reportage. Yet, as Houston Baker points out, by calling her narrative the life of *a* slave girl she generalizes her personal experience, implying that such sexual exploitation may define slavery for any, or even all, slave girls.[19] Jacobs's narrative strategies evince a desire to have it both ways, to hide her story, and hence her sexual vulnerability, within the general rubric of slavery's atrocities, and to rupture the normative abolitionist accounts of cruel masters and suffering slaves by interposing within it the private discourse of female sexuality.

Jacobs's two-part title, *Incidents in the Life of a Slave Girl, Written By Herself*, reveals more than convention, since the book is as much about the act of writing these incidents of sexual exploitation as it is about the incidents themselves. Jacobs's anxiety over literacy strikingly differentiates her text from the majority of slave narratives, in which command over letters frequently serves as a tool and symbol of liberation. Only rarely does Jacobs celebrate the cunning and skill that permitted Frederick Douglass to write his own pass or reveal the educational bravado with which William Wells Brown tricked white schoolchildren into teaching him letters by showing off the nonsense "writing" he had scratched with a stick into the dirt road.[20] Hiding in her grandmother's attic, Linda does send Dr. Flint taunting letters with misleading Northern postmarks. But in general the trickery and authority of literacy do not remain in her control, for at the very moments that she gains literacy she finds these new skills turned against her. Linda is taught to read and spell by the almost motherly mistress whose written will bequeaths her to the Flints, and when Dr. Flint discovers her teaching herself to write he twists this accomplishment to serve his own plans and begins to slip her threatening and lascivious notes. Thus Jacobs's abolitionist text must also be seen as a site of bondage and sexual degradation. Just as Linda's liaison with Mr. Sands succeeds in challenging the authority of her master at the cost of "womanly virtue," telling her sexual story both emancipates and exploits. The strained relations between the public record of slavery and the intimate whispers of sexuality are reenacted in the scene of writing.

In her introduction to this slave narrative, Lydia Maria Child states that the sexual dimensions of slavery have "generally been kept veiled" but that she, in her role as editor, "willingly take[s] the responsibility of presenting them with the veil withdrawn." In heralding the narrative as a form of undressing, a discursive striptease, Child also records the resistance that awaits the sexual exposure of reading and writing. She explains that her "sisters in bondage . . . are suffering wrongs so foul that our ears are too delicate to listen to them." At work here is not only the solipsism that replaces the suffering of the slave woman with the suffering of her auditor, but also a recognition, even in critique, that the act of narration is itself a sexual act—that though, as Child asserts, Jacobs's experiences may be called "delicate subjects," issues of delicacy are also entailed in their transmission. Urging female readers to the exertion of "moral influence" and exhorting male readers to actively "prevent" the implementation of the fugitive slave laws, Child concludes with a distinctly conservative vision of the gendering of abolitionist response. Out of keeping with her usual feminist posture, Child's insistence that the reading of this slave narrative will work to produce traditional gender norms testifies to her sense of the story's threatening indelicacy—its siege on sexual order and conventional morality (4).

Anxieties over the obstacles to transmission posed by the delicate ears of a Northern audience are directly thematized within Jacobs's text as she repeatedly restages the scene of telling: the abusive erotics of narration become the subject of her narration. The first of these restagings is initiated by the jealous interrogations of Linda's mistress, Mrs. Flint. In one of his many schemes of harassment, Dr. Flint decides to take his young daughter to sleep in his room as a pretext for requiring Linda's presence there throughout the night. The doctor's room and the mistress's room, the would-be scene of harassment and the scene of narration, vie with each other as the locus of Jacobs's text.

> After a while my mistress sent for me to come to her room. Her first question was, "Did you know you were to sleep in the doctor's room?"
> "Yes, ma'am."
> "Who told you?"
> "My master."
> "Will you answer truly all the questions I ask?"
> "Yes, ma'am."
> "Tell me, then, as you hope to be forgiven, are you innocent of what I have accused you?"
> "I am."
>
>   .   .   .   .

"If you have deceived me, beware! Now take this stool, sit down, look me directly in the face, and tell me all that has passed between your master and you."

I did as she ordered. As I went on with my account her color changed frequently, she wept, and sometimes groaned. She spoke in tones so sad, that I was touched by her grief. The tears came to my eyes; but I was soon convinced that her emotions arose from anger and wounded pride. She felt that her marriage vows were desecrated, her dignity insulted; but she had no compassion for the poor victim of her husband's perfidy. She pitied herself as a martyr; but she was incapable of feeling for the condition of shame and misery in which her unfortunate, helpless slave was placed. (33)

The scene has virtually no content: the accusation and the account given are not voiced within Jacobs's text. Instead of describing the events told, Jacobs represents the form of their telling, the dynamics of the discourse of female sexual experience. What Mrs. Flint requires from Linda is finally not a protestation of Linda's sexual innocence, but the titillation of being told all. Yet despite her request, Mrs. Flint refuses to listen to Linda's account; she replaces what Linda would say with her own groans, so that she becomes the martyred subject of the only story she is willing to hear. As in Child's introduction, the experience of the auditor all too easily supplants the sufferings of the slave.

For Linda, moreover, this enforced act of recounting her sexual victimization repeats the scene of sexual abuse. The descriptions of Dr. Flint's efforts to harass Linda provided within *Incidents* focus primarily on his corrupting words: "My master, whose restless, craving vicious nature roved about day and night, seeking whom to devour, had just left me, with stinging, scorching words; words that scathed ear and brain like fire" (18); "My master began to whisper foul words in my ear. . . . He peopled my young mind with unclean images, such as only a vile monster could think of" (27); "When I succeeded in avoiding opportunities for him to talk to me at home, I was ordered to come to his office, to do some errand. When there, I was obliged to stand and listen to such language as he saw fit to address to me" (32). Linda observes that Mrs. Flint's tears and groans derive from her own sense of martyrdom and not from sympathy with the position of her slave. Nevertheless, as this scene is portrayed, Mrs. Flint's position becomes that of the slave woman listening to Dr. Flint's "foul words." "Her color," Jacobs notes, "changed frequently." But though Linda's narration may thus seem to function as a medium of revenge, a way of wounding her cruel auditor, this inversion does not serve to empower Linda, to grant her the authority or dominance of the master. In speaking Dr. Flint's words, Linda both obeys the orders of her mistress, complying with Mrs. Flint's solipsistic and voyeuristic needs, and reveals the extent to which her master's words have indeed scathed her ear and brain. Linda, who met Dr. Flint's speeches with her own words of resistance, conforms to his language, yielding as it were to the dynamics of the sexual scene, only when she recreates it for Mrs. Flint. Rather than redress her sufferings, the act of voicing her sexual experiences enforces and realizes the abuses of which she speaks.[21]

Finally it is Mrs. Flint and not her husband who takes Linda to sleep "in a room adjoining her own."

> There I was an object of her especial care, though not of her especial comfort, for she spent many a sleepless night to watch over me. Sometimes I woke up, and found her bending over me. At other times she whispered in my ear, as though it was her husband who was speaking to me, and listened to hear what I would answer. If she startled me, on such occasions, she would glide stealthily away; and the next morning she would tell me I had been talking in my sleep, and ask who I was talking to. At last I began to be fearful for my life. (34)

As she bends over her sleeping slave, her mouth at Linda's ear, Mrs. Flint occupies precisely the position of erotic dominance repeatedly denied the doctor. This is the most explicitly and graphically sexual representation in the entire narrative; while Jacobs depicts Mrs. Flint in the dark, bending over Linda's supine body, she does not present either the doctor or the more sexually successful Mr. Sands in any similarly intimate posture. Since this scene, despite all of its overtly erotic content, purports to represent jealousy rather than lust, it falls safely within the bounds of acceptable feminine discourse. Modestly "veiled" by jealousy the scene offers no affront to "delicacy."

Such an explanation for the displacement of the role of rapist from husband to wife does not, however, fully account for Jacobs's description of these nocturnal encounters. In casting this scene of sexual domination between slave and mistress, rather than, as her plot would indicate, between slave and master, Jacobs collapses female sexual experience into the problems associated with feminine discourse and the telling of that experience. Mrs. Flint's midnight whisperings imitate both Dr. Flint's harassments and Linda's account of those harassments. The story Linda must tell and the act of telling it combine in this life-threatening figure. "Woman can whisper—her cruel wrongs into the ear of a very dear friend," Jacobs had written to Amy Post. Yet it is in this very image of an intimately whispering woman that Jacobs comes closest to depicting the scene of rape. In short, she identifies sexual oppression less with any physical act than with the representation of that act.

The rapes of narration and reenactment that Jacobs shows to be inherent in the discourse of sexuality occupy the place of the unspeakable event of male sexual violence and its institutionalization in the plantation economy, where illicit offspring become property. This does not mean, of course, that the compulsions of slavery and the threat of male violence have disappeared. After all, this nightmare scene explicitly reenacts Dr. Flint's efforts to harass Linda. He is never really absent from these apparently female interactions: in Linda's responses to the command that she tell all, and in Mrs. Flint's nocturnal visits, the doctor's lewd speech threatens, and indeed usurps, the identities of both women.[22] As Mrs. Flint whispers "as though it were her husband who was speaking," the discourse of female sexuality or female power finds itself hopelessly mired in the master's words.

Explicitly written for a Northern, white, female readership, *Incidents* bears a strained and strange relation to feminine domestic norms. The narrator frequently turns to address her readers, calling attention to her abolitionist purpose and to the fact that this textual account, like the scenes of narration presented within it, relies upon the responsive presence of an audience. This general tendency to address the reader becomes, however, unusually pronounced when Linda explains her attachment to Mr. Sands and her "plunge into the abyss" of sexual activity (53). While such passages of direct address usually function as a relatively detached form of commentary on the events described—a plea for action or an attack on Northern complicity not directly related to the incidents at hand—in the pages that discuss Linda's decision to become Mr. Sands's lover the reader's role seems less that of an audience than that of an essential actor in the scene. The plot of Linda's explanations to her judgmental readers largely overwhelms the plot of Mr. Sands's eloquence and Linda's gullible calculations. The presumed rejections and resistances of her readers quite literally replace the story of her sexual choices: "I will not try to screen myself behind the plea of compulsion from a master," she writes, "for it was not so,"

> Neither can I plead ignorance or thoughtlessness. . . . I knew what I did and I did it with deliberate calculation.
>   But, O, ye happy women, whose purity has been sheltered from childhood, who have been free to choose the objects of your affection, whose homes are protected by law, do not judge the poor desolate slave girl too severely! (54)

If Jacobs's narrative puts the white woman's expectations in the place of her own sexuality, she nevertheless insists that such displacements are finally untenable. After describing Mr. Sands's flattering attentions, and asserting the "something akin to freedom" in taking as a lover a man who is not her master, Linda concludes "there may be sophistry in all this; but the condition of a slave confuses all principles of morality, and, in fact, renders the practice of them impossible."

> Pity me, and pardon me, O virtuous reader! You never knew what it is to be a slave; to be entirely unprotected by law or

custom; to have the laws reduce you to the condition of a chattel, entirely subject to the will of another. . . . I know I did wrong. No one can feel it more sensibly than I do. The painful and humiliating memory will haunt me to my dying day. Still, in looking back, calmly, on the events of my life, I feel that the slave woman ought not to be judged by the same standard as others. (55–56)

Linda's stress on the wrongful humiliation of her past actions conforms to the moral code of her happy and virtuous readers.[23] Yet though she asks for their pity and their pardons, she also repeatedly and explicitly disqualifies them and their code of sexual morality for the task of judgment. It is not the protected reader, but only the slave woman, writing from the calm vantage of her experiences, who can articulate an appropriate standard. The sexual experience she decries and would repress provides the only available ground of judgment and therefore the only means of validation and liberation. If Linda's sexual relations with Mr. Sands tend to dissolve in this chapter into the narrative act of explaining and justifying those relations, the explanations offered invariably point back to the realm of experience. Asking for her readers' pity and yet denying their ability to comprehend her choices, Jacobs suggests that the experiences of slavery remain precisely what cannot be explained. Transgressing social norms, slavery threatens to foreclose communication. Just as Jacobs hopes that her narrative will redefine slavery, and perhaps even help to abolish it, slavery challenges the bounds of feminine discourse and the grounds of feminine judgment and hence redefines Jacobs's relation to her sexuality, her text, and the white women whose decorum would censor them both.

Within the text, Linda's attempts to tell this portion of her sexual history demonstrate the cultural pervasiveness of such censorship among black listeners as well as white. Newly arrived in Philadelphia, she is taken into the home of "a respectable-looking colored man," the Rev. Jeremiah Durham, where his questions reveal some of the limits of her Northern freedom.

> Mr. Durham observed that I had spoken to him of a daughter
> I expected to meet; that he was surprised, for I looked so
> young he had taken me for a single woman. He was approach-
> ing a subject on which I was extremely sensitive. He would
> ask about my husband next, I thought, and if I answered him
> truly, what would he think of me? He asked some further
> questions, and I frankly told him some of the most important
> events of my life. It was painful for me to do it; but I would not
> deceive him. If he was desirous of being my friend, I thought
> he ought to know how far I was worthy of it. "Excuse me, if I
> have tried your feelings," said he. "I did not question you
> from idle curiosity. I wanted to understand your situation, in
> order to know whether I could be of any service to you, or
> your little girl. Your straight-forward answers do you credit;
> but don't answer every body so openly. It might give some
> heartless people a pretext for treating you with contempt."
> (160)

Linda's sensitivity on this subject, her concern with what her
auditor will think, her insistence that such narrations are
painful to her, and her allusion to a scale of worthiness in
which the illegitimacy of her children functions as a demerit
all indicate her wish to comply with nineteenth-century standards of chastity. Yet despite these symptoms of internal censorship, Linda bristles at Rev. Durham's suggestion that she
suppress the sexual aspects of her history:

> That word *contempt* burned me like coals of fire. I replied,
> "God alone knows how I have suffered; and He, I trust, will
> forgive me. If I am permitted to have my children, I intend to
> be a good mother, and to live in such a manner that people
> cannot treat me with contempt." (161)

The words that had burned her under slavery were the
"scorching words" of Dr. Flint. The language of sexual harassment and the language of sexual suppression impose
comparable scars. Even before this quite sympathetic audience, Linda finds that the act of telling her sexual story subtly
reenacts that story.

Linda's response proposes the role of the "good mother"
as a substitute for chastity. Such a redefinition of sexual morality casts the children whose illegitimate birth attest to her

sexual activity as the signs and sources of her moral virtue. Abolitionist writings consistently offer the light-skinned child of the slave woman as proof of the miscegenating economy of slavery, so that the child stands as evidence of the gap between plantation life and the ideology of the sacrosanct bourgeois family. Inverting this system of bodily signs, Jacobs presents the slave-child, even the interracial slave-child, as a potential means of access to a virtuous, respectable domesticity. Rather than signifying her difference from the middle-class white woman, Linda recognizes her children as signs of her sameness, and as barriers against the contempt that comes with differentiation. This reinterpretation depends upon viewing the child not as a product of sexual activity, but as an object of maternal nature. Jacobs has used this defense before under antithetical circumstances. Threatened by the completion of the cabin where Dr. Flint proposes to keep her as his concubine, Linda asserts, "I will never go there. In a few months I shall be a mother" (56). Motherhood replaces sexuality.

Significantly, this maternal elision of sexuality characterizes Linda's attempt to tell her sexual history to her daughter Ellen. Her final restaging of the scene of sexual narration appears in a very brief chapter entitled "The Confession," only two chapters away from the end of the volume. But even here, with the book nearly completed, and with her daughter's loving acceptance of Linda's choices "making," as Hazel Carby argues, "external validation unnecessary and unwarranted," the act of telling her sexual story remains ambivalent.[24] In fact Linda hardly manages to tell her story at all:

> I recounted my early sufferings in slavery, and told her how nearly they had crushed me. I began to tell her how they had driven me into a great sin, when she clasped me in her arms, and exclaimed, "O, don't, mother! Please don't tell me any more."
> I said, "But my child, I want you to know about your father."
> "I know all about it, mother," she replied. (188–89)

As Ellen goes on to deny the claims of her father and affirm her love for her mother, the story of her parental allegiances silences the story of her mother's sexual experience. The ploy of denying parental sexuality emancipates through repression, granting respectability to the freed woman by forgetting the sexual vulnerability of the slave. Linda is empowered in this chapter not by her confession, as the title implies, but rather by the child's will to absolve by denial.

Jacobs hopes that the feminine discourse of domesticity and motherhood might serve to rectify the sexual story that is "the life of a slave girl." Her narrative, however, ultimately fails to displace the sexual experiences it describes. Instead it repeats them, as the act of telling this story results in rape, shame, contempt, and denial—results, that is, in the painful attributes of slavery's degrading sexuality. But if Jacobs's narration takes on the suffering and vulnerability of sexuality, it also commands a measure of its pleasures and its power. Before Child's introduction to *Incidents*, with its anxious but enticing promise of a story that would "unveil" the experiences of a slave girl, Jacobs places two epigraphs and a preface that locate the threat of sexual objectification differently.

The two epigraphs that introduce Jacobs's book discretely suggest that the reader shares in this story's sexual risk. "Northerners know nothing at all about Slavery," she quotes from a woman of North Carolina, "they have no conception of the depth of *degradation* involved in that word, SLAVERY." The epigraph promises a lesson in reading, in the belief that the comprehension of a word would produce abolitionist action. Yet, as her emphasis insists, all that would replace the "nothing" of ignorance and apathy must be recognized as *degradation.* Once fully read the word SLAVERY threatens to rape the "too delicate" ears of Jacobs's Northern audience. Indeed, the second epigraph to *Incidents* links the possibility of white women's political "rise" to Jacobs's ability to gain access to this eroticized narrative orifice: "Rise up, ye women that are at ease! Hear my voice, ye careless daughters! Give ear unto my speech" (Isaiah 32:9). P. Gabrielle Foreman calls attention to the subsequent lines of Isaiah pointedly not printed on Jacobs's page: "Tremble, you women who are at ease, Shudder you complacent ones. Strip and make yourself bare, and gird sackcloth upon your loins" (Isaiah 32:11). If Jacobs forbears from stripping her auditors, this suppressed threat nevertheless marks the potential reversibility of the circuits of narrative eroticism, destabilizing, as Foreman argues, "the very category of racially determined sexual objectification."[25]

Such reversals do not attempt to deny or evade the patterns of dominance and submission inherent in the erotics of narration, but they do imagine a form of telling that rather than merely unveil the slave girl who is its subject would also work to reveal its Northern audience. "I have not written my experiences in order to attract attention to myself," Jacobs states in her preface,

> on the contrary, it would have been more pleasant to me to have been silent about my own history. Neither do I care to excite sympathy for my own sufferings. But I do earnestly desire to arouse the women of the North to a realizing sense of the condition of two millions of women at the South, still in bondage, suffering what I suffered, and most of them far worse. (1)

In presenting herself to a Northern female readership as the representative of two million slave women, Jacobs makes her private history into a public and emblematically political document, but beyond this she defines the political purposes and forum for which she writes as female. The forbidden politics and the forbidden sexuality are conflated: throughout this statement her political goals assert an erotic urgency.[26] Reiterating Isaiah's injunction to "rise up," Jacobs forfeits a "pleasant" silence, and demurs "to excite sympathy" because of her "desire to arouse the women of the North." The arousal entailed in reading this "Life of a Slave Girl," the sexual charge of abolitionist politics, eroticizes Jacobs's Northern audience by equating their reading with the perverse interrogations of a Mrs. Flint. In constructing an equation between her jealous mistress, her Northern audience and, by extension, that suspect figure, the white critic, myself, Jacobs presents the sexual dynamics of narration with the "veil withdrawn." As she "desires" the arousal of her readers, she makes use of the erotic power of narration instead of being employed by it. Thus in telling the story of her own sexual exploitation Jacobs enlists both the sexual responses of her readers and the threat of their similar sexual vulnerability for her own abolitionist purposes. The act of narration may be a striptease, and so, like Linda's sexual relations with Mr. Sands, it may appear a source of shame. But such degradations may, nevertheless, prove tactical. Jacobs's conflation of sex and writing establishes both her sexual story and her telling of it as acts of defiance, as a means of resisting—however inadequately—the oppressions, even the sexual oppressions, of slavery.

4

At Home in the Body

*The Internal Politics of
Emily Dickinson's Poetry*

So I concluded that space & time are things of the body &
have little or nothing to do with our selves. My Country is
Truth. . . . I like Truth—it is a free Democracy.[1]

Emily Dickinson records these conclusions in a letter written
sometime near the end of both the Civil War and her own
years of greatest poetic production. In the face of a divided
nation she selects "Truth" as her country. During years suf-
fused with the abolitionist rhetoric of emancipating black
bodies and the corporeal horrors of the Civil War itself, she
allies freedom with the easy dismissal of the "things of the
body." In these lines Dickinson claims freedom for herself by
forfeiting any engagement with the nation and, even more
radically, by forfeiting her own body.

In proposing mass slave suicides as a means of eliminating
slavery, abolitionists suggest a comparable exchange of flesh
for freedom. Achieving freedom only through the bodily torture of the storehouse garret, Harriet Jacobs details just such
an exchange. In the stripping of flesh from the body on the
auction block, Walt Whitman seems willing to barter the
slave's body for a vision of unity. Dickinson's forfeiture
of her body is thus a familiar—if disquieting—ploy in the
nineteenth-century political discourse of emancipation. Dickinson herself, however, recognizes the limitations and instability of the fleshless liberty she claims in this letter. In her
poems this atemporal, incorporeal "free democracy" is constantly refigured as a quite different country, one bounded by

time, grounded in a mortal and sexual body, and characterized not by freedom but by bondage. Dickinson ultimately
locates "Truth" on the boundary between these two conceptions of nation, self, and liberty.

Dickinson never explicitly associates her concern over the
relation between embodiment and freedom with the contemporary political agitation over slavery. Indeed, for a member
of a family actively engaged in national politics, she is remarkably silent on such pressing public issues.[2] Dickinson's
social detachment has long been considered the paramount
characteristic of both her isolated adult life and her elusive,
nonreferential poetry.[3] In situating the problematics of Dickinson's verse in relation to the more publicly and politically
motivated writings discussed in earlier chapters, my work
modifies but does not disown this critical tradition. Rather I
am interested precisely in how the thematic connections between the treatment of liberty and embodiment in Dickinson's poems and in the political campaigns of feminism and
abolition become detached. This chapter assesses what has
happened when a concern with the corporeality of identity
that appears political and public in the writings of feminist-
abolitionists, Whitman, and Jacobs is fashioned by Dickinson into a poetic, ahistorical and ontological dilemma. My
concern is not simply to provide a historical context for
Dickinson's poems, but simultaneously to account for the
ways in which they resist and internalize this social and historical meaning.

Dickinson's assertion of a freedom detached from national
and physical bounds seeks to place her poetry "outside of
and apart from history," and so would seem to disassociate it
from the explicitly political concerns of this book.[4] Yet the
question of how political meaning adheres within individual
utterances has already proved problematic in earlier chapters. The tensions between narrative and lyric modes within
Whitman's poetic practice suggests that even for him the
project of reconciling history and poetry remains fundamentally unstable. In his attempt to reconcile personal and social
meaning, Whitman writes a poetry less of stabilizing union
than of desire. Conversely, in Jacobs's narrative, personal ex-

perience proves inseparable both from abolitionist politics and from the act of writing. If Whitman records the pain of a self never sufficiently incorporated within the social world, Jacobs records the pain of never sufficiently differentiating a self from its embeddedness in historical and narrative meanings. Thus Dickinson's celebration of a nationless, fleshless, and ahistorical liberty should be understood as an extreme articulation of the tensions between self and history already at stake in the writings of Whitman and Jacobs. Indeed, read in this context, Dickinson's strategies of social detachment demonstrate the doubleness of bodily definitions of personhood. Taken together these three confrontations with the corporeality of identity reveal both a uniquely differentiated identity—individual and private in nature—and simultaneously an identity constructed within a social matrix— inherently public and political.

The free democracy of truth that Dickinson claims in her letter thus stands in strained opposition to the divided nation in which she lived. In tracing her connections to and her detachment from the public discourses of emancipation, I do not wish to champion one nation or the other, but rather to recognize Dickinson's precarious perch between. From this middle place Dickinson does not aim, as Whitman does, to mediate between body and soul. The divisions within identity that her poems chart are not, for her, reconcilable. Indeed, what interests her about identity is precisely its unresolvable doubleness. Instead of forging mergers she seeks to describe a "Double Estate," one in which human identity is suspended between the irreconcilable but inseparable requirements of a body and a soul.

> I am afraid to own a Body—
> I am afraid to own a Soul—
> Profound—precarious Property—
> Possession, not optional—
>
> Double Estate—entailed at pleasure
> Upon an unsuspecting Heir—
> Duke in a moment of Deathlessness
> And God, for a Frontier.
> (1090)[5]

What frightens Dickinson about the double estate of body and soul is that it grants an identity both precarious and— without options, without freedom—inevitable. The identity provided by the compounding of body and soul can be neither assured nor escaped. Moreover, the double bind of human identity impinges on all attempts to imagine or give image to transcendence. Even the power and status of "Deathless-ness" comes contained within a temporal "moment." So, too, the "Frontier" that is God simultaneously suggests expanse and limit.

Dickinson figures the connection between self, body, and soul in explicitly proprietary terms: the relation that the "I" fears but cannot avoid is that of ownership. Conceptually, the horror of slavery lies in a master's legal claim to own a slave, body and soul. Dickinson's poem presents self-ownership as no less horrifying, since by commodifying the self it too de- nies freedom. In these transactions the self functions not only as owner but also as a passive subject to be controlled or pos- sessed, for though the "I" may come to own body and soul it does so from a position of powerlessness in which no alter- native status is possible and all the "pleasure" of this estate adheres elsewhere. For Dickinson, identity, like the condition of bondage, is a compulsory inheritance.[6] A proprietary or hereditary basis for identity undermines the possibility of a free and autonomous self. Indeed, after admitting its fear of self-ownership, the "I" disappears from the poem. Thus the double estate of body and soul that Dickinson describes in this poem ultimately calls both identity and voice into question: evading body and soul, from what possible posi- tion, with what possible agency, could the "I" of the opening lines speak?

Dickinson's description of identity as a double estate de- scribes body and soul as mutually confining: if the body shackles the soul, it is equally true that the soul binds the body. The equation between the body and bondage is not as simple or as unilateral as it initially appeared. Instead impris- onment proves to be as much spiritual or psychic as it is physical.

A Prison gets to be a friend—
Between its Ponderous face
And Ours—a Kinsmanship express—
And in its narrow Eyes—

We come to look with gratitude
For the appointed Beam
It deal us—stated as our food—
And hungered for—the same—

We learn to know the Planks—
That answer to Our feet—
So miserable a sound—at first—
Nor ever now—so sweet—

As plashing in the Pools—
When Memory was a Boy—
But a Demurer Circuit—
A Geometric Joy—

The Posture of the Key
That interrupt the Day
To Our Endeavor—Not so real
The Cheek of Liberty—

As this Phantasm Steel—
Whose features—Day and Night—
Are present to us—as Our Own—
And as escapeless—quite—

The narrow Round—the Stint—
The slow exchange of Hope—
For something passiver—Content
Too steep for looking up—

The Liberty we knew
Avoided—like a Dream—
Too wide for any Night but Heaven—
If That—indeed—redeem—

(652)

Dickinson begins this poem by describing the slow process by which confinement becomes familiar and so no longer simply oppressive. As the poem progresses, however, it becomes clear that the prison does not necessarily precede the resigned acceptance of "a Demurer Circuit / A Geometric Joy." The joy found in limits need not stem from a gradual accommodation to any physical or external constraints. Rather, Dickinson suggests, "the slow exchange of Hope" for a more passive "Content" may itself erect a prison. Thus the poem revolves around the double meaning of "Content": both as the quiet satisfaction of contentment and as an object enclosed or contained. In pretending that confinement may ultimately yield contentment, Dickinson raises the possibility that resigning oneself to such a pleasant complacency may actually enclose the self. Here it is the body, which once played free "plashing in the Pools," that has been bound by a "Demurer" soul.

But, characteristically, this poem invites the opposite interpretation as well. Personified, both the prison and liberty wear faces. Initially the "Ponderous face" of one and the "Cheek" of the other appear to be conventional literary devices. Yet the "Kinsmanship" of the prison's face and "Ours," or the way in which the "features" of the prison's steel bars "Are present to us—as Our Own" collapses this personification until the "Phantasm" of prison bars becomes recognizable as our own flesh, or until our own flesh becomes prison bars.

Liberty, however, keeps her alluring and elusive cheek to herself. The personification of liberty remains a literary trope; it is "Not so real" as the prison's face. Instead liberty glimmers on the borders of past and future, both embodied and disembodied: it belongs to a boyish memory of "plashing" physical abandon, spared both the responsibilities of age and the limitations of femininity, and it belongs to the incorporeal, and not quite convincing, dream of Heaven. In describing the links between liberty and bondage, in revealing the necessity for and the limits to both bodily and disembodied sources of identity, and in alternately allying both flesh and fleshlessness with bondage, Dickinson depicts the call for emancipation as problematic, even as she relocates it within her own identity, her own body, and her own utterance.

As the reclusive habits of Dickinson's adult life suggest, the relation between confinement and liberty was never, for her, simply a matter of oppositions. The allure of what one poem calls "a magic prison" (1602) informs Dickinson's efforts to redefine liberty. Martha Dickinson Bianchi's recollections of her Aunt Emily include these often cited scenes:

> I remember telling her how, when a child, I once had been sent up to the guest-room to sit quietly by myself as punishment—until I had regretted some trifling dereliction; but I had enjoyed the pretty room so much I had refused to come out when the ban was lifted, and how her eyes sparkled as she confided to me, joyously, "Matty, child, no one could ever punish a Dickinson by shutting her up alone."
>
> . . . .
>
> She would stand looking down, one hand raised, thumb and forefinger closed on an imaginary key, and say, with a quick turn of her wrist, "It's just a turn—and freedom Matty!"[7]

In these stories, freedom lies in being shut up alone. Dickinson inverts the mechanisms of discipline and claims confinement as a mode of liberation. In a manner reminiscent of Harriet Jacobs's tactics of escape, Dickinson asserts her liberty in retreat. Yet for Dickinson, as for Jacobs, such "loopholes of retreat" offer only the most provisional and contradictory of freedoms. Jacobs's escape into domestic space strains against her ultimate exclusion from the domestic, her inability ever to claim "a home of my own." In contrast, Dickinson's seclusion, her decision that she would "not cross my Father's ground to any House or town" is complicated by its perfect compliance with the notion of a separate feminine sphere bounded by male proprietorship.[8] Nineteenth-century domestic ideology praised woman's enclosure in the home not only as desirable and proper, but also as the celebrated source of feminine purity and moral power: female exclusion from the business of the nation was consistently figured as freedom. The rhetoric of the domestic ideal thus threatens to preempt the possibility of equating domestic enclosure with liberty, making it difficult to distinguish between escape from societal strictures and the rewards promised for docile submission to them. Aware of this contradiction, Dickinson explicitly associates the stoic notion of liberty-in-confinement with the domestic enclosure of the house, and thus signals an attempt to undo this preemption, and so to reclaim and reimagine domestic space.[9] Jacobs's exclusion from the domestic and Dickinson's confinement within it pose such radically different problems, that each can actually imagine using the domestic predicament of the other as a model for achieving domestic liberty. So Jacobs, dreaming of a home of her own, fantasizes liberty as living in and being serviced by the domestic, whereas Dickinson describes liberty as the ability to make the domestic—both by metaphorically figuring it and by exaggerating her housebound status—without having to actually inhabit or be defined by it. Thus their shared vision of liberty through confinement ultimately testifies less to their cultural contiguity than to the bleak and absolute differences in their social status.

Like Matty's description of her Aunt Emily gleefully locking herself into freedom with an imaginary key, the frequently anthologized "I dwell in Possibility" serves to celebrate the ties between domestic seclusion and imaginative or authorial liberty. Yet even here, I would argue, the relation is not so simple or so salutary.

> I dwell in Possibility—
> A fairer House than Prose—
> More numerous of Windows—
> Superior—for Doors—
>
> Of Chambers as the Cedars—
> Impregnable of Eye—
> And for an Everlasting Roof
> The Gambrels of the Sky—
>
> Of Visitors—the fairest—
> For Occupation—This—
> The spreading wide my narrow Hands
> To gather Paradise—
>
> (657)

The house of Possibility Dickinson praises in this poem is at once the space of poetry (fairer than Prose) and the realm of nature (with cedar chambers and a sky roof, not a house at all). As the metaphor of the house dissolves into poetry and nature the accolades of domestic liberty end in casting Possibility as an anti-house, inimicable to the domestic enclosures that would name it. "Impregnable," Dickinson's chambers prohibit entrance and yet suggest the secreted creativity of the womb. Her rooms are simultaneously closed and expansively fertile. The poetic and heavenly gathering with which the poem concludes entails a similar paradox: spread wide, her hands become a sieve with gaps between each finger. The anti-house, the impregnable chamber, the narrow hands spread wide all permit Dickinson to define domestic, feminine, narrowness as liberating. Dickinson represents poetic possibility as both domestic and unbounded; she celebrates domestic liberty, but the manner in which she does so demonstrates that it is a contradiction in terms. Dickinson locates freedom in domestic spaces, but she simultaneously figures normative domestic expectations as precisely what she wishes to escape.

Domestic ideology casts the home as the definitive marker and guarantor of female identity. Dickinson's metaphorics tend to reverse these signs: while she employs houses as useful images for the contours of her identity, she does not permit these structures to confine or define the self.[10] So she describes "Remembrance," that psychic collection of all the events and relations that have configured the self, as "something like a House." She insists that the relation between self and house remain on the level of simile, and that even as a simile it is at best approximate, merely *"something* like."

> Remembrance has a Rear and Front—
> 'Tis something like a House—
> It has a Garret also
> For Refuse and the Mouse.
>
> Besides the deepest Cellar
> That ever Mason laid—
> Look to it by its Fathoms
> Ourselves be not pursued—
>
> (1182)

The refuge this house offers is not protection from any external, public dangers; what threatens in this poem lurks in the infinite regress, the underground fathoms, of the house's own cellar. The orderliness of the house, with its proper place for everything, ultimately rests on top of the very horrors it proposes to domesticate. Though the nature of these buried horrors remains open and multiple, female sexuality is clearly implicated in the threat posed by "the *deepest* Cellar / That ever Mason *laid*." Moreover, the relation between cellar and house provides a telling depiction of the relation between female sexuality and domestic norms. Understood in terms of the bearing and rearing of children, female sexual experience provides the basis for the familial arrangements that characterize domesticity, and yet the possibility of an autonomous female sexual desire posits a powerful challenge to these social arrangements. In casting remembrance as a house, Dickinson reveals the equation between domestic order and repression. Yet in depicting the very foundations of the house, its cellar, as the repository for all the memories and desires that might challenge its domestic calm, Dickinson stresses the precariousness of such homely order. Her configuration of the self in terms of domestic architecture ultimately serves, quite literally as the cellar deepens, to undermine the domestic.

Yet in voicing the desperate desire that "Ourselves be not pursued," Dickinson acknowledges her dependence on such policies of repression. If Dickinson recognizes the confinements that characterize the domestic sphere as necessary, she nevertheless clearly balks against such regulatory "little duties":

> I tie my Hat—I crease my Shawl—
> Life's little duties do—precisely—
> As the very least
> Were infinite—to me—

Domesticity's pious insistence on the infinite value of even the least significant daily tasks (acting *because* the very least were infinite) collapses into a contrived and meaningless simulation (acting *as if* the very least were infinite). As the poem continues Dickinson punctures this domestic masquerade, disrupting her story of little duties with the "Existence" they cannot manage to contain.

> I put new Blossoms in the Glass—
> And throw the old—away—
> I push a petal from my Gown
> That anchored there—I weigh
> The time 'twill be till six o'clock
> I have so much to do—
> And yet—Existence—some way back—
> Stopped—struck—my ticking—through—
> We cannot put Ourself away
> As a completed Man
> Or Woman—When the Errand's done
> We came to Flesh—upon—
> There may be—Miles on Miles of Nought—
> Of Action—sicker far—
> To simulate—is stinging work—
> To cover what we are
> From Science—and from Surgery—
> Too Telescopic Eyes
> To bear on us unshaded—
> For their—sake—not for Ours—
> 'Twould start them—
> We—could tremble—
> But since we got a Bomb—
> And held it in our Bosom—
> Nay—Hold it—it is calm—
>
> Therefore—we do life's labor—
> Though life's Reward—be done—
> With scrupulous exactness—
> To hold our Senses—on—

$(443)^{11}$

Dickinson records how existence has "Stopped" beneath the sicker action of simulated living, and she imagines the "start" entailed in making this covered self visible. Her heart has been arrested ("struck—my ticking—through") or has gained the potential to explode ("a Bomb . . . held . . . in our Bosom"). I am stressing the opposition between the two moments in which, as Sharon Cameron puts it, "meaning disrupts both vacuous action and the sententia in which such action takes refuge," in order to make clear the array of emotion and experience that domesticity fails to contain or comprehend.[12] Yet it is equally important to note how the domestic vocabulary of "little duties" pervades the poem. The "Errand . . . We came to Flesh upon" remains an errand, despite its value as incarnation or bodily pleasure. The inability to "put Ourself away" recites a failure in housekeeping as much as it marks the abhorrence of a life that contains only such meaningless activities. If this poem asserts the emptiness of the domestic sphere, and the fragility of its easily exploded masquerade, the last stanza nevertheless insists that it is only submersion in these pointless daily tasks that preserves "our Senses"—any mind, any sensation, or any meaning—at all. For if the bomb of passion, anger, or loss were to explode it would destroy not just the despised domestic calm but also the woman who holds it against her breast.

The split in Dickinson's treatment of domestic space repeats in significant ways her sense of identity as a "double estate." Both her body and her domestic role appear to Dickinson as obstacles to the freedom she desires; but she also recognizes them as the inescapable conditions of her being, the necessary ground of her identity and of any "free democracy" to which she might lay claim. Moreover, as a nineteenth-century woman domesticated by biology, she may well have seen the two projects of remaking her body and her home into sites of liberation as one and the same. Her lexicon's five definitions of "home" include "the present state of existence" and illustrate this usage with a verse from 2 Corinthians, "Whilst we are at home in the body, we are absent from the Lord."[13] Such a definition assumes the earthly congruity of home and flesh in order to devalue both. For Dickinson, the double estate of identity can thus best be understood as a domestic problem: what it means to house a soul.

> The Body grows without—
> The more convenient way—
> That if the Spirit—like to hide
> Its Temple stands, alway,

Ajar—secure—inviting—
It never did betray
The Soul that asked its shelter
In solemn honesty

(578)

Even in this remarkably sanguine vision of the body's ability to shelter the soul, traces of doubleness remain as bodily shelter appears simultaneously "ajar" and "secure." Recording the body's valued role as a protective cover, Dickinson nevertheless intimates its potential to betray. Thomas Foster writes that "to be 'at home' in a female body was to be dispossessed metaphorically, in terms of political participation, and literally, in terms of property rights and home ownership."[14] For a woman to be at home in her body is at once a tautology—where else could she be but at home?—and a coercive contradiction, since both domesticity and embodiment are "not optional" but compulsory, and so, however familiar, never simply sites of refuge or freedom.

Dickinson's apparent willingness to forfeit her body for freedom, or her glee in choosing domestic isolation, indicates a desire to escape the constraints of body and home by simply asserting that she can do without them. "The Outer—from the Inner / Derives its Magnitude" she explains in one poem, comparing the invisible power of interiority to the "unvarying Axis / That regulates the Wheel— / Though Spokes—spin—more conspicuous" (451). The problem with such dismissals of the constraints of embodied, domestic existence is that they tend to leave the self not with freedom, but with nothing. The hub may center the wheel, but it is also formed by its intersecting spokes; without spokes there would be no axis. Moreover the pun on spokes needs to be taken seriously, for without them there would be no speech and no poems, either. Dickinson's desire for bodilessness, her insistence on the clear superiority of the "Inner" soul, constantly flounders on the unrecognizable and unspeakable nature of disembodied being.

This desire to dismiss the physical component of identity both carries a particular allure and poses particular problems for women, whose identities have been traditionally defined by their anatomy and by their domestic place. Significantly, 2 Corinthians posits body and home in opposition to the powerfully masculine presence of "the Lord." But what is a female self without a body and without a house?

> How many times these low feet staggered—
> Only the soldered mouth can tell—
> Try—can you stir the awful rivet—
> Try—can you lift the hasps of steel!
>
> Stroke the cool forehead—hot so often—
> Lift—if you care—the listless hair—
> Handle the adamantine fingers
> Never a thimble—more—shall wear—
>
> Buzz the dull flies—on the chamber window—
> Brave—shines the sun through the freckled pane—
> Fearless—the cobweb swings from the ceiling—
> Indolent Housewife—in Daisies—lain!
>
> (187)

Here Dickinson marks death and the body's inability adequately to express the self as a breakdown in the domestic order—indolent housekeeping. The recalcitrance of a body soldered, riveted, and hasped against interpretation keeps the self secret. The body's refusal to tell is matched, however, by the indifference of the audience that stands around the woman's corpse. The speaker's injunctions ("try—can you stir . . . try—can you lift") quickly lose the urgency of interest: "lift—if you care," they advise. In the face of the housewife's demise, care and engagement have become, at best, conditional. If Dickinson recognizes that the body does not reveal the self, she nevertheless figures it as deserving the respectful treatment owed to a self, or at least as deserving better care than the probing, stroking, and handling it receives here.

"Care" is, of course, precisely what fills a housewife's days. For Dickinson, however, the care that keeps windows clean and sweeps away cobwebs provides no better access to identity than that granted by the listless hair and adamantine fingers of the corpse. Dickinson satirizes the social perspective that, insistent on woman's domestic place, would label a dead woman "indolent." However, her own assessment of these domestic tasks remains mixed: she applauds as "brave" the sun that would shine through, and so overcome, the grime on unwashed windows, but she also, in perfectly balanced equity, finds the swinging cobwebs "fearless." The scorn shown the woman's body and the devaluation of her domestic labors rankle in this poem, even if Dickinson herself doesn't want to figure either as comprising female identity.

The problem is that if body and home can never adequately signify the female self it remains equally impossible to adopt any other signs. In a whimsical reversal of the prodding of the housewife's corpse, Dickinson attempts a similar assessment of a bodiless, postmortem soul:

> I felt my life with both my hands
> To see if it was there—
> I held my spirit to the Glass,
> To prove it possibler—
>
> I turned my Being round and round
> And paused at every pound
> To ask the Owner's name—
> For doubt, that I should know the Sound—
>
> I judged my features—jarred my hair—
> I pushed my dimples by, and waited—
> If they—twinkled back—
> Conviction might, of me—
>
> I told myself, "Take Courage, Friend—
> That—was a former time—
> But we might learn to like the Heaven,
> As well as our Old Home!"
>
> (351)

The senses—touch, sight, sound—cannot appraise a bodiless being. The absence of a body arrests both possession and language: the speaker repeatedly asks "the Owner's name / For doubt, that I should know the Sound." Her question signals the precariousness of any claim to self-ownership of a necessarily immeasurable self; if the thing claimed has no features and no dimensions, what does one own, after all? Bodilessness similarly defies the codification offered by language, reducing "name" to a nonconnotative "sound." Ultimately life without a body is so completely unrecognizable that Dickinson's effort to describe and affirm the soul in heaven collapses into the "Old Home" terms of a woman preening before a mirror.

The problem posited by this collapse is double, like identity itself. Featureless, with nothing to reflect in the poet's glass, the spirit must remain unimaginable. Yet judging features, jarring hair, and pushing dimples, the harsh, almost violent motions of feminine primping, hardly offer a promising means of assessing even a bodily identity. If the fact that a spirit has no reflection ensures that the soul remain fundamentally unknowable, unowned, and unnamed, the fact that a body can be reflected, and that a woman's body so often is, tends to trap female identity in the realm of mirrored appearances. In the face of this double threat to identity, the "I" of the poem remains disjunct from both its "spirit" and its "features"; so split, by the final stanza it becomes a plural "we."

The poem ends with the ambiguous promise that Heaven might come to seem like home. Home is not, for Dickinson, an unproblematic site of succor or freedom. Not surprisingly, neither is Heaven. Just as the dangers of home are implicated in Dickinson's discomfort with the claims of the body, it is bodilessness that makes Heaven desolate:

> Departed—to the Judgment—
> A Mighty Afternoon—
> Great Clouds—like Ushers—leaning—
> Creation—looking on—
>
> The Flesh—Surrendered—Cancelled—
> The Bodiless—begun—
> Two Worlds—like Audiences—disperse—
> And leave the Soul—alone—
>
> (524)

For all the trappings of a crowded performance—the ushers, the audiences, the looking on—Dickinson's scene of judgment echoes with emptiness.[15] "Departed" has no subject, since without a body there is nothing to come or go. Still, the poem begins rather as a joke, with the nonsense of weightless clouds "leaning" and of Creation somehow cordoned off in the bleachers. The joke sours, however, for imagining Heaven as a show implies that there would be something to see, and for a moment it seems as if death will be a striptease. The fantasy of a disembodied self surrendering its flesh reimagines the loss of the body in the imagery of bodily seduction. Dickinson knows that such images are a fraud, and she mentions the flesh's surrender only in order to negate it, replacing a sexual "surrendered" with a harshly absolute "cancelled." Thus the self-correction offered by this line enacts the stripping away of flesh that the poem describes. The canceling of the world of the body does not leave another, spiritual, realm intact, for not one but "Two Worlds" have dispersed. "The Bodiless—begun—" Dickinson writes, and the oddity of her grammar corresponds to the strangeness of such a situation: the adjective "bodiless" must serve as a noun because no thing exists that it could modify and not annihilate. If the soul remains as the lone residue of this canceling of flesh, its survival signifies not the soul's integrity, nor its import as an autonomous source of identity, but rather its devastation.

The problem persisted for Dickinson, and years later, after her father's death, her letters remain skeptical about whether a disembodied self might be "possibler":

> I dream about father every night, always a different dream, and forget what I am doing daytimes, wondering where he is. Without any body, I keep thinking, what kind can that be?[16]

Without physical bounds, without the markers of space and time that make location possible, "wondering *where* he *is*" proves absurd. Unlike the emphatically gendered threat of embodiment, the issues raised by a bodiless being stem precisely from the lack of any delimiting features. Thus even for a self "without any body" the only questions that can be asked are irrelevant queries about "kind," vain taxonomical efforts to contain the disembodied within the categories of the physical world. This failure of language to provide adequate terms in which to imagine a bodiless self reiterates the radical loneliness of the soul in "Departed—to the Judgment": to be "without any body" means being "without anybody," for community and communication require corporeality.

A bodiless self cannot be spoken, not only because corporeality makes complex claims on identity, but also because Dickinson understands language itself to be bound up with physicality. Though often quoted, the bodily grounding of Dickinson's definition of poetry has gone largely unremarked.

> If I read a book [and] it makes my whole body so cold no fire can ever warm me I know *that* is poetry. If I feel physically as if the top of my head were taken off, I know *that* is poetry. These are the only way I know it. Is there any other way.[17]

Poetry, Dickinson asserts, is written and measured in flesh. This definition accounts for much of the linguistic play of her poetic style: her characteristic depiction of abstract conceptions or emotions as if they were tangible presences. So she writes of "A nearness to Tremendousness" (963) implying that awe physically occupies space, or speaks of "A Quartz contentment" that is "like a stone" (341) precisely because such language redundantly insists on representing this emotion as matter: contentment might be like a stone, but quartz already is one. Such moments of rhetorical embodiment endow these abstractions with all the immediacy of bodily presence, and in doing so they suggest both Dickinson's yearning for the incorporeal and her sense that what has no body cannot be known or named.

Dickinson's definitions of poetry do not, however, take the act of rhetorical embodiment lightly. Behind the childlike fausse-naivete of her question lurks a frightening violence. Dickinson avers that she reads, and presumably writes, in an intensely, painfully corporeal way. Such a poetics reckons the extreme bodily costs of utterance, and so figures words and flesh as antagonistically if intimately enmeshed. Poetry may be created and assessed through the body, but it must also be understood as an attack on the body. In the very excess of its violence, however, Dickinson's poetics of freezings and scalpings demands to be treated metaphorically. She simultaneously insists that poetry cannot be divorced from the body, that indeed it necessarily entails a harrowing of flesh, and produces the body as a linguistic trope, since this definition can never be understood as palpably, physically true. On the one hand, in its violence, in its stress on rhetorical excess, Dickinson's poetics records her desire for disembodied speech, imagining a language and a self not chained to the "things of the body." On the other hand, it is precisely the vehement physicality of this attack on the flesh of writer and reader that marks such an ideal as unattainable, no matter how many bodies one's words might decapitate.

This violent representation of a poetry that would do away with flesh reflects Dickinson's sense of the body as an obstacle to freedom. Yet, in a pattern that has by now become familiar, Dickinson's fantasy of a fleshless liberty constantly collides with the sensual desire for a fully palpable freedom. The ambivalent attitude toward the body that characterizes Dickinson's sense of her own individual, sexual, and artistic liberty reiterates the contradictions that I have located in the period's political rhetoric of emancipation. The body constitutes a problem for nineteenth-century feminists and abolitionists because of the limitations it seems to set on freedom. Their confrontation with the corporeality of personhood clearly intends to emancipate. For Dickinson too, the issues raised by the body have implications for her conception of liberty; here, however, the body and the yearning at issue are not subjects of public debate; they are her own and all debate remains secreted within her poems. My point in this final section is less to note such parallels than to ask what becomes of the public call for emancipation once it has been remade into an internal and distinctly personal concern.

For Dickinson the problematic relation between liberty
and embodiment is best defined by the most extreme challenge to personhood—death—and the most personal of
attachments—love.

> What if I say I shall not wait!
> What if I burst the fleshly Gate—
> And pass escaped—to thee!
>
> What if I file this Mortal—off—
> See where it hurt me—That's enough—
> And wade in Liberty!
>
> They cannot take me—any more!
> Dungeons can call—and Guns implore
> Unmeaning—now—to me—
>
> As laughter—was—an hour ago—
> Or Laces—or a Travelling Show—
> Or who died—yesterday!
>
> (277)

In an attempt to compensate for the death of the beloved, this
poem imagines that liberty issues from fleshlessness. Yet
clearly the desire to "burst the fleshly gate" has a bodily, sexual content; the fantasy of having no body blends with the
fantasy of bodily union. The radical liberty of the poem's con-
jectures, the rebellious paradise of "what if," ultimately
points to a quite passionate, but quite conventional, mortal
love story. Dickinson's disembodied lovers want the same
things fully bodied ones do. Ultimately Dickinson figures
freedom not as fleshless but as so tangibly and sensually vis-
cous that one could "wade in Liberty."

Dickinson knows that the emancipation of dying is not so
pleasant or so easy. Although death promises immunity to
the threats posed by guns and dungeons, Dickinson's imagery suggests the instability of such a release, since the liberation of bursting the fleshly gate perversely mirrors the ex-
ploding guns and barred dungeons the lover wishes to
escape. Moreover, the poem suggests that death and bodilessness achieve liberty only by sloughing off all the limits
that constitute meaning. Dickinson compares the inability of
a disembodied self to comprehend limits or violence, even if

"implored," with the inability of the bereaved to find pleasure. Laughter, laces, and traveling shows are made "un-
meaning" by grief. Conversely, yesterday, when the beloved
was still alive, other people's deaths seemed insignificant.
The pathos of the poem lies in the speaker's belated recognition that death did have meaning yesterday. The fact of having been wrong then raises the possibility that this defiant
fantasy of fleshless liberty may prove equally misguided now.
In its last line the poem recalls who died today and with that
acknowledgment of loss exposes the delusion of ecstatic re-
union promised in the first stanza. Attempting to define the
unconcern of fleshless liberty, the poem relies on similes
from the temporalized world of "an hour ago" or "yesterday"
and so reinscribes the loss such fantasies had intended to
evade. By the poem's end liberty has collapsed back into
time, death, and mourning.

A later love poem, "Let Us play Yesterday," compares the
"Egg-life" of the days before the lovers' passion with the
speaker's feelings since "you troubled the Ellipse." In assessing these changes the poem turns, by its final stanzas, to the
implications of liberty:

> Can the Lark resume the Shell—
> Easier—for the Sky—
> Wouldn't Bonds hurt more
> Than Yesterday?
>
> Wouldn't Dungeons sorer grate
> On the Man—free—
> Just long enough to taste—
> Then—doomed new—
>
> God of the Manacle
> As of the Free—
> Take not my Liberty
> Away from Me—
>
> (728)

Dickinson's argument here, that confinement becomes harder
to bear once one has experienced freedom, presses oddly
against the banal prayer with which the poem ends. The concluding prayer assumes the speaker's present freedom,

though its conventional scansion and rhyme (Dickinson rhymes "Free" and "me" in the fifth stanza as well) and the implicit admission of God's ability, indeed proclivity, for taking away suggests that this "Liberty" is less free than the speaker supposes. If, as I have argued above, Dickinson perceives self-ownership as impinging on freedom, the liberty God may deign to grant appears even more suspect and less secure. This God is not "of the manacled," a God who tends to the oppressed, although the parallel structure of the lines may lead readers to expect such an abolitionist divinity. Rather, this is a "God of the manacle," a God equipped with shackles, who does not emancipate the abject but actually applies their chains. So framed, the liberty that the poem prays to retain seems liable to turn at any moment into a means of accentuating the manacled nature of human existence: the liberty pleaded for may well prove but the source of "sorer grate."

The dungeon and manacles of "Let Us play Yesterday," like the dungeons and guns of "What if I say I shall not wait," do not necessarily, or even primarily, refer to physical bondage. These markers of warfare and social control remain distinctly metaphoric, and so apolitical. The "dungeon" is not the punitive norm for nineteenth-century America. Dickinson defines freedom as internal, a concern not of society or the body but of the soul. Yet the issue of physical bondage cannot be so easily dismissed as merely imagistic, because what manacles the soul is, in large part, the body; the soul's bondage is literally physical. The pattern of bondage, liberty, and recapture reiterated by the string of questions in "Let Us play Yesterday" structures many of Dickinson's attempts to establish the conditions of personhood; in one of her best-known poems, Dickinson details this pattern to document the relation between bondage, identity, and sexuality.

> The Soul has Bandaged moments—
> When too appalled to stir—
> She feels some ghastly Fright come up
> And stop to look at her—

Salute her—with long fingers—
Caress her freezing hair—
Sip, Goblin, from the very lips
The Lover—hovered—o'er—
Unworthy, that a thought so mean
Accost a Theme—so—fair—

The soul has moments of Escape—
When bursting all the doors—
She dances like a Bomb, abroad,
And swings upon the Hours,

As do the Bee—delirious borne—
Long Dungeoned from his Rose—
Touch Liberty—then know no more,
But Noon, and Paradise—

The Soul's retaken moments—
When, Felon led along,
With shackles on the plumed feet,
And staples, in the Song,

The Horror welcomes her, again,
These, are not brayed of Tongue—

(512)

Dickinson describes both the experience of bandage/bondage and the experience of escape through the imagery of sexual contact and desire. Dickinson calls the soul "she," and in so gendering the soul endows it with a sexual body. Bandaged by female flesh, the soul becomes a spectacle. Indeed the soul cannot be distinguished from the flesh that wraps it, and its response to this ogling is purely tactile: "She *feels* some ghastly Fright come up / And stop to look at her." The ambiguous status of the "Fright"—at once gothic fiend, just another name for goblin, and a figure for the soul's own appalling fear—further exemplifies this tangling of the physical and the psychic. Sexual desire may be perverted as the goblin's caresses replace those of the lover and reduce the beloved to an object of lust; or sexual desire may itself prove frightful, demeaning the ostensible purity of the soul.

The body offers the soul moments of escape as well as bonds, and Dickinson opposes the sexual "thought so mean" with a vision of sexual intercourse as "Paradise." This second, idyllic scene of sexual embrace is not, however, attributed directly to the soul. In escape the soul appears explosive: "She dances like a Bomb," so that both the pleasure and the seductions of her movements threaten annihilation. The sexual content of the soul's dance is expressed through the comparisons of simile; the soul's escape is like the joy of a male bee in his feminized rose. Faced with such feminine passivity, the escaped Bee and the abusive Goblin appear strikingly similar.[18] The only possibility of an active female sexual pleasure that the poem will admit belongs to the terrifying and destructive image of the dancing bomb. The bee may "Touch Liberty" (and note the physicality of such freedom), but for the soul there is no liberty except self-immolation. The distinction between freedom and bondage that the poem proposes cannot be maintained. In the wake of bombs comes a need for bandages.

The felt difference between liberty and bondage that fuels abolitionist concern collapses in this poem. Nor will Dickinson uphold the differences among rapist, lover, and the autoerotic, bomb-like explosion. In fusing these distinctions Dickinson does not attribute bondage and sexual vulnerability to any particular object of oppression (slaves or women), nor can she see any means of reform or rescue; rather these politically resonant terms characterize the predicament of all who own a body and a soul. The impossibility of locating or maintaining the boundary between liberty and bondage, sexual abuse and sexual pleasure, reiterate the impossibility of extricating soul from body, or body from soul.

This recognition of the constraints embodiment imposes on identity also has ramifications for the writing of poetry. The bandaged, accosted, bursting, delirious bodies and souls of this poem are described in a vocabulary that simultaneously points to recent political concerns and yet appears blatantly literary. Dickinson explicitly identifies these scenes as metaphoric: set within a fantastic catalogue of goblins, frights, bees, and roses, the poem ranges among recognizably literary tropes from the gothic to the romantic. Thus in presenting bondage and sexual desirability as metaphors for the constraints on identity, Dickinson also raises questions about the implications and limits of metaphoric language. The soul's "plumed feet," feathered for a flight that shackles forbid, suggest the metric feet of poems. The "staples in the Song" rivet poetry with pain. These moments of recapture, this confinement of the soul, "are not brayed of Tongue." At stake in these depictions of the retaken felon are a sense of the divisions inherent in speech. The staples that pierce song also attest to the fragmentation of poetic utterance. If song were not disjunct from the social world, if it were not isolated and fragmented, there would be nothing for staples to bind and fasten. Instead song appears as a collection of dislocated body parts—some feet, a tongue. Dickinson stresses the animal quality of these bits of flesh: the feet are "plumed," the tongue would bray like a donkey. Like the soul, song comes wrapped in corporeality, and if it proves incapable of saying—or braying—the soul's fate, that is because it shares the soul's bonds.

"Dickinson's sparse language of public issues," Joanne Dobson observes, "is either referenced strikingly to the nature and potential of language itself, or it is strongly allusive or metaphoric, referring almost inevitably to personal rather than to public issues."[19] For Dickinson, the political imagery of emancipation counts not as politics but as imagery. Dobson is clearly right in her appraisal. Yet the internalization of the political entailed in Dickinson's location of her "free democracy" within the highly personal matrix of her own identity, body, and words may in itself constitute a significant critique of reformist discourse.

Dickinson's attitude toward the "Outer"-directed altruism of female reformers could be scathing. To her friend Jane Humphrey she reported:

> The Sewing Society has commenced again—and held its first meeting last week—now all the poor will be helped—the cold warmed—the warm cooled—the hungry fed—the thirsty attended to—the ragged clothed—and this suffering—tumbled down world will be helped to its feet again—which will be

quite pleasant to all. I dont attend—notwithstanding my high
approbation—which must puzzle the public exceedingly.

At the center of Dickinson's humorous attack on female phi-
lanthropy and social reform lie both an assertion of the inad-
equacy of such methods and a challenge to the female traits
of "cultivating meekness—and patience—and submission"
on which such reforms depend.[20] Inverting the conventional
philanthropic projects of providing the needy with warmth
and food, Dickinson's joke contains a commentary on the
Sewing Society's fear of the figures they sought to help. As
she slyly suggests, philanthropic concern with cooling the
warm and attending to the thirsty does not entail an effort to
alleviate the sufferings of others so much as an attempt to
tame the excesses of sexuality and alcohol and so to make the
poor respectable. If Dickinson's poetry is not overtly engaged
in social reform, neither is it complicit in this policy of repression. Like the ladies of the Sewing Society, Dickinson recognizes the dangers posed by bodily excess, but unlike these
reformers, and unlike many of the women engaged in
antislavery work, she does not project her fears onto the bodies of some poor "Other," safely cordoned off by class or race.
Rather, she recognizes this dangerous body as her own.

Dickinson's poems present the corporeality of identity not
in terms of the differences that rend society but rather as a
split within the self. Her poems lay bare the paradoxical complicity between the ideal of liberty and the structures of
bondage, between the sanctified appeal of the home and the
stultifying details of domestic repression, between sexual
pleasure and abjection or abuse, between the desire to be rid
of the body and the recognition of its definitional and sensual power. Revealing the instability of liberty, domesticity,
sexuality, and identity, such a position is uncompromisingly
radical. It also disables all programs of social reform. Thus
Dickinson's position is not detachedly depoliticized; it is actively antipolitical. Dickinson's critique cannot and should
not replace political action, yet by representing national issues and public divisions as nonsocial—lodged within the
interiority of the self—it does do the provocative political

work of illuminating the practices of appropriation and displacement by which reformers so often sought to deflect their anxieties about their own bodies, homes, and freedom. Recasting social divisions into a language for describing the self, Dickinson arrests such patterns of displacement—painfully laying claim to her own flesh and jeopardizing the precarious privilege that would have been secured by denial. She brings these political and national polemics home. " 'Sweet Land of Liberty' is a superfluous Carol till it concern ourselves—" Dickinson wrote to Mabel Loomis Todd. She signed the letter "America."[21]

Coda

Topsy-Turvy

I conclude with a domestic object, a doll that was widely popular in nineteenth-century America, north and south. Like all dolls, it was intended to teach little girls about domesticity. But this one, turned topsy-turvy, threatens to invert those lessons as well, or at least to reveal the issues of difference and dominance that lurk beneath proper feminine skirts. The topsy-turvy doll is two dolls in one: when the long skirts of the elegant white girl are flipped over her head, where her feet should be there grins instead the stereotyped image of a wide-eyed pickaninny.[1] Flipping between white missey and black pickaninny, the doll asserts the contiguity of these two figures; they are but opposite ends of the same domestic fate. Yet the doll also presents these figures as mutually effacing, since it is impossible to see the white and the black at the same time. To face one necessarily entails skirting the other.

Always either one color or the other, the topsy-turvy doll enacts the binary structure of difference, emblematizing a nation governed by the logical dualisms of segregation.[2] Moreover, as it blatantly figures absolute difference through a lifting of skirts, the topsy-turvy doll compactly embodies the concerns of this study: she stands as a cultural sign of the ways in which antebellum America conjoined racial issues with sexual ones. As a prop of racial divisions, the topsy-turvy doll is a remarkably prudish toy. She elides sexuality: there are no genitals underneath her skirt, not even hips or thighs. Indeed, one could say that from the waist down she has no body at all. Thus the doll's waist simultaneously cordons off her sexual body and marks the boundary between her alternative racial identities. If the ribbon around her waist articulates the difference between black and white, the claim to such an absolute differentiation depends upon banishing sexuality. But, of course, the possibilities of sexual relations are precisely what make untenable any clear and stable division between white and black. The appeal of such topsy-turvy transformations lies in their ability to mask and deny a national history of miscegenation.[3]

Despite the absence of pelvis or legs, it is not the case that there is nothing under the doll's skirts. Rather, the sexual organs of white woman and black have been displaced by the torso of the other. Thus the doll suggestively illustrates the patterns of displacements I have detailed throughout this study: here again, the sexual fears and desires of the white woman are refigured on the body of the black, while the black woman presents her sexual experience in the terms sanctioned by white models of feminine decorum.

The topsy-turvy doll tidily stitches the various concerns of this book into a single (if two-faced) artifact. The relations between the texts I have addressed are not, however, so easily sewn together. For one thing, the trajectory from didactic sentimental fiction to lyric poetry (and to two such different poets) is more complicated than the binary oppositions of a topsy-turvy arrangement. Though antislavery fiction, *Leaves of Grass, Incidents in the Life of a Slave Girl,* and Dickinson's untitled lyrics all can be seen to explore the relation—both political and aesthetic—between embodiment and representation, the cultural implications of their findings are remarkably disparate. Some of the larger ramifications of these differences are only visible now, at this study's end, when the arguments dispersed over various chapters can be seen in diverse relation to one another.

Sentimental writing, I argued in chapter 1, can be defined by its approach to the bodies of its readers. In particular, as a sentimental tale elicits tears and sighs, it enrolls the reader's bodily responses in the act of overcoming difference.

The sobs of character and reader work to blur the distinction between them. This literary strategy thus proves particularly pertinent for the political project of claiming personhood for the racially different body of the slave. Gothic or sensational texts, by contrast, may work equally strongly on the body of the reader, but the shivers and starts conjured by such writings serve to heighten rather than lessen a sense of bodily difference. The reader of gothic tales feels paranoid and isolated, not compassionate and connected; fearing the stab of phantom knives or the cool touch of unsuspected fingers, the reader remains vigilantly aware of the bounds of his or her body.

Viewed in these terms Harriet Jacobs's narrative—despite frequent evocations of sentimental literary conventions, from flowers and graves to motherhood, and equally frequent recourse to gothic "dungeons" and the suspense of sustained and repeated threats—leaves the bodies of its readers remarkably untouched. The story Jacobs tells is as horrible as Stowe's; it clearly hopes to make its readers angry and ashamed, but rarely, if ever, does it make them gasp or weep.[4] Even those moments when Linda fervently addresses her readers end in denying them the right to judge her sexual behaviors; the text's assumptions about its readers' bodily experiences disallow comprehension of or identification with Linda's choices. In recording how the act of narration reiterates the scene of sexual abuse, *Incidents in the Life of a Slave Girl* shows how the slave narrative is directed at the writer's own body.

Though manifest quite differently, the narratives of Frederick Douglass, Mary Prince, or Louisa Piquet similarly resist making identifying claims on the body of the reader. The flesh that feels in these texts is that of the slave. So Douglass, attesting to the power of slave songs, recalls the "tears" he frequently shed "while hearing them" and then, preempting the sympathetic effusions of a reader, adds: "The mere recurrence to those songs, even now, afflicts me; and while I am writing these lines, an expression of feeling has already found its way down my cheek."[5] Unlike the fictional Mary

French, whose liberating tears prove her whiteness and link her to her wet-eyed readers, Douglass insists that these tears—"an expression of feeling" he cannot control—are not the emancipatory effects of his moving prose but rather something afflicted upon him by the act of writing. Rarely playing on the body of the reader, the slave narrative replaces that body with the body of the author. This is a startling move, since generally the position of author gains its privilege precisely because the text produced occludes the specific physical body of the person who produced it.

Inverting this pattern, slave narratives, and perhaps all confessional or testimonial genres, rhetorically create an authorial body. Rather than attempt to assert the incorporeality of authorship, testimonial writing inscribes the author's bodily existence and experience. One purpose of the introductions and appendixes that flank Jacobs's narrative is to verify that these words were authentically produced by a black woman. The goal of the narrative itself is largely the same: to succeed in attaching a dark-skinned and female body to the recognition and respect—the personhood— awarded to authorship. These differing approaches to the body serve to delineate a generic and ethical gap. Unlike sentimental antislavery fiction, the aesthetic strategies of the slave narrative inhibit readerly appropriations, insisting that the bodily meaning of slavery cannot easily be shared.

I have suggested that in antislavery fiction the rhetorical strategies of embodiment serve a double ideological purpose: working to produce sympathetic identifications, they simultaneously enfranchise and exploit the body of the other. Walt Whitman's poetry is also predicated on the emancipatory potential of an identification with otherness. But in his poems the reader's body is not the privileged site of identification; rather, it is one of the many and various bodies these poems claim to absorb. The site of reconciliation is instead the lines of poetry that Whitman describes as identical to his flesh. Rather than occlude the author (as sentimental antislavery fiction does when it fashions the slave into a proxy for the unspeakable experiences and desires of the writer), or attest to the author's radical separateness (as the slave narrative does when it insists on the reader's inability to identify with the body of the writer), Whitman deploys the authorial body to encompass and mediate all otherness.

In Emily Dickinson's discoveries that the housewife's corpse cannot "tell" her identity and that the bodiless spirit must remain unknowable, she attests to the difficulties of sharing experience with bodies or without them. Thus it seems hardly surprising that her own modes of publication radically problematize the positions of author and reader.[6] Sent inside letters, her poems appear as forms of address to individual readers; in her increasing physical isolation they may be understood both as directed to specific bodies and as replacements for bodily contact. Copied into manuscript books to be kept in the privacy of her room, her poetry can be seen either as hoarded for the author's own reading or as addressing the hypothetical and amorphous readership of posterity.[7] Both the epistolary and the fascicle modes of publication situate Dickinson's poetry in an ambivalent relation to readerly bodies, simultaneously touching readers and distancing them.

The differing stances these texts take toward authors and readers all rest upon the assumption that words can and do act upon the body. Even this most basic assumption, however, is configured differently by each of the writers I have discussed. "Whoever touches this book touches a man," Whitman proclaims, asserting the perfect identity of body and text. For Harriet Jacobs the ways in which narration reenacts her sexual experiences mark the ways in which the culture continues to define her by those experiences. For Jacobs, the connection between her narrative and her body proves painful as well as empowering. For Whitman the pain lies in the inevitable failure of such connections. The desire that there be no difference between word and flesh informs much of Whitman's poetic practice, but it also, necessarily, remains thwarted. Thus his poetry registers both the desire to be fully embodied and the impossibility of realizing that desire; he simultaneously locates identity in the fact of embodiment and defines it as an infinitely flexible matter of representation.

The wish most adamantly expressed in Dickinson's work is, conversely, to get rid of the things of the body, to purge language of all corporeal stuff. Her desire for linguistic fleshlessness proves as unachievable as Whitman's fantasy of authoring full-bodied poems. Dickinson's inability to dismiss the body proves ambivalent: serving to confine identity and utterance, the body is nevertheless what makes them possible, meaningful, and pleasurable. Read together, Whitman and Dickinson's extreme and opposite poetic projects demonstrate how the bodiliness of personhood inevitably but inadequately informs not only all speech but also any attempt to construct a speaking subject.

To say this is to make a quite general, transhistorical, observation about the nature and limits of the relation between bodies and words. This relation, however, is manifested differently by the particular requirements of genre and politics in any historically specific act of representation. Thus Dickinson's use of the politically resonant imagery of embodiment, bondage, and liberty, and the analogies she suggests between self and society serve not, as they do for Whitman, to resolve national divisions but rather to internalize them, differentiating and illuminating her individual identity. Although she forfeits Whitman's expansive claims of representative immediacy—the posture of being America's poet—she also evades the appropriative potential of Whitman's poetic mergers. Likewise, as I argue at the end of chapter 4, Dickinson's focus on her own corporeality rejects reformist strategies of displacement: she does not procure her liberty with someone else's body.

A comparison with Jacobs, however, makes clear the ideological limits of Dickinson's strategy of internalization. While both women extract the cost of abolishing the distinction between the personal and the political from their own experience and their own flesh, the differences in genre and audience between the private, unpublished lyric and the polemically public slave narrative suggest the ultimately incommensurable nature of these costs. Slavery denies Jacobs the very right to claim personhood, and therefore the very internal identity out of which and about which Dickinson writes her poems.

In tracing the rhetorical and ideological impact of a corporeal conception of identity across genres from the sentimental to the lyric, I have discovered as much discontinuity as connection. Does the body inform the relation between character and reader? or is it the exclusive experience of the writer, painfully reiterated in the act of writing? or the always insufficient basis of authorial power? or the inescapable, and even pleasurable, limit to authorial liberty? The topsy-turvy doll makes the issue of bodily difference appear simple—a question of easy opposites. As these conflicting interpretations suggest, however, each attempt to articulate identity in corporeal terms bears a different relation to the body about which it would speak. Thus representing the body does not simplify what is being represented, nor does it make these representations into a uniform cultural phenomenon. The various chapters that make up this study do not finally trace a single subject through a variety of texts; rather, they demonstrate the instability of that subject. In fact, I would argue that a corporeal understanding of identity requires just such a dispersal of identity, since the one thing the body does bring to all of these discourses is the palpable pressures of difference.

Furthermore, the differences in where and how these various texts locate embodiment reveal the bodies represented not as guarantors of an extratextual reality but as themselves rhetorically constructed. I argue that the interests of antebellum feminists and abolitionists in claiming a bodily basis for political identity worked to unmask the exclusions implicit in a Constitution and a political system structured in the name of an incorporeal "we the people." But ultimately the body at stake in this critique must also be recognized as only a useful fiction. To recognize the insistence on bodiliness as itself a rhetorical tool does not solve the problems posed by the body, but it does clarify what these problems might be.

Emily Dickinson's fantasy of touching liberty expresses just such a useful fiction. In the desire for a liberty that would make tangible the more abstract promises of the nation's founders, in the conflation of sexual and political liberation so that caresses yield freedom, in the sentimental power to touch others and so change them, in the reciprocity of a touch that simultaneously affirms the physicality of liberty and of the self that reaches for it, thereby describing freedom as a condition of the body—in all these ways Dickinson's image that one might "touch liberty" gives voice to the complex of desires explored in this study. The line as a whole, however, attests to the limits of this politically and culturally powerful fantasy:

> Touch Liberty—then know no more,
> But Noon, and Paradise—
>
> (512)

At least as she frames it, a liberty that could be touched, a freedom and identity associated with the body, would limit or even obliterate all knowing and negate any temporal, earthly, and so physical reference for being. Paradise is where Uncle Tom ultimately gains his freedom; Angelina Grimké allegorizes the goals of abolition in a still unresurrected putrid corpse; Whitman sings his celebration of the slave's personhood by reducing the auctioned body to a stream of "red running blood"; for Jacobs, confined to the tight space of the garret, freedom proves literally crippling. That the rhetoric of bodily emancipation should come so wrapped up in the rhetoric of bodily annihilation attests to the sense of threat that results from the body's refusal to lie about difference. It therefore does much to explain the recoil from a political movement based on heeding the irreconcilable differences of identities that are bodily, to one focused on asserting the disembodied sameness of suffrage—one person, one vote. This investment in representative politics, and so in an abstract, incorporeal accounting of identity, clearly manifests a rhetoric of bodily denial. Moreover, it entails a suppression of the many and various actual bodies that do not conform to the hypothetical, constitutional "person" and so are silently and invisibly excluded from personhood. Thus the bodies at stake, though always products of representation, are not simply rhetorical. In evaluating this shift in the discourse of personhood it is important to remember that discourses can and do inflict physical violence.

Notes

INTRODUCTION

1. Angelina Grimké, *Appeal to the Christian Women of the South* (New York: American Anti-Slavery Society, 1836), 28, 33.

2. The image of the "body politic" may indeed prove more fundamental to the concept of the state than even its constant presence in Western political thought would imply. The anthropological work of Victor Turner and, after him, of Mary Douglas in *Natural Symbols: Explorations in Cosmology* (New York: Pantheon Books, 1970) argues that the human body functions as a "natural symbol" for all other systems, including the state, and suggests a dialectical relation in which society conditions how the body is perceived while the body symbolizes the social order. Such a dialectic is, obviously, inherent in my own work.

3. I am most specifically indebted to the work of Carole Pateman in *The Sexual Contract* (Stanford: Stanford University Press, 1988). Her critique of the ways in which the classical understandings of the social contract mask the sexual contract demonstrates how the assumption of disembodied and so sexless political actors serves to efface the fact of sexual subjugation and so protect patriarchal power. I find her argument important and persuasive but I also find it partial, as Pateman herself admits (221). In looking at both feminist and abolitionist arguments for the corporeality of identity, I wish to split the unitary "person" into a more disparate and unstable array of pieces than Pateman's gendered pair. For a discussion of contemporary case law that demonstrates how the assumption that the female body is just like the male body underlies legal theories of sexual equality, and consequently how female bodily "difference" serves to justify legal inequalities, see Zillah R. Eisenstein, *The Female Body and the Law* (Berkeley and Los Angeles: University of California Press, 1988).

4. In speaking of men as "created," Jefferson's phrasing already masks the bodiliness of identity. Rousseau's formulation that "men are born free" registers and then effaces sexual difference, making it even more evident that, as Anne Norton explains, "the freedom of men at their birth is dependent . . . on a conventional construction

of sexuality: the subordination of all women to all men" (*Reflections on Political Identity* [Baltimore: Johns Hopkins University Press, 1988], 38). Freedom may not require sexual bodies, but birth surely does.

5. See Ronald G. Walters's account of how Kelley made use of "this inadvertent wording" (*The AntiSlavery Appeal: American Abolitionism After 1830* [Baltimore: Johns Hopkins University Press, 1976], 10). My point, of course, is that Kelley and the Garrisonian faction in general were quite advertently engaged in redefining the conventional political terminology of "personhood."

Walters's position is that neither the schism itself, nor the "woman question" that prompted it, should be understood as a significant ideological divide within antislavery thought. Aileen S. Kraditor (*Means and Ends in American Abolition: Garrison and His Critics on Strategy and Tactics, 1834–1850* [New York: Pantheon, 1968]), Ellen DuBois ("Women's Rights and Abolition: The Nature of the Connection," in *Antislavery Reconsidered: New Perspectives on the Abolitionists*, ed. Lewis Perry and Michael Fellman [Baton Rouge: Louisiana State University Press, 1979]), and Blanche Glassman Hersh (*The Slavery of Sex: Feminist-Abolitionists in America* [Urbana: University of Illinois Press, 1978]), all mark this moment as formative for the development of a separate feminist movement, though their assessments of precisely how it matters differ significantly.

6. For the complete text and a record of how these phrases have been interpreted, see *The Constitution of the United States of America, Analysis and Interpretation: Annotations of Cases Decided by the Supreme Court of the United States to June 22 1964*, ed. Norman J. Small legislative reference service (Washington: U.S. Government Printing Office, 1964). For a discussion of antislavery women's reluctance to support the Fourteenth Amendment because of its gender bias, see Hersh, *Slavery of Sex*, 68. Ellen Dubois's chapter-length discussions of feminist stances on both amendments detail the risks to woman's suffrage of dependence on abolitionist Republicans, and therefore the need for an autonomous women's movement (*Feminism and Suffrage: The Emergence of an Independent Women's Movement in America, 1848–1869* [Ithaca, N.Y.: Cornell University Press, 1978]). "Indians not taxed" do feature in constitutional discussions of taxation, the apportioning of representatives, and so on, but here concepts of national identity are used to mask the racial implications of this category.

7. Sharon Cameron argues that an insistence on the corporeality of identity should be understood as a more general characteristic of American literature, not one specifically located in these few decades (*The Corporeal Self: Allegories of the Body in Melville and Hawthorne* [Baltimore: Johns Hopkins University Press, 1981]). Her discussion of the corporeal grounding of American literature focuses, however, on *Moby Dick* and Hawthorne's tales, and the majority of

her additional examples (Poe, Thoreau, Emerson, Brockden Brown, Whitman, Dickinson) also belong to the period with which I am concerned. Indeed, her examples from twentieth-century American literature, *The Sound and the Fury* and *Lolita*, are striking precisely because the voices and bodies of Caddy and Lolita are so conspicuously absent from these texts. In short, her arguments for the corporeal understanding of identity as a central concern of American literature are historically specific. Her own speculations on the reasons for the bodily focus of American texts is developmental, comparing "a child's first discovery that his body is his own, excluding other bodies, and the discovery of men struggling to distinguish their own literary subject." But the terms in which she explains this process resonate with the historically specific challenges posed by slavery:

> The mind works by analogies, deducing what it cannot see from what it can. The body is what one can see, is the thing (the only thing) that can be owned. Thus, given the particular concern with definition of one's own (national) space, with problems of territorial expansion, with a subject uniquely delineated, one's relation to one's own body (though far from being analogic), since it is the most palpable relationship we have, suggests analogies for these secondary problems of owned subject. (6–7)

I suggest that this developmental model of knowing the self first through the body was thrown into crisis in the middle of the nineteenth century because the agitation over slavery made it suddenly clear that one's own body could be owned by someone else.

8. See Norton (*Reflections on Political Identity*, especially chapter 3, "Representation: Presence and Absence") on the ways in which the same contradictions of absence and presence echo between political representation and semiotic representation.

9. The photograph of "Laura M. Towne, Dick, Maria, and 'seeker' Amoretta" is from the Schomburg Center for Research in Black Culture, and is reproduced in Margaret Washington Creel, *"A Peculiar People": Slave Religion and Community-Culture Among the Gullahs* (New York: New York University Press, 1988), 306. In her letter Towne goes on to describe these students' differing levels of educational skill (*The Letters and Diary of Laura M. Towne: Written from the Sea Islands of South Carolina, 1862–1884*, ed. R. S. Holland [Cambridge: Riverside Press, 1912], 172). An 1866 photograph from the Hooper School, portraying teacher Lizzie Langford and two of her students in the same pose, is from the Rufus and S. Willard Saxton Papers, Yale University Library, and is reproduced in Robert C. Morris, *Reading, 'Riting, and Reconstruction: The Education of Freedmen in the South, 1861–1870* (Chicago: University of Chicago Press, 1976), fig. 2.

10. Towne's *Letters and Diaries* give a detailed account of life at the Penn School, balancing such assertions of collective and proprietorial love (47) with scenes of genuine pleasure and affection: "Ellen and I took the little children into the creek to bathe, having dressed them in some of the 'theatricals' that came down here. There was more fun and mud than cleanliness" (83). For more general histories of freedmen's schools and the Northern women who largely staffed them see Jacqueline Jones, *Soldiers of Light and Love: Northern Teachers and Georgia Blacks, 1865–1873* (Chapel Hill: University of North Carolina Press, 1980), and Sandra E. Small, "The Yankee Schoolmarm in Freedmen's Schools: An Analysis of Attitudes," *The Journal of Southern History* 45 (August 1979). The complaint of Black ingratitude is quoted from James D. Anderson, *The Education of Blacks in the South, 1860–1935* (Chapel Hill: University of North Carolina Press, 1988), 12. Jones points to the ironic similarities between the posture of Northern teachers and that of the antebellum slave mistress, 148–49. In light of this comparison it is worth noting that James Mellon inaccurately captions the Penn School photograph, identifying teacher Harriet Murray as a plantation mistress: "while most slave children were prohibited from learning to read or write, their owners did occasionally read them bible stories." See *Bullwhip Days: The Slaves Remember*, ed. James Mellon (New York: Weidenfeld and Nicolson, 1988), plate 17.

11. See especially *Discipline and Punish: The Birth of the Prison*, trans. Alan Sheridan (New York: Vintage Books, 1979) and *The History of Sexuality*, vol. 1, trans. Robert Hurley (New York: Vintage Books, 1980). But see also Nancy Fraser on the philosophical and political limitations of Foucault's attempts to ground a new posthumanist social theory not on the humanist grounds of subjectivity and reciprocal rights, but rather on the body and its pleasures ("Foucault's Body Language: A Posthumanist Political Rhetoric?" in *Unruly Practices: Power, Discourse and Gender in Contemporary Social Theory* [Minneapolis: University of Minnesota Press, 1989]).

12. See Emily Martin, *The Woman in the Body: A Cultural Analysis of Reproduction* (Boston: Beacon Press, 1987) and Elaine Scarry, *The Body in Pain: The Making and Unmaking of the World* (New York: Oxford University Press, 1985). Two other participants in these debates have greatly influenced my work. In many of her essays (soon to be published in book form), Hortense Spillers has most specifically related the problematics of embodiment to the conditions of American slavery. Her oppositional terminology of "body" and "flesh" attempts to keep track of the difference between a socially and rhetorically constructed "body" and the real physical stuff of "flesh." I am suggesting, however, that the problem is precisely that such distinctions cannot be systematically maintained. The predicaments of flesh ground all conceptions of the body, while this rhetorically constructed body informs the experience of flesh.

Sharon Cameron's discussion of literal versus allegorical appre-
hensions of the body in *The Corporeal Self* suggests the significance of
these concerns not only for understanding the body but also for understanding representation. Her account of how allegorical tropes
cover up literal violence—marking the human dismemberments
narrated as safely not real—reveals a doubleness in literary language akin to the doubleness of the body. As her work insists, the
contradictory nature of a rhetoric of embodiment disables both the
conventional distinction between body and soul or, I would add, between a natural and a socially constructed body, and that between
the literal and allegorical dimensions of language. Following Cameron, my work addresses the ways in which the problems posed by
the body become problems of representation.

13. As Nancy Armstrong and Leonard Tennenhouse remind us,
representation is structured by dominance and suppression and so
is inherently violent. This is as true of academic discourse as it is of
political or literary texts. To describe the ways in which black and female bodies were put to use in antebellum writings requires recognizing the extent to which I too use this flesh to authorize my words.
See "Introduction: Representing Violence or 'How the West was
Won' " (*The Violence of Representation: Literature and the History of Violence*, ed. Armstrong and Tennenhouse [New York: Routledge, 1989]).

14. Jean Fagan Yellin's *Women and Sisters: The Antislavery Feminists in American Culture* (New Haven: Yale University Press, 1989)
was published after I had largely completed this manuscript. She
too works to trace feminist-abolitionist rhetoric into the sphere of
high culture—specifically through Hiram Power's *Greek Slave*,
Nathaniel Hawthorne's *Scarlet Letter*, and Henry James's *The Bosto-
nians*. Her examples of such cultural osmosis bolster the claims I
wish to make here. I want to stress, however, the differences between our analyses of the patterns of appropriation inherent in such
cultural intersections. Yellin describes the ease with which symbols
of resistance can be absorbed and deformed by the dominant ideology; she records the process by which oppositional discourse is silenced. Thus antislavery feminists' fundamentally positive figura-
tions of the supplicant slave woman are appropriated by the cultural
elite and made to serve decidedly unliberating purposes. In contrast, I find traces of oppression and appropriation within the abolitionist's symbols of social protest and, along with the political erasures, traces of political resistance—intentional or not—embedded
in the aesthetic concerns of lyric poetry. I doubt, however, that the
more ambivalent relation I am suggesting is any better. If such a
reading does not allow cultural absorption completely to silence
oppositional discourse, it also unmasks the political purity of the
oppositional register.

15. For discussions of how slavery figures in white, canonical literature of the period, see the essays by Eric J. Sundquist and Walter

Benn Michaels in *The American Renaissance Reconsidered: Selected Papers from the English Institute, 1982–83,* ed. Walter Benn Michaels and Donald E. Pease (Baltimore: Johns Hopkins University Press, 1985); Carolyn L. Karcher, *Shadow Over the Promised Land: Slavery, Race, and Violence in Melville's America* (Baton Rouge: Louisiana State University Press, 1980); and most recently Yellin's *Women and Sisters.*
Scholars of African-American literature have been concerned with the impact of slavery for much longer and in importantly different terms. Hazel Carby and Deborah McDowell discuss some of the paradoxes of the ties between slavery and the African-American novel in their contributions to *Slavery and the Literary Imagination: Selected Papers from the English Institute, 1987,* ed. Deborah E. McDowell and Arnold Rampersand (Baltimore: Johns Hopkins University Press, 1989). For various examples of how the slave narrative and a "racial" history of slavery can be used to ground discussions of African-American literary traditions, see the other essays in this volume as well as *The Slave's Narrative,* ed. Henry Louis Gates Jr. and Charles Davis (New York: Oxford University Press, 1985); Hazel Carby, *Reconstructing Womanhood: The Emergence of the Afro-American Woman Novelist* (New York: Oxford University Press, 1987); Valerie Smith, *Self-Discovery and Authority in Afro-American Narrative* (Cambridge: Harvard University Press, 1987); Houston A. Baker Jr., *Blues, Ideology, and Afro-American Literature: A Vernacular Theory* (Chicago: University of Chicago Press, 1984) and William L. Andrews, *To Tell a Free Story: The First Century of Afro-American Autobiography, 1760–1865* (Urbana: University of Illinois Press, 1986).
16. For useful compendiums of essays about new historicism see *The New Historicism,* ed. H. Aram Veeser (New York: Routledge, 1989); Marjorie Levinson et al., *Rethinking Historicism: Critical Readings in Romantic History* (Oxford: Basil Blackwell, 1989); and *The New Cultural History,* ed. Lynn Hunt (Berkeley: University of California Press, 1990). That such arguments are of more than academic interest—though their influence in the reshaping of academic curricula would be their foremost consequence—is ironically evinced by the fervor with which they have been debated, not just within universities but from pulpits, in government offices, and in the popular press.

CHAPTER 1

1. Lydia Maria Child, *Anti-Slavery. Catechism* (Newburyport: Charles Whipple, 1836), 17.
2. Ibid., 16.
3. That the husband's confidence in her racial purity is expressed in terms of white lineage "since the flood" ridicules the most frequently deployed Biblical defense of slavery, which dated

the divine sanctioning of racial subjugation from the curse Noah pronounced on Ham's son Canaan (Genesis 9:25). Ham's fault, coincidentally, was the disrespect of looking upon the body of his drunken and naked father. For a discussion of the antebellum debate over the significance of this passage, see Ron Bartour, " 'Cursed be Canaan, a Servant of Servants shall he be unto his Brethren': American Views on 'Biblical Slavery,' 1835–1865, a Comparative Study," *Slavery and Abolition* 4 (May 1983).

4. On the simple level of events, the intersections are legion: the Grimké sisters, antislavery lecturers of the 1830s, were the first women to give public lectures before "mixed" or "promiscuous" audiences, and Angelina Grimké was the first American woman to speak before a legislative body (censured for such unfeminine activity, the Grimké's increasingly addressed the issue of woman's rights within their antislavery discourse); in the 1830s and 1840s, Susan B. Anthony and Lucy Stone worked as paid agents of the American Anti-Slavery Society, lecturing on both abolition and woman's rights; Elizabeth Cady Stanton and Lucretia Mott first met at the World's Anti-Slavery Convention of 1840, where the female delegates were refused seats; and legend has it that the idea of a woman's rights convention—not realized until 1848—was first discussed in the London hotel rooms of these excluded women.

5. Andrew Sinclair, "Woman or Slave," in *The Better Half: the Emancipation of the American Woman* (New York: Harper and Row, 1965).

6. Carroll Smith-Rosenberg, "Beauty, the Beast and the Militant Woman," in *Disorderly Conduct: Visions of Gender in Victorian America* (New York: Oxford University Press, 1985); and Barbara J. Berg, *The Remembered Gate: Origins of American Feminism: the Woman and the City, 1800–1860* (New York: Oxford University Press, 1978).

7. DuBois, "Women's Rights and Abolition."

8. Hersh, *Slavery of Sex.*

9. Smith-Rosenberg, "Puberty to Menopause: the Cycle of Femininity in Nineteenth Century America," in *Disorderly Conduct.*

10. Included in Aileen S. Kraditor, *Up from the Pedestal: Selected Writings in the History of American Feminism* (Chicago: Quadrangle Books, 1968), 190–91. This fantasy was published as an editorial in the *Herald,* thus providing the very news copy it gleefully imagines.

11. The diagnosis is that of Dr. Samuel A. Cartwright in "Diseases and Peculiarities of the Negro Race," *De Bow's Review* (1851), excerpted in *Advice among Masters: the Ideal in Slave Management in the Old South,* ed. James O. Breeden (Westport, Conn.: Greenwood Press, 1980), 173. Breeden identifies Cartwright as among the "leading scientific spokesmen" of "the campaign to defend the South's sectional interests and to promote southern nationalism," and thus a consciously biased interpreter of anatomy.

12. Lydia Maria Child included these quotations, along with many similar items gleaned from the Southern press, in *The Patriarchal Institution as Described by Members of Its Own Family* (New York: The American Anti-Slavery Society, 1860). She added the italics as a form of commentary. The first quote mentioned here is cited by Child from an advertisement for the runaway slave of Anthony M. Minter (A.M.) in the *Free Press*, Alabama, September 18, 1846 (13). She takes the second from an advertisement posted by John A. Rowland, jailer, to publicize his capture of a presumed runaway, in the Fayetteville, North Carolina, *Observer*, June 20, 1838 (11).

13. Angelina Grimké, *An Appeal to the Women of the Nominally Free States: Issued by an Anti-Slavery Convention of American Women Held by Adjournment from the 9th to the 12th of May 1837* (New York: W. S. Doss, 1837).

14. For a more general analysis of how the idealization of freedom that characterizes Western thought relies upon the historical and factual presence of slavery, see Orlando Patterson, *Slavery and Social Death* (Cambridge: Harvard University Press, 1982).

15. See Hersh, *Slavery of Sex*, chapters 1, 2, and 6, for a summary of the analogies drawn by feminist abolitionists. Examples of the first two follow. A more frivolous example of the analogy can be found in Amelia Bloomer's defense of the short skirts and pantaloons that carry her name: "I suppose in this respect we are more mannish, for we know that in dress as in all things else, we have been and are slaves, while man in dress and all things else is free."

16. Sarah Grimké, *Letters on the Equality of the Sexes and the Condition of Women. Addressed to Mary S. Parker, President of the Boston Female Anti-Slavery Society* (Boston: Isaac Knapp, 1838), 13, 75.

17. Elizabeth Cady Stanton, letter to the National Woman's Rights Convention, Cooper Institute, dated Seneca Falls, November 24, 1856; included in the appendixes of *The History of Woman Suffrage*, ed. Elizabeth Cady Stanton, Susan B. Anthony, and Matilda Joslyn Gage (New York: Fowler and Wells, 1881), 1:860.

18. See Barbara Welter, "The Cult of True Womanhood, 1820–1860," *American Quarterly* 18 (Summer 1966) and Berg, "Towards the Woman-Belle Ideal," in *The Remembered Gate*, for compendiums of all the virtues a "True Woman" was expected to possess. One of the charges consistently brought against the Grimké sisters' antislavery lectures was that of indelicacy. In their *Pastoral Letter* of 1837, directed at the Grimkés, the Massachusetts Congregationalist clergy "especially deplore the intimate acquaintance and promiscuous conversation of females with regard to things 'which ought not to be mentioned.' " The unmentionables, of course, were the rape and concubinage of slave women and the nullity of slave marriage. See Kraditor, *Up from the Pedestal*, 51–52, and Sarah Grimké's response to the pastoral letter in her third *Letter on the Equality of the Sexes*.

19. Margaret Fuller, "Woman in the Nineteenth Century" (1844) in *The Writings of Margaret Fuller*, ed. Mason Wade (New York: Viking Press, 1941), 123.

20. The most famous instance of this turn is Sojourner Truth's refrain "a'n't I a woman" at the Akron Woman's Rights Convention on May 29, 1851.

> "Dat man ober dar say dat womin needs to be helped into carriages, and lifted ober ditches, and to hab de best place everywhar. Nobody eber helps me into carriages, or ober mud-puddles, or gibs me any best place!" And raising herself to her full height, and her voice to a pitch like rolling thunder, she asked, "And a'n't I a woman? Look at me! Look at my arm! (and she bared her right arm to the shoulder, showing her tremendous muscular power) . . ."

For this audience her body makes her argument. "Reminiscences of Frances D. Gage: Sojourner Truth," in Stanton, Anthony, and Gage, *History of Woman Suffrage*, 1:116.

21. For a fascinating account of the cultural uses and meanings of this emblem, see Yellin, *Women and Sisters*.

22. *The Liberator*, January 7, 1832, quoted in Hersh, *Slavery of Sex*, 10–11.

23. Whether Garrison knew it or not, there is no etymological slippage at all. Cattle refers not only to the bovine, but more generally to "movable property or wealth," that is, to chattel; both forms derive from *capitale*. Capital is accumulated currency, "stock in trade," and the classification of slaves as livestock recognizes that their status as things (however vital) implies exchangeability. The evolving connotations of these words encapsulate centuries of economic history, which my discussion collapses and necessarily simplifies. See the *OED*, s.v. "cattle."

24. Quoted in Hersh, *Slavery of Sex*, 66, from Stone's letter to Anthony dated September 11, 1856.

25. Hersh, *Slavery of Sex*, 16. Her figures are taken from the records of the Massachusetts society. Angelina Grimké asserted in 1836 that there were a total of sixty Female Anti-Slavery Societies in the Northern states, though I have found no other evidence to corroborate this figure (*Appeal to Christian Women*, 23).

26. Grimké, *Appeal to Christian Women*, 23. This fairly conservative portrait of Female Anti-Slavery Societies, though accurate in its depiction of the majority of the women involved in antislavery work, does not necessarily characterize all of the authors whose stories I discuss here, just as it does not fit the Grimkés and other public lecturers and political organizers. In particular, Lydia Maria Child and Carolyn Wells Healey Dall saw their fiction-writing as a distinctly political, indeed revolutionary, form of action. Nevertheless, even the most overtly political women plied their needles for

the cause while urging this more conventional form of political activity on their female audiences, and less daring women constituted the major readership for all of these stories as well as the authors of many of them.

27. There has as yet been no systematic study of the history of antislavery stories. Carolyn Karcher postulates that Child's story "The St. Domingo Orphans," published in her *Juvenile Miscellany* for September of 1830, may well have initiated the genre. Though antislavery stories appeared in *The Liberator* from 1831 and in many other antislavery papers, the major forum for their publication was provided by giftbooks and collections of literature for children, since these permitted longer narratives than most newspapers could afford. The earliest antislavery giftbook of which I am aware—*Oasis* (1834)—was produced by Child; it held mostly her own stories, accompanying them with two articles by her husband, David Child, and a handful of disparate pieces by abolitionist friends.

Later antislavery giftbooks, and most notably the *Liberty Bell* (1839–1858), follow this model of female production and control. Even though men contributed a large percentage of the material in such collections, they supplied argumentative pieces and poetry but rarely stories. For example, while two-thirds of the more than two hundred contributors to the *Liberty Bell* were men, only two (Edmund Quincy and an anonymous "Southron," presumably male) wrote stories.

Karcher suggests, and my own findings support her contention, that the antislavery stories written by men generally differ from those by women in thematic terms: men's tend to focus more on slave rebellions than on sexual exploitation, while in women's, miscegenation, concubinage, rape and—I would add—the breakup of families predominate. The thematics of escape is shared in works by both sexes. There are, of course, individual instances that contradict these generalizations. See Carolyn L. Karcher, "Rape, Murder, and Revenge in 'Slavery's Pleasant Homes': Lydia Maria Child's Antislavery Fiction and the Limits of Genre," *Women's Studies International Forum* 9 (1986).

28. Most obvious among these followers is *Liberty Chimes*, published in 1845 by the Ladies Anti-Slavery Society of Providence, Rhode Island. But also see the somewhat more successful giftbook *Autographs of Freedom*, edited by Julia Griffith for the Rochester, New York, Ladies Auxiliary in 1853 and 1854; it is unique in containing a number of pieces by ex-slaves, including Frederick Douglass, and for the closing of each selection with a facsimile of the author's signature—hence the title. Antislavery giftbooks were also occasionally produced by men; for example, Richard Sutton Rost compiled *Freedom's Gift* (Hartford, Conn.: S. S. Cowels, 1840) predominantly

as a showcase for Garrison. Many of the poems and fictional pieces, however, were contributed by women.

29. Before 1846 they were known as the "Massachusetts Anti-Slavery Fair." From 1847 until their replacement by "soirées" in 1858, they were more grandly entitled the "National Anti-Slavery Bazaar." The first *Liberty Bell* was released on October 29th, 1839, but the fair and publication were subsequently moved to the more lucrative Christmas season, and later editions are all dated early December. The only missed years were 1840, 1850, 1854, 1855, and 1857, so a total of fifteen volumes were published. All except the last, which reprinted some earlier selections, consisted entirely of new material. See Ralph Thompson, "*The Liberty Bell* and Other Anti-Slavery Gift-Books," *New England Quarterly* 7 (March 1934). The relation between the *Bell* and other sale items is nicely illustrated by "An English Child's Notion of the Inferiority of the Colored Population in America," in which a mother recounts her daughter's explanation of the words this five-year-old had stitched on a sampler she was making for the Boston fair. The child sent her sampler, and the mother sent this anecdote—presumably accompanied by her own needlework (*Liberty Bell* 8 [1847]: 49).

30. The average of the Fair's profits is taken from Jane H. Pease and William H. Pease, "The Boston Bluestocking, Maria Weston Chapman," *Bound with Them in Chains: A Biographical History of the Anti-Slavery Movement* (Westport, Conn.: Greenwood Press, 1972), 45; and the information on the finances of *The Liberty Bell* comes from Thompson, "Anti-Slavery Gift-Books," 158–59. Thompson queries the committee's boast, arguing that many volumes were distributed free, and hence at a loss, but even if the committee's figures are inflated there is no reason to believe that the books were not economically successful, especially considering that the cost of each printing was donated.

31. Quoted by Pease and Pease, *Bound with Them,* 34–35, from a letter by Chapman dated January 27, 1846.

32. The point, of course, is that the sentimentality required by the genre necessarily undermines any aspirations toward realism. For a far more sophisticated and interesting variation on this critique see Walter Benn Michaels's argument that Stowe's claims to realism mask an essentially romantic belief in inalienable property ("Romance and Real Estate," in *American Renaissance Reconsidered*).

33. The examples are endless, but to choose three from the stories discussed in this chapter: "The Slave-Wife," by Frances Green, *Liberty Chimes* (Providence, R.I.: Ladies Anti-Slavery Society, 1845) is presented as told by a friend who met Laco Ray, the slave husband, after his escape to Canada. Reprinting "Mary French and Susan Easton" anonymously in *The Slave's Friend* (New York:

American Anti-Slavery Society, 1836), Child added this italicized introduction: *"Perhaps some of my little readers may remember seeing, about a year and a half ago, advertisements in the newspapers . . . ."* "Mark and Hasty," by Matilda G. Thompson, in *The Child's Anti-Slavery Book* (New York: Carlton and Porter, 1859) is prefaced with a note that the "facts" of this St. Louis story "were communicated to the author by a friend residing temporarily in that city." Fiction had, of course, long been viewed with suspicion in Puritan America, and the practice of defending tales with the claim that they were "founded on fact" had become, by the eighteenth century, a conventional attribute of storytelling. Because, however, antislavery stories proposed to alter attitudes and behavior—to change the facts of American slavery—their claims to a factual basis served a double purpose, countering not only the general prejudice against frivolous or decadent fictionality but also the specific charge that fiction had no bearing on political realities.

34. Harriet Beecher Stowe, preface to *Uncle Tom's Cabin* (New York: The Library of America, 1982), 10; *A Key to Uncle Tom's Cabin*, vol. 2 of *The Writings of Harriet Beecher Stowe* (Boston: Riverside Press, 1896), 255–56. My evocation of Stowe here, and throughout this paper, is admittedly opportunistic, as her position within the contemporary critical canon allows me to assume a familiarity with the problematics of her work obviously lacking for most of the other texts I cite. Thus her more accessible and discussed novels provide an entry into the issues confronted in their more obscure precursors and also a means of situating these stories within contemporary critical discourse. Implicit in my work, moreover, is the assumption that Stowe's achievement needs to be read and evaluated within a genre of antislavery fiction initiated at least two decades before the success of *Uncle Tom*. I deemphasize the importance of distinguishing between novel and story, at least for the issues of corporeality and the effort to redefine personhood with which I am here concerned; the anecdotal structure of Stowe's novels, with their focus on repeated and distinct tableaus, diminishes the violence of this critical strategy.

35. Child, "Mary French and Susan Easton" in *Juvenile Miscellany* (Boston: Allen and Ticknor) 3d series, 6 (May 1834): 196.

36. In *"Cage aux folles*: Sensation and Gender in Wilkie Collins's *The Woman in White"* (*Representations* 14 [Spring 1986]), D. A. Miller argues that the nervous sensations that characterize the reading of sensation novels are associated, within the novels themselves, with femininity. This insight and the implications Miller elaborates from it prove equally suggestive for the similarly gendered weeping that characterizes the reading of sentimental fiction. The gendering of physical response bears somewhat different meanings, however, in sentimental and sensation fiction. For while the feminine nervous-

ness instigated by thrillers produces the sense of confinement and incarceration of femininity, the tears ushered by sentimental fiction flow outward as mechanisms of escape.

37. Analyzing the "power" of *Uncle Tom's Cabin*, Jane Tompkins finds that in sentimental fiction "not words, but the emotions of the heart bespeak a state of grace, and these are known by the sound of a voice, the touch of a hand, but chiefly in moments of greatest importance, by tears" ("Sentimental Power: *Uncle Tom's Cabin* and the Politics of Literary History," in *Sensational Designs: The Cultural Work of American Fiction 1790–1860* [New York: Oxford University Press, 1985], 131–32). Tompkins is most centrally interested in that "state of grace" expressed by emotions that are themselves spoken through bodily signs. So in her catalogue of scenes marked by weeping, Tompkins defends these tears in terms of the message of "salvation, communion, reconciliation" that they suggest; in contrast, I am concerned here less with what the tears may say than with Stowe's recourse to bodily symptoms as the most efficacious means of saying.

38. Harriet Beecher Stowe, *Dred: A Tale of the Great Dismal Swamp*, vol. 3 of *Writings*, 190–91.

39. *The Slave's Friend* (New York: American Anti-Slavery Society, 1836–1838), a penny monthly for children, makes its lessons in reading more explicit. The first article of the first number of the 1837 edition shows a picture of two girls—one black and one white—peering together at a large book, followed by three pages of detailed analysis explaining how to interpret the scene. It concludes by pointing to the dog in the lower corner of the print and informing its young readers that "when you see a dog in a picture like this, it is an emblem, or sign of Fidelity" (3). The signs are sure; one need only learn the vocabulary.

40. Stowe, *Dred*, 247–48.

41. Green, "Slave-Wife, 82.

42. Child, "Mary French," 202.

43. The fantasy of colorlessness in fact amounts to the same thing, for though the pinkish-yellowish-gray of "white" skin is indeed a color, white (as defined in the first entry of *Webster's New Collegiate Dictionary*) means "free from color."

44. Child's struggle with this problem can be traced through her revisions of the story as she prepared it for republication in *The Slave's Friend* of 1836. In this later version "the streak whiter than the rest of [Mary's] face" is replaced by a streak that is "lighter," a substitution that masks the problem but does not really avoid it.

45. One source of difficulty is that black and white have come to symbolize the moral dichotomy between good and evil. For antislavery discourse such symbolism is profoundly troubling and frequently results in absurdly paradoxical rhetoric in which the positive

valuation of the black man is depicted in terms of whiteness. For example, the vignette of "The Apple and the Chestnut" presents a "white man" taunting a "poor colored man" by comparing his own race to an apple and the black's to a chestnut. The black man replies with a witticism that, by inverting the intended insult, ultimately deepens it: "O, Massa, what you say is true. The chestnut has dark skin just like poor black man, but its kernel is all white and sweet. The apple, though it looks so pretty, has many little black grains at the heart." Attempting to explain the moral of this exchange, the narrator only intensifies the contradictions: "Now little boys and girls can't be abolitionists until they get rid of all these black grains in their hearts" (*The Slave's Friend* 1 [1836]: 3). Such logic suggests that the ability to liberate the black people depends upon first expunging blackness.

46. Eliza Lee Follen, "A Melancholy Boy," *The Liberty Bell* 5 (1844): 94–95.

47. The only notable exception to this trend is Jules Zanger, "The 'Tragic Octoroon' in Pre-Civil War Fiction," *American Quarterly* 18 (Spring 1966), which discusses some of the strategic uses of this figure in abolitionist writing. His most useful insight for my purposes is that the octoroon "represented not merely the product of the incidental sin of the individual sinner, but rather what might be called the result of cumulative institutional sin, since the octoroon was the product of four [*sic*] generations of illicit, enforced miscegenation made possible by the slavery system" (66).

48. Caroline Wells Healey Dall, "Amy," *Liberty Bell* 10 (1849): 6, 8, 11, 12. In "The Inalienable Love" (*Liberty Bell* 15 [1858]), Dall makes this point explicit, asserting that if she were to write her story with the "nervous strength" of the slave's narration, "all the women in the land would tear the pages out of the fair volume" (87).

49. The opposite, and most conservative, pattern of racial and sexual pairings is demarcated by another frequently told story of miscegenation, one that romanticizes the relation between a white man and a darker woman. In its most prevalent form, a beautiful, refined quadroon loves a white gentleman only to lose him through either death or marriage. This loss entails, in addition to the statutory broken heart, a fall from a life of luxury and endearments into one of slavery and sexual exploitation. Even in these stories, however, where the power of the white man and the exclusion of the black man seem most absolute, miscegenation works to interrogate white male supremacy. These are stories about the unequal positions of men and women within a love relation, where the inherent similarities between the nearly white quadroon and the white woman emphasize the ways in which the quadroon's inability to control her fate is only an extreme example of the victimization of all women in a society that considers love a fair exchange for power.

50. The examples of this last passion are myriad. See especially Harry's incestuous worship of his half-sister and mistress Nina Gordon in Stowe's *Dred,* and Jan's rivalry with both the husband and the son of his beloved mistress Maria in Child's "Jan and Zaida," *Liberty Bell* 14 (1856).

51. See the discussion of the revolutionary force of Child's stand on miscegenation in both Karcher's article "Rape, Murder, and Revenge" and in her introduction to Lydia Maria Child's *Hobomok and Other Writings on Indians* (New Brunswick, N.J.: Rutgers University Press, 1986). In *Hobomok,* as in Catharine Sedgwick's *Hope Leslie* (New Brunswick, N.J.: Rutgers University Press, 1987), the marriages of white women and Native American men are (somewhat equivocally) endorsed, suggesting once again the difference in antebellum racial attitudes toward the noble savage and the slave.

52. Child, *An Appeal in Favor of that Class of Americans Called Africans* (1836; facsimile reprint, New York: Arno Press, 1968), 196–97.

53. Harriet E. Wilson's *Our Nig: or, Sketches from the Life of a Free Black* (New York: Vintage Books, 1983) is not essentially an antislavery fiction; in Mag Smith's marriage to the "kind-hearted African" Jim it does, however, narrate this most socially unacceptable of unions. It is worth noting that such a story, when finally written, was first penned by a black woman, not a white.

54. Green, "Slave-Wife," 87, 94, 103, 107.

55. Matilda G. Thompson, "Aunt Judy's Story: A Story from Real Life," *The Child's Anti-Slavery Book,* 113, 115, 112, 117. For a more extended example of this narrative strategy, see Jane Elizabeth Jones, *The Young Abolitionists, or, Conversations on Slavery* (Boston: Anti-Slavery Office, 1848). This juvenile novel begins with a series of conversations between a mother and her three children and then dramatizes these lessons in abolition as the family helps to hide a group of fugitive slaves.

56. I do not mean to deny that abolitionists found the domestication of slavery politically useful, but only to suggest that despite its strategic efficacy the practice had costs for women, children, and slaves. For a brilliant analysis of how the strategy worked see Philip Fisher, "Making a Thing into a Man: The Sentimental Novel and Slavery," *Hard Facts: Setting and Form in the American Novel* (New York: Oxford University Press, 1985). Fisher argues that the domestication of slavery in *Uncle Tom's Cabin,* and particularly the distillation of the horrors of slavery into the recurring image of the separation and destruction of slave families, performs the cultural work of "making a thing into a man," and so proves efficacious in restructuring popular attitudes toward the slave. The notion of the slave as thing, object, property is replaced in domestic antislavery fiction with the imaginative conception of the slave as person, because this

fiction makes the slave familiar by putting him or her within the ordinary and emotionally accessible realm of the family. Furthermore, Fisher points out that setting the destruction of the black slave family within the context of the white slave-owning family makes "the contradiction between the inevitable sentimental nature of the family and the corrosive institution of slavery . . . the central analytic point of Stowe's novel" (101). I would add that the juxtaposition of the institutions of slavery and family also reveals the corrosive dimension of the family itself.

Gillian Brown's article "Getting in the Kitchen with Dinah: Domestic Politics in *Uncle Tom's Cabin*" (*American Quarterly* 36 [Fall, 1984]) preceded the publication of *Hard Facts* and is positioned largely in response to Jane Tompkins's evaluation of Stowe's use of domestic values as the source of sentimental power and the ideal replacement for political and commercial power. However, it can also serve as a critique of Fisher on this point, questioning his essentially positive reading of the family. Brown argues that the comparison between slavery and family in *Uncle Tom's Cabin* reveals the economic basis of existing familial relations and that Stowe's utopian vision of a society governed by familial mores is therefore predicated on a restructuring of the family. Stowe, she asserts, "seeks to reform American society not by employing domestic values but by reforming them. . . . Stowe's domestic solution to slavery, then, represents not the strength of sentimental values but a utopian rehabilitation of them, necessitated by their fundamental complicity with the market to which they are ostensibly opposed" (507). The obvious difference between Stowe's work, as Brown interprets it, and that of Coleman and Thompson is that the latter do not self-consciously embrace the feminist project of rehabilitating domesticity, a fact that makes their unwitting display of the similarities between slavery and family all the more disturbing.

57. Coleman and Thompson, "A Few Words About American Slave Children," *The Child's Anti-Slavery Book*, 10, 9.

58. "The Difference Between a Slave and a Child," *The Child's Book on Slavery, or Slavery Made Plain* (Cincinnati: American Reform Tract and Book Society, 1857), 31.

59. Ibid., 30, 28.

60. Such displacements into the moral realm are quite common in abolitionist discourse. For example, see Rev. Charles Beecher's very similar argument in the American Anti-Slavery Society tract, "The God of the Bible against Slavery." Quoting from a decision by Judge Ruffin that distinguishes between the structures of authority associated with slavery and those associated with the family by reference to the differing "ends" of the two systems ("the happiness of youth" versus "the profits of the master"), Beecher characterizes slavery as "intrinsically and unchangeably selfish" and the parent-

child relation as "intrinsically benevolent." Reprinted in Beecher, *Anti-Slavery Tracts*, ser. 1 (1855–1856, reprinted, Westport Conn.: Negro University Press, 1970) tract 17, 5–7.

61. See David Brion Davis, *The Problem of Slavery in Western Culture* (Ithaca, N.Y.: Cornell University Press, 1966) especially chapters 6 and 7, "The Legitimacy of Enslavement" and "The Ideal of the Christian Servant," and chapter 10, "Religious Sources of Antislavery Thought: Quakers and the Sectarian Tradition."

62. See Smith-Rosenberg's introductions to parts 1 and 2 of *Disorderly Conduct*.

63. Consider, for example, the minister Laco Ray consults in "The Slave-Wife" or the whole collection of church apologists for slavery in *Dred*. Along with Mrs. Shelby from *Uncle Tom*, compare Mrs. Nelson and Mrs. Jennings in *The Child's Anti-Slavery Book*, who cannot prevent the sale of Mark in "Mark and Hasty"; a less harsh reading of Edith's delicacy might also cast her in this role.

64. Stowe, *Uncle Tom's Cabin*, 415.

65. Tom's soul, however, is not completely disentangled from the commercial realm, for in responding to his taunts, Tom engrafts the New Testament vocabulary of redemption based on Christ's sacrificial payment onto Legree's assertion that the money he paid for Tom establishes his ownership. In claiming God as his purchaser, Tom excludes himself from the conflict and recasts it as a dispute between masters. See Michaels's discussion of the ways in which Stowe found that the body and even the soul "could not be guaranteed against capitalistic appropriation" ("Romance and Real Estate," 176).

66. C., "A Thought upon Emancipation," *Liberty Chimes*, 80. I do not want to discredit the heroic potential of slave suicides. Surely the will to take one's own life may be the last, and in some situations perhaps the only means of expressing a will at all. What is suspect here is not the slave's motives for suicide but the abolitionist's desire for and glorification of such deaths.

CHAPTER 2

1. *Family Notes and Autobiography: Brooklyn and New York*, vol. 1 of *The Collected Writings of Walt Whitman: Notebooks and Unpublished Prose Manuscripts*, ed. Edward F. Grier (New York: New York University Press, 1984), 67. Grier dates this notebook (it survives only in microfilm, Library of Congress Collection item 80) as being used between 1847 and 1854. Consequently, in his judgment, these lines are probably the earliest extant instances of Whitman's new poetic form. See both his introduction to the "albot Wilson" notebook in this volume and his "Walt Whitman's Earliest Known Notebook" (*PMLA* 83 [October, 1968]: 1453–56). In so dating this manuscript Grier endorses

Emory Halloway's claim that with these lines "begin the first preserved attempts that Whitman made at creating the verse form
which he was to employ in 'Leaves of Grass' " (*The Uncollected Poetry
and Prose of Walt Whitman* [New York: Doubleday, Page and Co.,
1921], 2:69). For the less convincing argument for a later dating of
notebook and passage see Floyd Stovall, "Dating Whitman's Early
Notebooks," *Studies in Bibliography* 24 (1971): 197–204.
   2. *Walt Whitman's Leaves of Grass: the First (1855) Edition*, ed. Malcolm Cowley (New York: Penguin Classics, 1986) ll. 422–23. Whitman sets these words as two lines through the edition of 1871,
after which he had them printed as a single long line. In the inter-
vening editions Whitman made changes in punctuation and, more
notably, in capitalization, first capitalizing *soul* in the 1860 edition,
and then in 1867 giving *body* an initial capital as well.
   Unless otherwise specified all citations from *Leaves of Grass* refer
to the 1855 edition, for which I use Cowley's text and line numbers.
Since in the 1855 edition the poems were not given titles, for convenience I generally employ the titles Whitman used in the final
"deathbed" edition of 1881. My commentary on later emendations
and on post–1855 poems relies on *Leaves of Grass: A Textual Variorum
of the Printed Poems*, 3 vols., ed. Sculley Bradley et al. (New York:
New York University Press, 1980).
   3. Indeed, in a discussion of the "Body Language" of the 1855
Leaves of Grass, Helen Vendler writes that "readers who seek in
Whitman the poet of social protest find an authentic Whitman. But
they do not find the primary one. The primary Whitman, psycho-
logically speaking, is the Whitman who, at some point in his thir-
ties, opened a new circuit between the energies of sexuality and the
energies of language . . ." ("Body Language: *Leaves of Grass* and the
Articulation of Sexual Awareness," *Harpers* 273 [October 1986]: 64).
Vendler's stratification of authentic Whitmans into primary and
lesser figures exemplifies the disjunction between political and
bodily or sexual interpretations that characterizes the vast majority
of Whitman criticism. Thus for Vendler, discussing the sexuality of
Whitman's poetry entails dismissing its political import.
   Conversely, the most interesting discussions of the politics of
Whitman's poetry generally disregard issues of corporeality. See
Mitchell Breitwieser, "Who Speaks in Whitman's Poems?" in *The
American Renaissance: New Dimensions*, ed. Harry Garvin (Lewisburg,
Penn.: Bucknell University Press, 1983); Kenneth Burke, "Policy
Made Personal: Whitman's Verse and Prose—Salient Traits," in
Leaves of Grass: One Hundred Years After, ed. Milton Hindus (Stanford:
Stanford University Press, 1955); and Allen Grossman, "The Poetics
of Union in Whitman and Lincoln: An Inquiry toward the Relation-
ship of Art and Policy," in Michaels and Pease, *American Renaissance
Reconsidered*. Thus, for example, in Grossman's brilliant discussion

of the "poetics of union" he hardly refers to sexual union. I argue that a central aim of Whitman's poetics is precisely to mediate between such exclusively bodily or abstractly political conceptions of identity and of poetic utterance. Michael Moon's study, *Disseminating Whitman: Revision and Corporeality in "Leaves of Grass"* (Cambridge: Harvard University Press, 1991) provides a wonderful and rare exception to this pattern; it does so by focusing on the politics of bodily control evident in cultural attitudes toward male/male desire.

4. Allen Grossman says of these lines (and of Whitman's early formal experiments in "Resurgemus," "Blood-Money," and "Wounded in the House of Friends") that "the 'open' line as formal principle appears simultaneously with the subject of liberation and is the enabling condition of the appearance of that subject" ("The Poetics of Union," 192). Although my analysis is deeply indebted to Grossman's insights, I wish to stress the difference between our readings: my focus on Whitman's identification of the role of the poet with that of the mediator lays the basis for a quite different conception of Whitman's poetics and produces a more reciprocal understanding of the relation between the form and subject of these lines than that Grossman describes.

5. See Whitman's own description of the creole Margaret in *Franklin Evans,* cited below.

6. Leslie Fiedler, *Love and Death in the American Novel,* rev. ed. (New York: Stein and Day, 1966), 301.

7. *Franklin Evans,* in *The Collected Writings of Walt Whitman: The Early Poems and the Fiction,* ed. Thomas L. Brasher (New York: New York University Press, 1963), 206. All subsequent citations refer to this edition.

8. My thanks to Eve Kosofsky Sedgwick, who, on hearing a version of this chapter, pointed out the suppression of *fustigate.*

9. Evans's description of Margaret as "dark and swarthy" provides the most pointed instance of the manufacturing of difference I am discussing here. His penchant for explaining her emotional vehemence as a sign of her African ancestry functions similarly; see his references to "the fiery disposition of her nation" (210), "the spirit of her fiery race" (213), and the observation that "her heart had still a remnant of the savage" (224). Margaret's progressive darkenings culminate in the scene in which, standing outside Mrs. Conway's sickroom window, her entire body is absorbed into the blackness of the night so that only "those glittering things, which were human eyes" remain visible (225).

10. Though the fact of their cohabitation is mentioned, the days between the wedding and the awakening of Evans's disgust are carefully elided: "It needs not that I should particularize the transactions of the next few days" (207).

11. Later, when Louis's death from the Southern disease drives the maddened Margaret to confession and suicide, Evans merely reports the events, not even stating how she killed herself. (Piercing dagger or strangling noose perhaps?) In a story built out of oppositions and mediation, once Mrs. Conway's death collapses the triangle of their relations, Margaret's suicide becomes redundant and uninteresting. For this story of mergings, the single term remains outside the structures of linkage and therefore unrepresented and indeed largely meaningless.

12. See Sharon Cameron, *Lyric Time: Dickinson and the Limits of Genre* (Baltimore: Johns Hopkins University Press, 1979).

13. Breitwieser draws the related conclusion:

> The word *I* in *Leaves of Grass* is the self-designation of two entities, one a single member of the wide spectrum of American possibility, the other a reverse prism that, after such single members have painfully resigned their warped centrality, collects them and emits the plain friendly light of day: "He judges not as the judge judges but as the sun falling around a helpless thing." What we call "Whitman" is always both the blessing sun and one of the naked helpless things it blesses. ("Who Speaks in Whitman's Poems," 142)

The difference between our readings is that I would divide Whitman's "I" still further, not stopping with the impersonal all-encompassing "I" and the single individual but going on to note how even the naked, helpless things are self-divided, encompassing a staggering multiplicity.

14. This passage is one of the four excerpts from Whitman's work anthologized in *The Penguin Book of Homosexual Verse*, ed. Stephen Coote (Harmondsworth: Penguin Books, 1983). For Coote, at least, the erotic appeal of the drowning has become the defining characteristic of these lines.

15. F. O. Matthiessen was, I believe, the first to identify this event: "Thus merged with the night, his series of flickering pictures expands into a few that take up whole paragraphs: of a swimmer being drowned; of a ship being wrecked—a reconstruction of his memory of the *Mexico* as it is broken to pieces on Hampstead beach in 1840." *American Renaissance: Art and Expression in the Age of Emerson and Whitman* (New York: Oxford University Press, 1941), 572. Matthiessen's account of the expansion of flickering pictures into whole paragraphs describes the generic instability I am discussing as an instance of losing poetic control: Whitman apparently forgets that he is writing a dream.

16. The money paid "for their blood" that identifies this oppressive relation as slavery rewrites the poem "Blood-Money" that Whitman published in the New York *Tribune Supplement* of March 22, 1850, probably as a commentary on Webster's support of the fugitive slave law. "Blood-Money" equates the sale of slaves with the sil-

ver Judas took for the body of Jesus and so offers an explicitly political version of this Luciferian moment.

17. Manuscript drafts reveal that the process of erasing the particular contents of slavery begins with the initial composition of this passage: an early version refers to "Black Lucifer." *Notes and Fragments Left by Walt Whitman*, ed. R. M. Bucke (London: Talbot, 1899), item 40.

18. Fredric Jameson defines mediation as "the classical dialectical term for the establishment of relationships between, say, the formal analysis of a work of art and its social ground, or between the internal dynamics of the political state and its economic base" (*The Political Unconscious: Narrative as Socially Symbolic Act* [Ithaca, N.Y.: Cornell University Press, 1981], 39; Jameson discusses this concept of mediation on 39–44 and 225–26). My work obviously entails such an effort to relate Whitman's poetic practice to the contemporaneous political problematics of slavery. In his own work, however, Whitman is engaged in a similar project of mediation, both in his placement of the poet between master and slave and in the political and social impact of poetry that such a stance assumes.

19. As, for instance, I basically do in my reading of "The Sleepers." Breitwieser's discussion of Whitman's use of the word "I" helpfully demonstrates how Whitman's poetry exaggerates and so confronts the mobile nature of deictic signs and the consequent precariousness of written assertions of presence. His analysis focuses on the linguistic implications of Whitman's extravagant transpositions of first person utterance, mine on the significance of Whitman's mobile "I" for his definition of identity and his conception of embodiment.

20. For a more general discussion of this dynamic see Tenney Nathanson's analysis of the pathos inherent in Whitman's "intense literalism," the poet's acute insistence that all sorts of external things, steamships as well as human flesh, are literally present in his poems ("Whitman's Tropes of Light and Flood: Language and Representation in Early Editions of *Leaves of Grass*," *ESQ* 31 [1985]: 118).

CHAPTER 3

1. Harriet A. Jacobs, *Incidents in the Life of a Slave Girl, Written by Herself*, ed. Lydia Maria Child (1861). Reprint, ed. Jean Fagan Yellin (Cambridge: Harvard University Press, 1987). Jacobs's letters to Post of 1852[?] and June 21, 1857, are included in the "Correspondence" section of Yellin's edition (232, 242). Amy Post clearly saw these statements as significant, quoting the latter in her postscript to *Incidents* as evidence of how Jacobs's "sensitive spirit shrank from publicity" (203).

In the correspondence Jacobs's own practices of punctuation, capitalization, and spelling have been retained. I follow Yellin, however, in inserting an additional space where a period and the subsequent capital letter have been omitted (see Yellin's "Note on this Edition," xxxiv). All quotations from *Incidents* refer to the Yellin edition and are given parenthetically within the text.

2. Henry Louis Gates Jr., "Introduction," *Figures in Black: Words, Signs, and the "Racial" Self* (New York: Oxford University Press, 1987), xxiv.

3. Harriet Jacobs to Amy Post, February 14, 1853, in Yellin, *Incidents*, 233.

4. Harriet Jacobs to Amy Post, April 4, 1853, in Yellin, *Incidents*, 235.

5. Henry Louis Gates Jr. explains that Frederick Douglass was "the representative colored man of the United States" in part because he was "the most presentable" ("The Trope of a New Negro and the Reconstruction of the Image of the Black," *Representations* 24 [Fall 1988]: 128).

6. Harriet Jacobs to Amy Post, April 4, 1853, in Yellin, *Incidents*, 235. In her letter to Post of October 9, 1853, Jacobs writes, "Mrs Stowe never answered any of my letters after I refused to have my history in her key   perhaps it is for the best at least I will try and think so," and then discusses her "scribbling" of antislavery pieces for the *New York Tribune* in preparation for writing her history herself (236). As such letters indicate, Jacobs understood her own writing as a means of responding to Stowe's treatment.

7. The evaluations of Jacobs's deportment are from Lydia Maria Child's editorial introduction to *Incidents* (3). Amy Post provides a similar, if warmer, assessment in an appended postscript to the volume: "the author of this book is my highly-esteemed friend. . . . [When introduced] I immediately became much interested in Linda; for her appearance was prepossessing, and her deportment indicated remarkable delicacy of feeling and purity of thought" (203). Thus Jacobs's story is framed by the testimony of well-bred abolitionist women to her fine character and manners.

8. See Dorothy Sterling, *We Are Your Sisters: Black Women in the Nineteenth Century* (New York: W. W. Norton, 1984), 84.

9. Before Yellin's superb work in documenting Jacobs's authorship of *Incidents*, Jacobs's existence was almost completely concealed by her book. Some critics argued that though the basic story might have been that of a fugitive slave, the book itself was merely an imitation of a slave narrative written by its purported editor, Lydia Maria Child. See, for example, John Blassingame, *The Slave Community: Plantation Life in the Antebellum South* (New York: Oxford University Press, 1979), 367–82, as well as Yellin's discussion of Blassingame and this critical trend in Yellin, "Written By Her-

self: Harriet Jacobs's Slave Narrative," *American Literature* 53 (November 1981): 479–86.

Even among those critics who upheld the text's authenticity as a slave narrative, Linda Brent was generally noted as its author, with significant results. For example, Annette Niemtzow's perceptive comparison of *Incidents* and *Narrative of the Life of Frederick Douglass an American Slave, Written by Himself* (New York: Signet, 1968), includes a discussion of these texts' different attitudes toward names: "male slaves needed names and control of naming to achieve adult identity; for women, bound to give up their names, the issues of adulthood were different" ("The Problematic of Self in Autobiography: The Example of the Slave Narrative," in *The Art of the Slave Narrative: Original Essays in Criticism and Theory,* ed. John Sekora and Darwin T. Turner [Macomb, Ill.: Western Illinois University, 1982], 104–5). Niemtzow is clearly unaware that "Linda Brent," the name she ascribes to the author of *Incidents,* is itself an instance of the control over naming she associates with the narratives of male slaves.

10. Taken together, Annette Niemtzow's and Valerie Smith's discussions of *Incidents* can be read as a debate over the relation of Jacobs's text to generic norms. In their analyses of *Incidents,* both critics examine the influence of domestic fiction, and particularly the Richardsonian plot of seduction, on the form of the slave narrative. Niemtzow ultimately presents these conventions as disabling. She argues that, finding no space for her experiences as a female slave in the fundamentally male genre of the slave narrative, Jacobs evokes the female seduction story, only to be imprisoned within its white and middle-class definitions of femininity. Smith, on the other hand, argues that in her juxtaposition and manipulation of these two genres—that of the male slave and that of the free woman—Jacobs radically critiques and transforms them both. Niemtzow, 104–8, and Smith, "Form and Ideology in Three Slave Narratives," *Self Discovery and Authority in Afro-American Narrative* (Cambridge: Harvard University Press, 1987), 28–43.

11. See Hortense Spillers's discussion of the paradox by which the "peculiar institution" both denies slaves a "private realm" and makes them "the very stuff of domesticity as planter-aristocrats envisioned it" ("Changing the Letter: The Yokes and Jokes of Discourse, or, Mrs. Stowe, Mr. Reed," in McDowell and Rampersand, *Slavery and the Literary Imagination,* 25).

12. My thanks to my Amherst College students Jonathan Flatley, who helped me to think of Jacobs as "poaching" on the private, and Margaret Stohl, whose paper on *Incidents* taught me a good deal about Jacobs's use of domestic space and specifically that the peephole looked out but not in.

13. Margaret Horniblow's testament is among the many documents Yellin has discovered. In a codicil she wills "that my negro

girl Harriet be given to my niece Mary Matilda Norcom Daughter of Dr. James Norcom, and I further give & bequeathe to my said niece my bureau & work table & their contents." Not recognized as a neighbor, Jacobs is rather in the category of "negro girl," a possession little different from a work table. Yellin prints a facsimile of the codicil (*Incidents*, 213).

14. As Hazel Carby notes, "Any feminist history that seeks to establish the sisterhood of white and black women as allies in the struggle against the oppression of all women must also reveal the complexity of the social and economic differences between women." Carby's reading of *Incidents* examines Jacobs's treatment of this problem specifically in terms of Linda's relations to her various mistresses (" 'Hear My Voice, Ye Careless Daughters': Narratives of Slave and Free Women before Emancipation," *Reconstructing Womanhood*, 53). See also her discussion of the "sisterhood" of Linda's mother and mistress (51–53).

15. Angela Davis has made similar observations about the power of the slave woman who, in tending to the needs of the slave community, "was performing the *only* labor of the slave community which could not be directly and immediately claimed by the oppressor" ("Reflections on the Black Woman's Role in the Community of Slaves," *Black Scholar* 3 [December 1971]: 7).

16. Jacobs details the privations of plantation domesticity:

> If the dinner was not served at the exact time on that particular Sunday, [Mrs. Flint] would station herself in the kitchen, and wait till it was dished, and then spit in all the kettles and pans that had been used for cooking. She did this to prevent the cook and her children from eking out their meager fare with the remains of the gravy and other scrapings. The slaves could get nothing to eat except what she chose to give them. Provisions were weighed out by the pound and ounce, three times a day. I can assure you she gave them no chance to eat wheat bread from her flour barrel. She knew how many biscuits a quart of flour would make, and exactly what size they ought to be.
>
> Dr. Flint was an epicure. The cook never sent a dinner to his table without fear and trembling; for if there happened to be a dish not to his liking, he would either order her to be whipped, or compel her to eat every mouthful of it in his presence. The poor, hungry creature might not have objected to eating it; but she did object to having her master cram it down her throat till she choked. (12)

In Mrs. Flint's domestic economy, the household wisdom so prized by nineteenth-century matrons produces deprivation, not the bounty its proponents promised. Mrs. Flint spitting into the pots or Dr. Flint force-feeding the cook literally invert the normative and life-sustaining processes of consumption: the kettle, instead of containing food for the body, becomes a receptacle for excretions from the body; the cook, instead of preparing the meal, is choked by

it. Food withheld, contaminated, or crammed down the throat becomes punitive, its nutritive value perverted into a sign of dominance and submission. Significantly, many of the women who wrote
for the abolitionist cause also wrote treatises on household management, thus casting the well-ordered, thrifty, but bountiful free-
home as a mechanism of political reform. See, for example, Catherine Beecher and Harriet Beecher Stowe, *The American Woman's
Home: Or, Principles of Domestic Science* (New York: J. B. Ford and Co.,
1869) and Lydia Maria Child, *The Frugal Housewife* (Boston: Carter,
Hendee, 1830).

17. For a reading of how these three stories interact with each
other and with the chapter's explicitly gendered title, "The Slave
Who Dared to Feel like a Man," see Smith, *Self-Discovery*, 34–35.

18. The questions that accompany Child's request for a longer
and more explicit account of the Southern outrages that followed
Turner's rebellion make clear the titillating violence inherent in
antislavery's appeal.

> My object in writing at this time is to ask you to write what you can
> recollect of the outrages committed on the colored people, in Nat
> Turner's time. You say the reader would not believe what you saw "in-
> flicted on men, women, and children, without the slightest ground of
> suspicion against them." What *were* those inflictions? Were any tor-
> tured to make them confess? And how? Were any killed? Please write
> some of the most striking particulars, and let me have them to insert.
> (Lydia Maria Child to Harriet Jacobs, August 13, 1860, in Yellin, *In-
> cidents*, 244).

Ambivalent in her assessment of the allure of cruelty, Child also
included suggestions such as grouping the more gruesome stories
of neighborhood atrocities together in one chapter "in order that
those who shrink from 'supping upon horrors' might omit them"
(Yellin, *Incidents*, xxii). To note that two of these digressive chapters
were suggested by Child only illustrates the discontinuities entailed
in coupling the requirements of a personal narrative to the needs of
abolitionist politics.

19. Baker, *Blues, Ideology, and Afro-American Literature*, 52. In general, Jacobs does not extend this concern to "any slave boy." She associates sexual vulnerability primarily with the body of the female
slave; thus, while admitting that "slavery is terrible for men," she
contends that "it is far more terrible for women. Supperadded to the
burden common to all, *they* have wrongs, and sufferings, and mor-
tifications peculiarly their own" (*Incidents*, 77). Though she relates
stories of white women whose offspring are fathered by their slaves,
she does not present such incidents as evidence of the oppression of
these enslaved men, but rather as a sign of the moral laxity inherent
to slaveholding (51–52). The one exception is the story of Luke, who

was forced to wear nothing but his shirt so as to be always ready for the whip, and who was made to submit to "the strangest freaks of despotism. . . . Some of these freaks were of a nature too filthy to be repeated." Yet what Jacobs labels most freakish about Luke's ordeal is undoubtedly that he has been fashioned into a slave girl. The feminization that characterizes Luke's enslavement is reversed as the story of his eventual escape includes the symbolic castration of his now dead master: Luke requests and receives his master's old trousers, their pockets secretly loaded with bills (192–93).

20. Douglass's story of writing "protections" is not of course without its ambivalences: on discovery of the escape plan, he and his friends must destroy the evidence by eating the forged passes along with their biscuits (*Narrative*, 94–97). Such scenes of bodily incorporation, however, ultimately reiterate Douglass's sense of writing as replacing and filling the slave body: "My feet have been so cracked with the frost, that the pen with which I am writing might be laid in the gashes" (43). William Wells Brown, "The Life and Escape of William Wells Brown," in *Clotel, or, The President's Daughter* (New York: University Books, 1969), 38. Also see Brown's barter of barley sugar for lessons in spelling (36–37).

21. The recognition that the act of telling about sexual abuse may prove largely indistinguishable from the abuses told is common among the narratives of slave women. Stories of interracial rape and sexual compulsion might well fuel abolitionist zeal, but they also necessarily cater to the voyeurism of Northern audiences. For a particularly explicit example of these dynamics, see the Rev. H. Mattison's interview of Louisa Piquet, published as an antislavery tract in 1861. Piquet speaks about her experiences under slavery in the hope of gaining subscriptions to a fund for the purchase of her mother. While Mattison is supportive of her efforts, his questions pruriently focus on the more pornographic aspects of her story: how thin her dress when she was whipped, what parts of her body were scarred by the cowhide, whether she was stripped at the auction, and of course, what her sexual relations were with her various masters (Rev. H. Mattison, *Louisa Piquet, The Octoroon: A Tale of Southern Life*, included in *Collected Black Women's Narratives*, ed. Anthony G. Barthelemy, Schomburg Library of Nineteenth Century Black Women Writers [New York: Oxford University Press, 1988]).

22. My analysis owes much to Hortense Spillers's treatment of this passage in "Mama's Baby, Papa's Maybe: An American Grammar Book," *Diacritics* 17 (1988): 65–81. Spillers discusses the analogy between the position of the jealous mistress and that of the master and concludes, as I do, that such an analogy provides neither the white woman nor the slave woman with a position of authority: "Neither could claim her body and its various productions—for quite different reasons, albeit—as her own" (77). My reading differs

from Spillers's, however, in the attempt to relate this scene to the more general dynamics of a discourse of female sexuality.

23. Jacobs's concern with bourgeois standards of feminine virtue was characteristic of early black feminists. Linda Gordon and Ellen Dubois note that since the problems of maintaining respectability common to all nineteenth-century women were especially severe for the black woman, "the black women's movement conducted a particularly militant campaign for respectability, often making black feminists spokespeople for prudery in their communities" ("Seeking Ecstasy on the Battlefield: Danger and Pleasure in Nineteenth-Century Feminist Sexual Thought," *Feminist Studies* 9 [Spring 1983]: 10). At stake in such campaigns, and in Jacobs's narrative project, is both an acknowledgment of the black woman's position as the one recognized site of sexuality in a purportedly asexual female world, and the desire that it were otherwise.

24. Carby, *Reconstructing Womanhood*, 61.

25. I thank P. Gabrielle Foreman for allowing me to quote from her manuscript "Manuscript in Signs," 7.

26. Jacobs is not alone in suggesting the erotic power of anti-slavery work. For example, in an article published in the 1854 gift-book *Autographs for Freedom* the white feminist-abolitionist, Jane Swisshelm, describes William Lloyd Garrison's abolitionist fervor in just these terms: "It is necessary to his existence that he should work—work for the slave; and in his work he gratifies all the strongest instincts of his nature, more completely than even the grossest sensualist can satisfy *his*, by unlimited indulgence!" That Swisshelm should draw such an analogy is no doubt indicative of the relation between politics and sexuality in her own life and mind. Nevertheless, it is important to note that her discussion of the sexual dimension of political work is explicitly framed in terms of male, not female, experience. See Ronald Walters, "The Erotic South: Civilization and Sexuality in American Abolitionism," *American Quarterly* 25 (May 1973): 177–201; Walters quotes Swisshelm on 178.

CHAPTER 4

1. One of the "snatches" Joseph Lyman copied out and preserved from Emily Dickinson's letters to him. Richard Sewall provisionally dates these passages "about 1865" (*The Lyman Letters: New Light on Emily Dickinson and Her Family,* ed. Richard B. Sewall [Amherst: The University of Massachusetts Press, 1965], 71).

2. Throughout the 1850s and 1860s the Dickinson home, eminent in the town of Amherst, was a decidedly politicized space. Nevertheless, the family's political loyalties and class position did not foster a reformist zeal. When discussing "the 'great questions' of public policy which agitate the country," Edward Dickinson, the

poet's father, felt sufficiently untouched by the agitation to signal his distance from the great questions with quotation marks. Whatever his concern over the great questions, Edward Dickinson's years of party politics belonged to the most divisive period of sectional debate. His record is that of an inveterate Whig: he supported the Compromise of 1850 as a means of preserving the Union and voted for Daniel Webster through all fifty-three ballots at the Whig National Convention of 1852. His one term in Congress coincided with the debate over the Kansas-Nebraska Act, which he called an "unnecessary, unjust & iniquitous bill"; the morning after its passage, he served as host for a meeting at which the founding of a new "Republican" party was discussed. This was the limit, however, of his antislavery activity. He refused to run for Lieutenant Governor of Massachusetts on the Constitutional Unionist ticket of 1861, and in declining the nomination he urged the party to "denounce as subversive to all constitutional guarantees, if we expect to reconstruct or restore the Union, the heretical dogma that immediate and universal emancipation of slaves should be proclaimed by the government as a means of putting an end to the war." See Millicent Todd Bingham, *Emily Dickinson's Home: Letters of Edward Dickinson and His Family* (New York: Harper and Brothers Publishers, 1955), 244–45, 390–98; and Jay Leyda, *The Years and Hours of Emily Dickinson* (New Haven: Yale University Press, 1960) 1:337, 303–4. A discussion of the class implications of Edward Dickinson's politics is forthcoming in Robert Gross, "Squire Dickinson and Squire Hoar" (manuscript).

Whatever his shortcomings as a reader of her poems, Dickinson's epistolary mentor, Thomas Wentworth Higginson, was a publicly recognized reformer, consistent and adamant in his support of both feminist and abolitionist causes. When she began their correspondence, he was serving as the colonel of the Twenty-ninth Regiment, the first corps of black soldiers in the Union army. For biographies of Higginson see Anna Mary Wells, *Dear Preceptor: The Life and Times of Thomas Wentworth Higginson* (Boston: Houghton Mifflin, 1963) and Tilden G. Edelstein, *Strange Enthusiasm: A Life of Thomas Wentworth Higginson* (New Haven: Yale University Press, 1968).

3. Analysis of Dickinson's resistance to referential readings has proved the most fertile and sophisticated approach to her poetry. See, for example, Robert Weisbuch's precise discussions of Dickinson's "sceneless poetry" and her "extreme subordination of subjects to structures" (*Emily Dickinson's Poetry* [Chicago: University of Chicago Press, 1972], 24). Interestingly, this critical tradition has not served to dismiss Dickinson's elusive subjects. Thus Leyda's invaluable compilation of data on Dickinson's world proposes to supply the "omitted center" of her writing in order "to get at the truth of Emily Dickinson" (*Years and Hours*, xxi, xix); and Barton St. Armand's *Emily Dickinson and Her Culture: The Soul's Society* (Cam-

bridge: Cambridge University Press, 1984) strives to situate her poems among the stuff of New England culture, from scrapbooks to gravestones. Similarly, a great deal of work has been done to explain Dickinson's poetry in terms of her sexual and psychological experience: the apparent "scenelessness" of her poetry and the mythic isolation of her life reinforce each other in eliciting circular readings that use poems and life to decode one another. See, for example, the countless searches for the identity of Dickinson's lover, as well as John Cody, *After Great Pain: The Inner Life of Emily Dickinson* (Cambridge: Belknap Press, 1971); Barbara Antonina Clarke Mossberg, *Emily Dickinson: When a Writer is a Daughter* (Bloomington: Indiana University Press, 1982); and Vivian R. Pollak, *Dickinson: The Anxiety of Gender* (Ithaca, N.Y.: Cornell University Press, 1984).

The task of situating the poems in terms of a larger social nexus is more difficult, and Shira Wolosky's *Emily Dickinson: A Voice of War* (New Haven: Yale University Press, 1984) remains the only book-length study to attempt such a historical grounding. Wolosky is surely right to heed the fact that Dickinson's "flood years" of astounding poetic production coincide with the fighting of the Civil War, but she is less persuasive in explaining what that coincidence might tell us about Dickinson's poems.

4. Karl Keller uses this phrase to explain what he considers the uniquely apolitical nature of Dickinson's poetry: "It is not at all possible, I believe, to refer to her writings as political in any sense, whereas those of the others almost always are in some sense or other," (*The Only Kangaroo Among the Beauty: Emily Dickinson and America* [Baltimore: Johns Hopkins University Press, 1979], 122).

5. *The Poems of Emily Dickinson*, ed. Thomas Johnson, 3 vols. (Cambridge: Belknap Press, 1955). All citations of Dickinson's poetry refer to Johnson's edition, and I rely on his numbering system to identify each poem. I use the first lines of Dickinson's poems as titles.

6. Harriet Jacobs describes Linda Brent as just such an "unsuspecting Heir" of her slave status: "When I was six years old my mother died; and then, for the first time, I learned by the talk around me, that I was a slave" (*Incidents*, 6).

7. Martha Dickinson Bianchi, *Emily Dickinson Face to Face* (Boston: Houghton Mifflin Co., 1932), 65–66.

8. Letter number 330, dated June 1869. In *The Letters of Emily Dickinson*, ed. Thomas Johnson and Theodora Ward, 3 vols. (Cambridge: Belknap Press, 1958), 2:460.

9. Feminist critics have long argued over whether Dickinson's domestic imagery and housebound days are signs of creative entrapment or of emancipation. If Dickinson is the "helpless agoraphobic" (583) of Sandra Gilbert and Susan Gubar's account, should her domestic enclosure and "secret art" (634) be understood as

an extreme literalization of the nineteenth-century emblem of female creativity, so that Dickinson actually becomes the fictional "madwoman in the attic"? (*The Madwoman in the Attic: The Woman Writer and the Nineteenth-Century Literary Imagination* [New Haven: Yale University Press, 1979]). Or should her domestic seclusion be understood as, in Adrienne Rich's words, "a necessary economy" that permitted, or indeed liberated, Dickinson to write poetry? ("Vesuvius at Home: The Power of Emily Dickinson" [1975], *On Lies, Secrets, and Silence: Selected Prose 1966–1978* [London: Virago, 1980]). Wendy Martin's *An American Triptych: Anne Bradstreet, Emily Dickinson, Adrienne Rich* (Chapel Hill: University of North Carolina Press, 1984) concurs in this interpretation of Dickinson's self-empowering position and then uses it to inform her reading of Rich's own poetic strategies.

The problem with this debate lies in the either/or structure of its readings, in which "home" can mean only one—freeing or incarcerating—thing. Helen McNeil's work on Dickinson offers a wonderful corrective to this debate by demonstrating that Dickinson's houses mean differently in different poems. Although my work is indebted to McNeil's multifaceted understanding of Dickinson's domestic imagery, I want also to emphasize how we differ. For McNeil, Dickinson's elastic and innovative uses of the house to detail "the borderline between inner and outer, between what one has generated and what is given, between present and past" contrasts with a depiction of the body as a site of "easy dualism" unmarked by culture or time (*Emily Dickinson* [New York: Pantheon, 1986], 114). My own work in this chapter presents Dickinson's house and body in a mutually destabilizing network of imagery.

10. Jean Mudge's discussion of the ways in which Dickinson's actual Amherst houses leave their marks on her poetry is of interest here (*Emily Dickinson and the Image of Home* [Amherst: University of Massachusetts Press, 1975]). See also the appendix in which Mudge selectively lists Dickinson's recurrent "vocabulary of space." Mudge does not comment, but it seems worth noting that Dickinson's most commonly used spatial words are "away" (216 uses), "go" (152 uses), "without" (140 uses), and "out" (114 uses), only then followed by "home" (86 uses) and "within" (also 86 uses): in this count the vocabulary of escape far exceeds that of enclosure (229).

11. Ralph Franklin argues that the lines from " 'Twould start them" to "it is calm" do not belong in this poem, but instead form a concluding stanza to "A Pit—but Heaven over it" (1712). I do not find the placement of these lines in poem 1712 wholly convincing: at least, I find Franklin's reliance on the repetition of " 'Twould start" in both this passage and in poem 1712 no more compelling than the repetition of "held," "hold," and "hold" in the passage and the last lines of "I tie my hat." See Franklin, *The Editing of Emily Dickinson: A Reconsideration* (Madison: University of Wisconsin Press, 1967), 40–

46, and his facsimile reproduction of fascicle 24 in *The Manuscript Books of Emily Dickinson*, 2 vols. (Cambridge: Belknap Press, 1981), 1:533–60.

12. Cameron, *Lyric Time*, 77. Cameron goes on to situate these disjunctions as an instance of sexual passion or love transformed into a fury as capable of rupturing sanity as it has proved able to rend the poem's narrative facade. I find this a powerful reading and only want to supplement it by giving attention to the domestic nature of these "vacuous actions."

13. The Dickinson family owned a copy of the 1844 edition of Noah Webster. The volume's other definitions of home are "a dwelling house," "one's own country," "the place of constant residence," and "grave, death; or a future state." See Mudge's discussion of these entries in *Image of Home*, 11–12.

14. Thomas Foster, "Homelessness at Home: Placing Emily Dickinson in (Women's) History," in *Engendering Men: The Question of Male Feminist Criticism*, ed. Joseph A. Boone and Michael Cadden (New York: Routledge, 1990), 243–44.

15. For a discussion of God as master of ceremonies, including a reading of this poem, see Cynthia Griffin Wolff, *Emily Dickinson* (New York: Alfred A. Knopf, 1986), 326–31.

16. Letter number 471 written to her cousins Louise and Frances Norcross, dated August 1876 (*Letters*, 2:559).

17. Letter number 342a of Thomas Wentworth Higginson to his wife, in which he lists samples of Emily Dickinson's conversation at their first meeting (*Letters*, 2:473–74). After leaving Amherst he sent her "another sheet about E.D." that included the question "Could you tell me what home is?" (letter 342b, *Letters*, 2:475).

18. The identification of Bee and Goblin is further supported by another poem that Dickinson placed in the same fascicle with "The Soul has Bandaged moments." "If you were coming in the Fall" ends, "It goads me, like the Goblin Bee— / That will not state—its sting" (511). See *Manuscript Books*, fascicle 17, 1:353–77.

19. Joanne Dobson, *Dickinson and the Strategies of Reticence* (Bloomington: Indiana University Press, 1989), 79. Dobson details Dickinson's rhetorical use of public issues, especially poverty, throughout her fourth chapter, " 'The Grieved—are many—I am told—': The Woman Writer and Public Discourse."

20. Letter number 30, dated 23 January 1850 (*Letters*, 1:84).

21. Letter number 1004, dated summer 1885. The patriotism of "Carol" and signature refer to Todd's present state of "exile"—on vacation in Europe (*Letters*, 3:882).

Coda

1. Shirley Samuels writes about the ways in which this doll both postulates and refuses racial reversibility ("The Identity of Slavery,"

in *The Culture of Sentiment: Race, Gender, and Sentimentality in Nineteenth-Century America*, ed. Shirley Samuels [New York: Oxford University Press, 1992]).

2. The structures of racial difference embodied by topsy-turvy dolls may even be evoked explicitly within antislavery fiction. I suspect, for example, that Harriet Beecher Stowe's "Topsy" may well take her name from these dolls; such a source makes her pairing with the angelic Little Eva poignant indeed. See *Uncle Tom's Cabin* (New York: The Library of America, 1982), chapters 18–20. Pairs of "Topsy" and "Little Eva" dolls were marketed by both Sears and Montgomery Ward during the 1930s, and as late as 1950 topsy-turvy versions of Stowe's characters were still being manufactured (Doris Y. Wilkinson, "The Toy Menagerie: Early Images of Blacks in Toys, Games and Dolls" in *Images of Blacks in American Culture: A Reference Guide to Information Sources*, ed. Jessie Carney Smith [New York: Greenwood Press: 1988], 283).

3. The interpretation I am detailing here corresponds to what I believe to be the prevalent and hegemonic cultural function of these dolls within antebellum society. Signs are rarely, however, univalent, and the doll suggests culturally subversive meanings as well. In particular, as one head emerges from the skirts of the other, she can be seen as enacting an interracial birthing (marking past acts of miscegenation). Or, conjoined as they are, the paired figures may suggest the more radical challenge of interracial lesbianism. Such readings demonstrate how even the most conservative and absolute structural dualisms remain inherently unstable and so open to subversion.

4. My thanks to Laura Wexler, who in talking with me about the inhibition of sentimental response to *Incidents* helped me elaborate this contrast.

5. Douglass, *Narrative*, 32.

6. Outside the epistolary and fascicle models of private publication discussed here, at least ten Dickinson poems were printed by the popular press, some of them more than once. The evidence for contemporary interest in publishing Dickinson's poems is sufficient to suggest that the infrequency of public publication reflects an aesthetic decision. Thus the readers of these few Dickinson poems in the *Springfield Republican* and elsewhere ought not to be viewed as her primary or intended readership; they are rather the readership she chose to do without. See Karen Dandurand, "Publication of Dickinson's Poems in Her Lifetime," *Legacy* 1 (Spring 1984) and her "New Dickinson Civil War Publications," *American Literature* 56 (March 1984).

7. My thanks to Joseph Harrison, whose work on Dickinson's manuscript books as strategies for "canonical self-inscription" informs these alternatives.

Select Bibliography

Allen, Gay Wilson. *The Solitary Singer: A Critical Biography of Walt Whitman*. New York: Macmillan, 1955.

Allen, Pamela P. *Reluctant Reformers*. Washington, D.C.: Howard University Press, 1974.

Anderson, James D. *The Education of Blacks in the South, 1860–1935*. Chapel Hill: University of North Carolina Press, 1988.

Andrews, William L. *To Tell a Free Story: The First Century of Afro-American Autobiography, 1760–1865*. Urbana: University of Illinois Press, 1986.

————, ed. *Six Women's Slave Narratives*. Schomburg Library of Nineteenth-Century Black Women Writers. New York: Oxford University Press, 1988.

Arac, Jonathan. *Critical Genealogies: Historical Situations for Postmodern Literary Studies*. New York: Columbia University Press, 1987.

Armstrong, Nancy, and Leonard Tennenhouse, eds. *The Violence of Representation: Literature and the History of Violence*. New York: Routledge, 1989.

Aspiz, Harold. *Walt Whitman and the Body Beautiful*. Urbana: University of Illinois Press, 1980.

Autographs of Freedom. Rochester: New York Ladies Auxiliary, 1853–1854.

Baer, Helen G. *The Heart is Like Heaven: The Life of Lydia Maria Child*. Philadelphia: University of Pennsylvania Press, 1964.

Baker, Houston A., Jr. *Blues, Ideology, and Afro-American Literature: A Vernacular Theory*. Chicago: University of Chicago Press, 1984.

————. *The Journey Back*. Chicago: University of Chicago Press, 1980.

Barthelemy, Anthony G., ed. *Collected Black Women's Narratives*. The Schomburg Library of Nineteenth-Century Black Women Writers. New York: Oxford University Press, 1988.

Bartour, Ron. " 'Cursed be Canaan, a Servant of Servants shall he be unto his Brethren': American Views on 'Biblical Slavery,' 1835–1865, a Comparative Study." *Slavery and Abolition* 4 (May 1983).

Baym, Nina. *Novels, Readers, and Reviewers: Responses to Fiction in Antebellum America*. Ithaca, N.Y.: Cornell University Press, 1985.

Beaver, Harold. "Homosexual Signs." *Critical Inquiry* 8 (Fall 1981).

Beecher, Catherine, and Harriet Beecher Stowe. *The American Woman's Home: Or, Principles of Domestic Science.* New York: J. B. Ford and Co., 1869.

——. *The Evils Suffered by American Women and American Children: The Causes and the Remedy.* New York: Harper and Brothers, 1846.

Beecher, Charles. "The God of the Bible against Slavery." *Anti-Slavery Tracts,* Ser. 1, Nos. 1–20, 1855–1856. Reprinted Westport, Conn.: Negro University Press, 1970.

Benhabib, Seyla, and Drucilla Cornell, eds. *Feminism as Critique: On the Politics of Gender.* Minneapolis: University of Minnesota Press, 1987.

Berg, Barbara J. *The Remembered Gate: Origins of American Feminism: the Woman and the City, 1800–1860.* New York: Oxford University Press, 1978.

Bianchi, Martha Dickinson. *Emily Dickinson Face to Face.* Boston: Houghton Mifflin Co., 1932.

Bingham, Millicent Todd. *Emily Dickinson's Home: Letters of Edward Dickinson and His Family.* New York: Harper and Brothers Publishers, 1955.

Blassingame, John. *The Slave Community: Plantation Life in the Antebellum South.* New York: Oxford University Press, 1979.

Bloom, Harold, "Whitman's Image of Voice: To the Tally of My Soul." *Modern Critical Views: Walt Whitman.* Edited by Harold Bloom. New York: Chelsea House Publishers, 1985.

Boydston, Jeanne, Mary Kelley, and Anne Margolis, eds. *The Limits of Sisterhood: The Beecher Sisters on Women's Rights and Woman's Sphere.* Chapel Hill: University of North Carolina Press, 1988.

Breeden, James O., ed. *Advice among Masters: the Ideal in Slave Management in the Old South.* Westport, Conn.: Greenwood Press, 1980.

Breitwieser, Mitchell. "Who Speaks in Whitman's Poems?" *The American Renaissance: New Dimensions.* Edited by Harry Garvin. Lewisburg, Penn.: Bucknell University Press, 1983.

Brodhead, Richard H. "Sparing the Rod: Discipline and Fiction in Antebellum America." *Representations* 21 (Winter 1988).

Brown, Gillian. *Domestic Individualism: Imagining Self in Nineteenth-Century America.* Berkeley: University of California Press, 1990.

——. "Getting in the Kitchen with Dinah: Domestic Politics in 'Uncle Tom's Cabin.' " *American Quarterly* 36 (Fall 1984).

Brown, William Wells. *Clotel, or, the President's Daughter.* New York: University Books, 1969.

Burke, Kenneth. "Policy Made Personal: Whitman's Verse and Prose—Salient Traits." *Leaves of Grass: One Hundred Years After.* Edited by Milton Hindus. Stanford: Stanford University Press, 1955.

Cameron, Sharon. *The Corporeal Self: Allegories of the Body in Melville and Hawthorne.* Baltimore: Johns Hopkins University Press, 1981.

———. *Lyric Time: Dickinson and the Limits of Genre.* Baltimore: Johns Hopkins University Press, 1979.

Capps, Jack L. *Emily Dickinson's Reading, 1836–1886.* Cambridge: Harvard University Press, 1966.

Carby, Hazel. "Ideologies of Black Folks: The Historical Novel of Slavery." *Slavery and the Literary Imagination: Selected Papers from the English Institute, 1987.* Edited by Deborah E. McDowell and Arnold Rampersand. Baltimore: Johns Hopkins University Press, 1989.

———. *Reconstructing Womanhood: The Emergence of the Afro-American Woman Novelist.* New York: Oxford University Press, 1987.

Cavitch, David. *My Soul and I: The Inner Life of Walt Whitman.* Boston: Beacon Press, 1985.

Chapman, Maria Weston. *Right and Wrong in Boston.* Boston: Dow and Jackson's Anti-Slavery Press, 1839.

Child, Lydia Maria. *Anti-Slavery Catechism.* Newburyport: Charles Whipple, 1836.

———. *An Appeal in Favor of that Class of Americans Called Africans.* 1836. Facsimile reprint. New York: Arno Press, 1968.

———. "The Black Saxons." *Liberty Bell* 2 (1841).

———. *Fact and Fiction: A Collection of Stories.* New York: C. S. Francis, 1846.

———. *The Frugal Housewife.* Boston: Carter, Hendee, 1830.

———. *The History of the Condition of Women in Various Ages and Nations.* 2 vols. Boston: John Allen, 1835.

———. *Hobomok and Other Writings on Indians.* Edited by Carolyn L. Karcher. New Brunswick, N.J.: Rutgers University Press, 1986.

———. "Jan and Zaida." *Liberty Bell* 14 (1856).

———. *Lydia Maria Child: Selected Letters, 1817–1880.* Edited by Milton Meltzer, Patricia Holland, and Francine Krasno. Amherst: The University of Massachusetts Press, 1982.

———. "Mary French and Susan Easton." *Juvenile Miscellany.* Boston: Allen and Ticknor 3d ser., 6 (May 1834).

———. *The Oasis.* Boston: Allen and Ticknor, 1834.

———. *The Patriarchal Institution as Described by Members of Its Own Family.* New York: The American Anti-Slavery Society, 1860.

———. "The Quadroons." *Liberty Bell* 3 (1842).

———. "Slavery's Pleasant Homes: A Faithful Sketch." *Liberty Bell* 4 (1843).

The Child's Book on Slavery, or, Slavery Made Plain. Cincinnati: American Reform Tract and Book Society, 1857.

Clinton, Catherine. *The Plantation Mistress: Another Side of Southern Slavery, 1780–1835.* New York: Pantheon Books, 1982.

Coleman, Julia, and Matilda Thompson. *The Child's Anti-Slavery Book.* New York: Carlton and Porter, 1859.

Conrad, Susan P. *Perish the Thought: Intellectual Women in Romantic America.* New York: Oxford University Press, 1976.

Constitution of the United States of America, Analysis and Interpretation: Annotations of Cases Decided by the Supreme Court of the United States to June 22 1964. Legislative Reference Service. Edited by Norman J. Small. Washington: U.S. Government Printing Office, 1964.

Coote, Stephen, ed. *The Penguin Book of Homosexual Verse.* Harmondsworth, England: Penguin Books, 1983.

Cott, Nancy F. *The Bonds of Womanhood: 'Woman's Sphere' in New England, 1780–1835.* New Haven: Yale University Press, 1977.

Creel, Margaret Washington. *"A Peculiar People": Slave Religion and Community-Culture Among the Gullahs.* New York: New York University Press, 1988.

Dall, Caroline Wells Healey. "Amy." *The Liberty Bell* 10 (1849).

———. "The Inalienable Love." *The Liberty Bell* 15 (1858).

Dalton, Karen C. Chambers. " 'The Alphabet is an Abolitionist': Literacy and African Americans in the Emancipation Era." *Massachusetts Review* 32 (Winter 1991–1992).

Dandurand, Karen. "New Dickinson Civil War Publications." *American Literature* 56 (March 1984).

———. "Publication of Dickinson's Poems in Her Lifetime." *Legacy* 1 (Spring 1984).

Davis, Angela. "Reflections on the Black Woman's Role in the Community of Slaves." *Black Scholar* 3 (December 1971).

———. *Women, Race, and Class.* New York: Vintage Books, 1983.

Davis, David Brion. *The Problem of Slavery in Western Culture.* Ithaca, N.Y.: Cornell University Press, 1966.

———. *The Slave Power Conspiracy and the Paranoid Style.* Baton Rouge: Louisiana State University Press, 1969.

De Groot, Joanna. " 'Sex' and 'Race': the Construction of Language and Image in the Nineteenth Century." *Sexuality and Subordination: Interdisciplinary Studies of Gender in the Nineteenth Century.* Edited by Susan Mendus and Jane Rendall. New York: Routledge, 1989.

De Lauretis, Teresa. "Feminist Studies/Critical Studies: Issues, Terms, and Contexts." *Feminist Studies/Critical Studies.* Bloomington: Indiana University Press, 1986.

Dickinson, Emily. *The Letters of Emily Dickinson.* 3 vols. Edited by Thomas Johnson and Theodora Ward. Cambridge: Belknap Press, 1958.

———. *The Manuscript Books of Emily Dickinson.* 2 vols. Edited by Ralph Franklin. Cambridge: Belknap Press, 1981.

———. *The Poems of Emily Dickinson,* 3 vols. Edited by Thomas Johnson. Cambridge: Belknap Press, 1955.

Diehl, Joanne Feit. *Dickinson and the Romantic Imagination.* Princeton: Princeton University Press, 1981.

Dobson, Joanne. *Dickinson and the Strategies of Reticence: The Woman Writer in Nineteenth-Century America*. Bloomington: Indiana University Press, 1989.

Douglas, Ann. *The Feminization of American Culture*. New York: Alfred A. Knopf, 1977.

Douglas, Mary. *Natural Symbols: Explorations in Cosmology*. New York: Pantheon Books, 1970.

———. *Purity and Danger: An Analysis of the Concepts of Purity and Taboo*. London: Routledge and Kegan Paul, 1985.

Douglass, Frederick. *Narrative of the Life of Frederick Douglass an American Slave, Written by Himself*. New York: Signet, 1968.

Dubois, Ellen. *Feminism and Suffrage: The Emergence of an Independent Women's Movement in America, 1848–1869*. Ithaca, N.Y.: Cornell University Press, 1978.

———. "Women's Rights and Abolition: The Nature of the Connection." *Antislavery Reconsidered: New Perspectives on the Abolitionists*. Edited by Lewis Perry and Michael Fellman. Baton Rouge: Louisiana State University Press, 1979.

Edelstein, Tilden G. *Strange Enthusiasm: A Life of Thomas Wentworth Higginson*. New Haven: Yale University Press, 1968.

Eisenstein, Zillah R. *The Female Body and the Law*. Berkeley: University of California Press, 1988.

Ellison, Mary. "Resistance to Oppression: Black Women's Response to Slavery in the United States." *Slavery and Abolition* 4 (Spring 1983).

Erkkila, Betsy. "Walt Whitman: The Politics of Language." *American Studies* 24 (Fall 1983).

Fetterly, Judith, ed. *Provisions: A Reader from Nineteenth-Century American Women*. Bloomington: Indiana University Press, 1985.

Fiedler, Leslie. *Love and Death in the American Novel*. Rev. ed. New York: Stein and Day, 1966.

Fisher, Philip. "Democratic Social Space: Whitman, Melville, and the Promise of American Transparency." *Representations* 24 (Fall 1988).

———. "Making a Thing into a Man: The Sentimental Novel and Slavery." *Hard Facts: Setting and Form in the American Novel*. New York: Oxford University Press, 1985.

Flanders, Mrs. G. *The Ebony Idol*. 1860. Reprint. Miami: Mnemosyne Publishing Co., 1969.

Follen, Eliza Lee. "A Melancholy Boy." *The Liberty Bell* 5 (1844).

Foreman, P. Gabrielle. "The Spoken and the Silenced in 'Incidents in the Life of a Slave Girl' and 'Our Nig.' " *Callaloo* 13 (Spring 1990).

———. "Manifest in Signs." Manuscript.

Foster, Frances Smith. *Witnessing Slavery*. Westport, Conn.: Greenwood Press, 1979.

Foster, Thomas. "Homelessness at Home: Placing Emily Dickinson in (Women's) History." *Engendering Men: The Question of Male Feminist Criticism.* Edited by Joseph A. Boone and Michael Cadden. New York: Routledge, 1990.

Foucault, Michel. *Discipline and Punish: The Birth of the Prison.* Translated by Alan Sheridan. New York: Vintage Books, 1979.

———. *The History of Sexuality.* Vol. 1. Translated by Robert Hurley. New York: Vintage Books, 1980.

———. *Language, Counter-Memory, Practice: Selected Essays and Interviews.* Edited and translated by D. F. Bouchard. Ithaca, N.Y.: Cornell University Press, 1980.

Fox-Genovese, Elizabeth. *Within the Plantation Household: Black and White Women of the Old South.* Chapel Hill: University of North Carolina Press, 1988.

Franklin, Ralph. *The Editing of Emily Dickinson: A Reconsideration.* Madison: University of Wisconsin Press, 1967.

Fraser, Nancy. *Unruly Practices: Power, Discourse and Gender in Contemporary Social Theory.* Minneapolis: University of Minnesota Press, 1989.

Frederickson, George M. *The Black Image in the White Mind.* New York: Harper and Row, 1971.

Freedom's Gift. Hartford, Conn.: S. S. Cowels, 1840.

Fuller, Margaret. *The Writings of Margaret Fuller.* Edited by Mason Wade. New York: Viking Press, 1941.

Gatens, Moira: "Towards a Feminist Philosophy of the Body." *Crossing Boundaries: Feminisms and the Critique of Knowledges.* Edited by Barbara Caine, E. A. Grosz, and Maria de Lepervanche. Boston: Allen and Unwin, 1988.

Gates, Henry Louis, Jr. *Figures in Black: Words, Signs, and the "Racial" Self.* New York: Oxford University Press, 1987.

———, ed. *'Race' Writing and Difference.* Chicago: University of Chicago Press, 1986.

———. "The Trope of a New Negro and the Reconstruction of the Image of the Black." *Representations* 24 (Fall 1988).

Gates, Henry Louis, Jr., and Charles Davis, eds. *The Slave's Narrative.* New York: Oxford University Press, 1985.

Genovese, Eugene. *Roll, Jordan, Roll: The World the Slaves Made.* New York: Pantheon Books, 1974.

Giddings, Paula. *When and Where I Enter: The Impact of Black Women on Sex and Race in America.* New York: William Morrow, 1984.

Gilbert, Sandra, and Susan Gubar. *The Madwoman in the Attic: The Woman Writer and the Nineteenth-Century Literary Imagination.* New Haven: Yale University Press, 1979.

Gilman, Sander C. "Black Bodies, White Bodies: Toward an Iconography of Female Sexuality in Late Nineteenth Century Art, Medicine, and Literature." *Critical Inquiry* 12 (Fall 1985).

Gordon, Linda, and Ellen Dubois. "Seeking Ecstasy on the Battle-field: Danger and Pleasure in Nineteenth-Century Feminist Sexual Thought." *Feminist Studies* 9 (Spring 1983).

Green, Frances. "The Slave-Wife." *Liberty Chimes*. Providence, R.I.: Ladies Anti-Slavery Society, 1845.

Greene, Eliza. "Emily Dickinson was a Poetess." *College English* 34 (Fall 1972).

Grier, Edward F. "Walt Whitman's Earliest Known Notebook." *PMLA* 83 (October 1968).

Grimké, Angelina. *Appeal to the Christian Women of the South*. New York: American Anti-Slavery Society, 1836.

————. *An Appeal to the Women of the Nominally Free States: Issued by an Anti-Slavery Convention of American Women Held by Adjournment from the 9th to the 12th of May 1837*. New York: W. S. Doss, 1837.

————. *Letters to Catherine E. Beecher, in Reply to an Essay on Slavery and Abolition Addressed to A. E. Grimké*. Boston: Isaac Knapp, 1838.

Grimké, Sarah. *An Epistle to the Clergy of the Southern States*. New York, 1836.

————. *Letters on the Equality of the Sexes and the Condition of Women. Addressed to Mary S. Parker, President of the Boston Female Anti-Slavery Society*. Boston: Isaac Knapp, 1838.

Gross, Robert. "Squire Dickinson and Squire Hoar." Manuscript.

Grossman, Allen. "The Poetics of Union in Whitman and Lincoln: An Inquiry toward the Relationship of Art and Policy." *The American Renaissance Reconsidered: Selected Papers from the English Institute, 1982–83*. Edited by Walter Benn Michaels and Donald Pease. Baltimore: Johns Hopkins University Press, 1985.

Gutman, Herbert. *The Black Family in Slavery and Freedom 1750–1925*. New York: Vintage Books, 1977.

Gwin, Minrose C. "Green-eyed Monsters of the Slavocracy: Jealous Mistresses in Two Slave Narratives." *Conjuring: Black Women, Fiction, and Literary Tradition*. Edited by Marjorie Pryse and Hortense Spillers. Bloomington: Indiana University Press, 1985.

Hersh, Blanche Glassman. *The Slavery of Sex: Feminist-Abolitionists in America*. Urbana: University of Illinois Press, 1978.

Homans, Margaret. *Women Writers and Poetic Identity: Dorothy Wordsworth, Emily Brontë, and Emily Dickinson*. Princeton: Princeton University Press, 1980.

hooks, bell. *Ain't I a Woman: Black Women and Feminism*. Boston: South End Press, 1981.

Hunt, Lynn, ed. *The New Cultural History*. Berkeley: University of California Press, 1990.

Jacobs, Harriet A. *Incidents in the Life of a Slave Girl, Written by Herself*. Edited by Lydia Maria Child. 1861. Reprint. Edited by Jean Fagan Yellin. Cambridge: Harvard University Press, 1987.

Jacobus, Mary, Evelyn Fox Keller, and Sally Shuttleworth. *Body/Politics: Women and the Discourses of Science.* New York: Routledge, 1990.

Jameson, Fredric. *The Political Unconscious: Narrative as Socially Symbolic Act.* Ithaca, N.Y.: Cornell University Press, 1981.

Johnson, Barbara. *A World of Difference.* Baltimore: Johns Hopkins University Press, 1987.

Jones, Jacqueline. *Soldiers of Light and Love: Northern Teachers and Georgia Blacks, 1865–1873.* Chapel Hill: University of North Carolina Press, 1980.

Jones, Jane Elizabeth. *The Young Abolitionists, or, Conversations on Slavery.* Boston: Anti-Slavery Office, 1848.

Jordan, June. "For the Sake of a People's Poetry: Walt Whitman and the Rest of Us." *Passion: New Poems, 1977–1980.* Boston: Beacon Press, 1980.

Juhasz, Suzanne. *Feminist Critics Read Emily Dickinson.* Bloomington: Indiana University Press, 1983.

———. *"The Undiscovered Continent": Emily Dickinson and the Space of the Mind.* Bloomington: Indiana University Press, 1983.

Kaplan, Justin. *Walt Whitman: A Life.* New York: Simon and Schuster, 1980.

Karcher, Carolyn L. "Rape, Murder and Revenge in 'Slavery's Pleasant Homes': Lydia Maria Child's Antislavery Fiction and the Limits of Genre." *Women's Studies International Forum* 9 (Fall 1986).

———. *Shadow Over the Promised Land: Slavery, Race, and Violence in Melville's America.* Baton Rouge: Louisiana State University Press, 1980.

Keller, Karl. *The Only Kangaroo Among the Beauty: Emily Dickinson and America.* Baltimore: Johns Hopkins University Press, 1979.

Kelley, Mary. *Private Woman, Public Stage: Literary Domesticity in Nineteenth-Century America.* New York: Oxford University Press, 1984.

Kennon, Donald R. " 'An Apple of Discord': The Woman Question at the World's Anti-Slavery Convention of 1840." *Slavery and Abolition* 5 (Winter 1984).

Kirk, Jeffrey. "Marriage, Career, and Feminine Ideology in Nineteenth-Century America: Reconstructing the Marital Experience of Lydia Maria Child, 1828–1874." *Feminist Studies* 2 (Winter-Spring 1975).

Kraditor, Aileen S. *Means and Ends in American Abolition: Garrison and His Critics on Strategy and Tactics, 1834–1850.* New York: Pantheon, 1968.

———. *Up from the Pedestal: Selected Writings in the History of American Feminism.* Chicago: Quadrangle Books, 1968.

Law, Sylvia A. "Rethinking Sex and the Constitution." *University of Pennsylvania Law Review* 132 (June 1984).

Lebsock, Suzanne. *The Free Women of Petersburg.* New York: W. W. Norton, 1984.

Lerner, Gerda. *The Creation of Patriarchy.* New York: Oxford University Press, 1986.

———. *The Grimké Sisters from South Carolina: Pioneers for Women's Rights and Abolition.* New York: Schocken Books, 1967.

———. *The Majority Finds Its Past.* New York: Oxford University Press, 1979.

Levinson, Marjorie, Marilyn Butler, Jerome McGann, and Paul Hamilton. *Rethinking Historicism: Critical Readings in Romantic History.* Oxford: Basil Blackwell, 1989.

Levy, David. "Racial Stereotypes in Anti-Slavery Fiction." *Phylon* 26 (Summer 1970).

Leyda, Jay. *The Years and Hours of Emily Dickinson.* New Haven: Yale University Press, 1960.

Liberty Bell. Boston: Massachusetts Anti-Slavery Fair, 1839–1858.

Liberty Chimes. Providence: the Ladies Anti-Slavery Society of Providence, Rhode Island, 1845.

Lumpkin, Katharine Du Pre. *The Emancipation of Angelina Grimké.* Chapel Hill: University of North Carolina Press, 1974.

Lutz, Alma. *Crusade for Freedom: Women of the Antislavery Movement.* Boston: Beacon Press, 1968.

McDowell, Deborah E. and Arnold Rampersand, eds. *Slavery and the Literary Imagination: Selected Papers from the English Institute, 1987.* Baltimore: Johns Hopkins University Press, 1989.

McNeil, Helen. *Emily Dickinson.* New York: Pantheon, 1986.

Martin, Biddy. "Feminism, Criticism, Foucault." *New German Critique* 27 (Fall 1982).

Martin, Emily. *The Woman in the Body: A Cultural Analysis of Reproduction.* Boston: Beacon Press, 1987.

Martin, Wendy. *An American Triptych: Anne Bradstreet, Emily Dickinson, Adrienne Rich.* Chapel Hill: University of North Carolina Press, 1984.

Matthiessen, F. O. *American Renaissance: Art and Expression in the Age of Emerson and Whitman.* New York: Oxford University Press, 1941.

Mellon, James, ed. *Bullwhip Days: The Slaves Remember.* New York: Weidenfeld and Nicolson, 1988.

Meltzer, Milton. *Tongue of Flame: The Life of Lydia Maria Child.* New York: Crowell, 1965.

Michaels, Walter Benn, and Donald E. Pease, eds. *The American Renaissance Reconsidered: Selected Papers from the English Institute, 1982–83.* Baltimore: Johns Hopkins University Press, 1985.

———. "Romance and Real Estate," in *The American Renaissance Reconsidered: Selected Papers from the English Institute, 1982–83.* Edited by Walter Benn Michaels and Donald E. Pease. Baltimore: Johns Hopkins University Press, 1985.

Michie, Helena. *The Flesh Made Word: Female Figures and Women's Bodies.* New York: Oxford University Press, 1986.

Miller, Cristanne. *Emily Dickinson: A Poet's Grammar.* Cambridge: Harvard University Press, 1987.

Miller, D. A. "*Cage aux folles:* Sensation and Gender in Wilkie Collins's *The Woman in White.*" *Representations* 14 (Spring 1986).

Moody, E. Prior. "Mrs. Stowe's Uncle Tom." *Critical Inquiry* 5 (Summer 1979).

Moon, Michael. "Disseminating Whitman." *South Atlantic Quarterly* 88 (Winter 1989).

——. *Disseminating Whitman: Revision and Corporeality in "Leaves of Grass."* Cambridge: Harvard University Press, 1991.

Morris, Robert C. *Reading, 'Riting, and Reconstruction: The Education of Freedmen in the South, 1861–1870.* Chicago: University of Chicago Press, 1976.

Morse, Ruth. "Impossible Dreams: Miscegenation and Building Nations." *Southerly* 48 (1988).

Mossberg, Barbara Antonina Clarke. *Emily Dickinson: When a Writer is a Daughter.* Bloomington: Indiana University Press, 1982.

Mudge, Jean McClure. *Emily Dickinson and the Image of Home.* Amherst: University of Massachusetts Press, 1975.

Nathanson, Tenney. "Whitman's Tropes of Light and Flood: Language and Representation in Early Editions of 'Leaves of Grass.' " *ESQ* 31 (Spring 1985).

Niemtzow, Annette. "The Problematic of Self in Autobiography: The Example of the Slave Narrative." *The Art of the Slave Narrative: Original Essays in Criticism and Theory.* Edited by John Sekora and Darwin T. Turner. Macomb, Ill: Western Illinois University, 1982.

Norton, Anne. *Alternative Americas: A Reading of Antebellum Political Culture.* Chicago: University of Chicago Press, 1986.

——. *Reflections on Political Identity.* Baltimore: Johns Hopkins University Press, 1988.

Olney, James. " 'I was Born': Slave Narratives, Their Status as Autobiography and Literature." *Callaloo* 7 (Winter 1984).

Pateman, Carole. *The Sexual Contract.* Stanford: Stanford University Press, 1988.

Patterson, Orlando. *Slavery and Social Death.* Cambridge: Harvard University Press, 1982.

——. "Slavery: The Underside of Freedom." *Slavery and Abolition* 5 (Fall 1984).

Pearce, Harvey. "Whitman Justified: The Poet in 1855." *Critical Inquiry* 8 (Fall 1981).

Pease, Donald. *Visionary Compacts: American Renaissance Writings in Cultural Context.* Madison: University of Wisconsin Press, 1987.

Pease, Jane H., and William H. Pease. "The Boston Bluestocking, Maria Weston Chapman." *Bound with Them in Chains: A Biograph-*

ical History of the Anti-Slavery Movement. Westport, Conn.: Greenwood Press, 1972.

Perry, Lewis. *Radical Abolitionism: Anarchy and the Government of God in Antislavery Thought.* Ithaca, N.Y.: Cornell University Press, 1973.

Pike, Mary Hayden. *Ida May: A Story of Things Actual and Possible.* Boston: Phillips, Sampson and Co., 1854.

Pollak, Vivian R. *Dickinson: The Anxiety of Gender.* Ithaca, N.Y.: Cornell University Press, 1984.

Porter, David T. *The Art of Emily Dickinson's Early Poetry.* Cambridge: Harvard University Press, 1966.

———. *Dickinson: The Modern Idiom.* Cambridge: Harvard University Press, 1981.

Reynolds, David S. *Beneath the American Renaissance: The Subversive Imagination in the Age of Emerson and Melville.* New York: Knopf, 1988.

Rich, Adrienne. "Vesuvius at Home: The Power of Emily Dickinson." In *On Lies, Secrets, and Silence: Selected Prose 1966–1978.* London: Virago, 1980.

St. Armand, Barton Levi. *Emily Dickinson and Her Culture: The Soul's Society.* Cambridge: Cambridge University Press, 1984.

Samuels, Shirley, ed. *The Culture of Sentiment: Race, Gender, and Sentimentality in Nineteenth-Century America.* New York: Oxford University Press, 1992.

———. "The Identity of Slavery." In *The Culture of Sentiment: Race, Gender, and Sentimentality in Nineteenth-Century America.* Edited by Shirley Samuels. New York: Oxford University Press, 1992.

Scarry, Elaine. *The Body in Pain: The Making and Unmaking of the World.* New York: Oxford University Press, 1985.

Scott, Joan. "Deconstructing Equality-Versus-Difference: Or, the Uses of Post Structuralist Theory for Feminism." *Feminist Studies* 14 (Spring 1988).

Sedgwick, Catharine. *Hope Leslie.* Edited by Mary Kelley. New Brunswick, N.J.: Rutgers University Press, 1987.

Sekora, John, and Darwin T. Turner, eds. *The Art of the Slave Narrative.* Macomb, Ill.: Western Illinois University Press, 1982.

Sewall, Richard B. *The Life of Emily Dickinson.* 2 vols. New York: Farrar, Straus and Giroux, 1974.

———, ed. *The Lyman Letters: New Light on Emily Dickinson and Her Family.* Amherst: University of Massachusetts Press, 1965.

Sinclair, Andrew. *The Better Half: the Emancipation of the American Woman.* New York: Harper and Row, 1965.

Sklar, Kathryn Kish. *Catharine Beecher: A Study in American Domesticity.* New Haven: Yale University Press, 1973.

The Slave's Friend. New York: American Anti-Slavery Society, 1836–1838.

Small, Sandra E. "The Yankee Schoolmarm in Freedmen's Schools: An Analysis of Attitudes," *The Journal of Southern History* 45 (August 1979).

Smith, Valerie. *Self-Discovery and Authority in Afro-American Narrative*. Cambridge: Harvard University Press, 1987.

Smith-Rosenberg, Carroll. *Disorderly Conduct: Visions of Gender in Victorian America*. New York: Oxford University Press, 1985.

Sommer, Doris. "Supplying Demand: Walt Whitman as the Liberal Self." *Reinventing the Americas: Comparative Studies of Literature of the U.S. and Spanish America*. Edited by Gale Chevigny and Gary Laguardia. Cambridge: Cambridge University Press, 1986.

Spelman, Elizabeth V. "Theories of Race and Gender: The Erasure of Black Women." *Quest* 5 (1979).

———. "Woman as Body: Ancient and Contemporary Views." *Feminist Studies* 8 (Fall 1982).

Spillers, Hortense. "Changing the Letter: The Yokes and Jokes of Discourse, or, Mrs. Stowe, Mr. Reed." *Slavery and the Literary Imagination: Selected Papers from the English Institute, 1987*. Edited by Deborah E. McDowell and Arnold Rampersand. Baltimore: Johns Hopkins University Press, 1989.

———. "Mama's Baby, Papa's Maybe: An American Grammar Book." *Diacritics* 17 (1988).

———. "Notes on an Alternative Model: Neither/Nor." *The Left Year 2: An American Socialist Yearbook*. Edited by Mile Davis, Manny Marabel, Fred Pfeil, and Michael Sprinker. London: Verso, 1987.

Stanton, Elizabeth Cady, Susan B. Anthony, and Matilda Joslyn Gage, eds. *The History of Woman Suffrage*. 6 vols. New York: Fowler and Wells, 1881–1922.

Sterling, Dorothy. *We Are Your Sisters: Black Women in the Nineteenth Century*. New York: W. W. Norton, 1984.

Stovall, Floyd. "Dating Whitman's Early Notebooks." *Studies in Bibliography* 24 (1971).

Stowe, Harriet Beecher. *A Key to Uncle Tom's Cabin*. Vol. 2 of *The Writings of Harriet Beecher Stowe*. Boston: Riverside Press, 1896.

———. *Dred: A Tale of the Great Dismal Swamp*. Vol. 3 of *The Writings of Harriet Beecher Stowe*. Boston: Riverside Press, 1896.

———. *Uncle Tom's Cabin*. New York: The Library of America, 1982.

Sundquist, Eric J. "Slavery, Revolution and the American Renaissance." *The American Renaissance Reconsidered: Selected Papers from the English Institute, 1982–83*. Edited by Walter Benn Michaels and Donald E. Pease. Baltimore: Johns Hopkins University Press, 1985.

———, ed. *New Essays on Uncle Tom's Cabin*. Cambridge: Cambridge University Press, 1986.

Thompson, Ralph. " 'The Liberty Bell' and Other Anti-Slavery Gift-Books." *New England Quarterly* 7 (March 1934).

Tompkins, Jane. "Sentimental Power: 'Uncle Tom's Cabin' and the Politics of Literary History." *Sensational Designs: The Cultural Work of American Fiction, 1790–1860.* New York: Oxford University Press, 1985.

Towne, Laura M. *The Letters and Diary of Laura M. Towne: Written from the Sea Islands of South Carolina, 1862–1884.* Edited by R. S. Holland. Cambridge: Riverside Press, 1912.

Veeser, H. Aram, ed. *The New Historicism.* New York: Routledge, 1989.

Vendler, Helen. "Body Language: 'Leaves of Grass' and the Articulation of Sexual Awareness." *Harpers* 273 (October 1986).

Walker, Julia. "Emily Dickinson's Poetic of Private Liberation." *Dickinson Studies* 45 (June 1983).

Walters, Ronald G. *The Antislavery Appeal: American Abolitionism After 1830.* Baltimore: Johns Hopkins University Press, 1976.

————. "The Erotic South: Civilization and Sexuality in American Abolitionism." *American Quarterly* 25 (May 1973).

Washington, Mary Helen. *Invented Lives: Narratives of Black Women, 1860–1960.* Garden City, N.Y.: Anchor Press, 1987.

Weisbuch, Robert. *Emily Dickinson's Poetry.* Chicago: University of Chicago Press, 1972.

Weld, Theodore Dwight, Angelina Grimké Weld, and Sarah Grimké. *The Letters of Theodore Dwight Weld, Angelina Grimké, and Sarah Grimké, 1822–1844.* 2 vols. Edited by Gilbert H. Barnes and Dwight L. Dumond. New York: Da Capo, 1970.

Wells, Anna Mary. *Dear Preceptor: The Life and Times of Thomas Wentworth Higginson.* Boston: Houghton Mifflin, 1963.

Welter, Barbara. "The Cult of True Womanhood, 1820–1860." *American Quarterly* 18 (Summer 1966).

Whitman, Walt. *The Collected Writings of Walt Whitman: The Early Poems and the Fiction.* Edited by Thomas L. Brasher. New York: New York University Press, 1963.

————. *The Collected Writings of Walt Whitman: Notebooks and Unpublished Prose Manuscripts.* Vol. I: *Family Notes and Autobiography: Brooklyn and New York.* Edited by Edward F. Grier. New York: New York University Press, 1984.

————. *Leaves of Grass: A Textual Variorum of the Printed Poems.* 3 vols. Edited by Sculley Bradley, Harold W. Blodget, Arthur Golden, and William White. New York: New York University Press, 1980.

————. *Notes and Fragments Left by Walt Whitman.* Edited by R. M. Bucke. London: Talbot, 1899.

————. *The Uncollected Poetry and Prose of Walt Whitman.* Edited by Emory Halloway. New York: Doubleday, Page and Co., 1921.

————. *Walt Whitman's Leaves of Grass: The First (1855) Edition.* Edited by Malcolm Cowley. New York: Penguin Classics, 1986.

Wilkinson, Doris Y. "The Toy Menagerie: Early Images of Blacks in Toys, Games and Dolls." *Images of Blacks in American Culture: A Reference Guide to Information Sources.* Edited by Jessie Carney Smith. New York: Greenwood Press, 1988.

Wilson, Harriet E. *Our Nig: or, Sketches from the Life of a Free Black.* New York: Vintage Books, 1983.

Wolff, Cynthia Griffin. *Emily Dickinson.* New York: Alfred A. Knopf, 1986.

Wolosky, Shira. *Emily Dickinson: A Voice of War.* New Haven: Yale University Press, 1984.

Yellin, Jean Fagan. *The Intricate Knot: Black Figures in American Literature, 1776–1863.* New York: New York University Press, 1972.

———, ed. *Incidents in the Life of a Slave Girl, Written by Herself,* by Harriet A. Jacobs, edited by Lydia Maria Child. 1861. Reprint. Cambridge: Harvard University Press, 1987.

———. *Women and Sisters: The Antislavery Feminists in American Culture.* New Haven: Yale University Press, 1989.

———. "Written By Herself: Harriet Jacobs's Slave Narrative." *American Literature* 53 (November 1981).

Zanger, Jules. "The 'Tragic Octoroon' in Pre-Civil War Fiction." *American Quarterly* 18 (Spring 1966).

Ziff, Larzer. "Whitman and the Crowd." *Critical Inquiry* 10 (Summer 1984).

Index

Abolitionism: and apologies for slavery, 92; and cattle metaphor, 21, 151n23; and claim of personhood for slave, 1, 135, 157–58n56; and decomposition metaphor, 2–3, 8; and divisions from feminism, 5; and domesticity, 11, 42, 43–45, 157–58n56, 158–59n60; dominant-culture appropriation of, 147n14; female auxiliary societies for, 23–24, 151nn25,26; and incorporeality, 3, 4; moral displacements of, 45–46, 98–99, 158–59n60; and obliteration of blackness, 31–32, 48, 155nn43,44,45; and sexual exploitation, 92, 168n21; and sexuality, 169n26; structures of dominance in, 6–7; and violence, 167n18. *See also* Antislavery stories; Feminist-abolitionist intersection

Abstract political identity. *See* Incorporeality

Amalgamation: in antislavery stories, 30, 32–41; and class, 38; and feminist-abolitionist intersection, 33–34, 36; and maternity, 101; and mediation, 59–60; and merger, 52, 68; and miscegenation laws, 36–38; and obliteration of blackness, 32; and sexual exploitation of female slaves, 34–35; and topsy-turvy doll, 134, 174n3. *See also* Interracial bodies

American Anti-Slavery Society, 4, 144n5

"Amy" (Dall), 34–36, 159n63

Anthony, Susan B., 149n4

Anti-Slavery Catechism (Child), 15

Antislavery stories, 24–44, 153n29; amalgamation in, 30, 32–41; and bodies as texts, 26, 27–28; bodily nature of, 26–27, 154–55n36, 155n37; and domesticity, 41–43, 167n16; and female gender roles, 24; as female political action, 24, 151n26, 152n27; and ironies of representation, 24–25; male authorship of, 152n27; market value of, 24–25, 153n30; moral displacements in, 45–48; obliteration of blackness in, 31–32, 48, 155nn43,44,45; portrayal of heroes in, 28–30, 38; realism in, 25–26, 153n33; in Sunday school primers, 42–46

An Appeal in Favor of that Class of Americans Called Africans (Child), 36–38

"The Apple and the Chestnut," 156n45

Appropriation, 9; and feminist-abolitionist intersection, 17, 19, 34; and genre, 147n14; and representation, 43, 147n13; of slave body, 18–19

"Aunt Judy's Story" (Coleman & Thompson), 42–43

Authorship. *See* Writing

Baker, Houston, 92

Beecher, Rev. Charles, 158n60

Benjamin (*Incidents in the Life of a Slave Girl*), 91–92

Bianchi, Martha Dickinson, 111

Bisexuality, 66

Black body. *See* Slave body

Black feminism, 169n23

"Blood-Money" (Whitman), 161n4, 162n16
Bloomer, Amelia, 150n15
Bodies: authorial, 135–37; and discourse, 8, 54–55; vs. flesh, 146n12; intelligible vs. docile-useful, 7; reclaiming of, 18; self-ownership of, 19, 23, 33, 41, 126; and sentimental fiction, 26–29, 134–35, 154n36, 155n37; social construction of, 7–8, 146n12; as symbol of body politic, 3, 143n2; as texts, 15, 18, 26, 27–29, 54. *See also* Corporeal identity; Disembodiment; Interracial bodies
Bodily specificity. *See* Difference
"The Body grows without," (Dickinson), 116–17
Body politic, 1–2, 3, 143n2. *See also* Incorporeality
Breastfeeding, 90–91
Breeden, James O., 149n11
Breitweiser, Mitchell, 162n13, 163n19
Brent, Linda. See *Incidents in the Life of a Slave Girl*
Brown, Gillian, 157n56
Brown, William Wells, 93

Cameron, Sharon, 115–16, 144n7, 147n12, 173n12
Carby, Hazel, 101, 166n14
Cartwright, Samuel A., 149n11
Chapman, Maria Weston, 24, 25
Child, David, 152n27
Child, Lydia Maria, 14–15; fiction of, 26, 30–31, 151n26, 152n27, 153–54n33, 155n44, 157n50; and Harriet Jacobs, 86, 92, 93–94, 94, 102, 167n18; on miscegenation laws, 36–38
The Child's Anti-Slavery Book (Coleman & Thompson), 42–44, 159n63
The Child's Book on Slavery, or Slavery Made Plain, 44–45
Clusy ("The Slave-Wife"), 39–41
Coleman, Julia, 42–44, 158n56
Commercial realm: and antislavery stories, 24–25, 153n30; and

breastfeeding, 90–91; and soul, 46, 159n63. *See also* Ownership; Slave body; Slavery
Constitution, 1, 4–5, 144n6. *See also* Incorporeality; Personhood
Conway, Mrs. (*Franklin Evans*), 60, 61–62, 63
Corporeal identity: ambivalence about, 2–3; and annihilation of personhood, 33; commodification of, 90–91; differences in, 9–10, 139; and domesticity, 116–17, 173n13; and female gender roles, 17–18, 118; as fiction, 139–40; vs. incorporeality, 1, 3, 143n3, 143n4; in *Leaves of Grass*, 55–56; and liberty, 110, 123–24; nineteenth-century development of, 1–2, 5, 144n7; and ownership, 52, 53; and political identity, 4–5, 51–52, 107; and representation, 12, 46, 122–23, 128–29, 137–38, 147n12; and sentimental fiction, 26; and soul, 46–48, 50–51, 81, 107, 108, 159n63; as threatening, 84; and violence, 123. *See also* Difference; Disembodiment; Embodiment, poetics of; Identity; Incorporeality
The Corporeal Self: Allegories of the Body in Melville and Hawthorne (Cameron), 144n7, 147n12
"Crossing Brooklyn Ferry" (Whitman), 53
Cruikshank, George, 47
Cult of true womanhood. *See* Female gender roles

Dall, Carolyn Wells Healey, 34–36, 151n26, 156n48
Davis, Angela, 166n15
Death. *See* Disembodiment; Violence
Delicacy. *See* Female gender roles
"Departed—to the Judgment" (Dickinson), 120–21
Dickinson, Edward, 169n2
Dickinson, Emily, 105–31; on confinement, 108–11, 171n9; on corporeal identity, 122–23, 128–29;

on disembodiment, 105, 117–22,
124–25, 138–39; on repressiveness
of domesticity, 114–16, 172n12;
on dual identity, 11, 107–8, 116–
17; on liberty, 105, 111–13, 123–
24, 125–26, 140, 172n10; and
modes of publication, 137, 174n6;
nonreferentiality of, 11–12, 106,
170n3; political detachment of,
11–12, 106–7, 129–31, 169n2,
171n4
Difference, 2, 9–10; and amalgamation, 30, 52; and annihilation of
personhood, 15, 143n3; equality
in, 30; and genre, 64, 134; and
interracial bodies, 30; manufacturing of, 59–60, 161n9; and mediation, 59–60, 161n9; and modern feminism, 12–13; obliteration
of, 20; and physical contact, 77;
and political identity, 4–5; and
separation, 71–73; as threatening,
8–9; and topsy-turvy doll, 133;
and violence, 70–71, 77. *See also*
Corporeal identity; Merger, poetics of
Discourse, 7, 9. *See also*
Representation
Disembodiment: absurdity of, 119–
20, 121–22; and decomposition
metaphor, 2–3, 8; as desolate,
120–21; and domesticity, 118–19;
and genre, 138–39; and liberty,
105, 117–18, 128, 140–41; and
obliteration of blackness, 48; and
poetics of embodiment, 56–57,
75; and poetics of merger, 68;
and sexuality, 121, 124–25; and
slave suicide, 48–49, 105, 159n66;
and violence, 123. *See also* Incorporeality; Personhood, annihilation of
Dobson, Joanne, 129
Domestic fiction. *See* Sentimental fiction
Domesticity: and antislavery stories, 41–43, 167n16; and corporeal
identity, 116–17, 173n13; and
deprivation, 166n16; and disembodiment, 118–19; exclusion

from, 87–91, 111, 112, 165n11,
166n16; and female auxiliary societies, 23–24; and female gender
roles, 111–12, 113, 118–19; and
female slaves, 87–88, 165n11; and
liberty, 11, 87, 111–13, 172n10;
and maternity, 89–91, 101; reform
of, 158n56; as repressive, 11, 42,
43–45, 114–16, 157n56, 158n60,
171n9, 173n12; and sexuality,
114, 173n12. *See also* Female
gender roles
Douglas, Mary, 143n2
Douglass, Frederick, 93, 135–36,
164n5, 168n20
Dred (Stowe), 27–29, 157n50, 159n63
Dubois, Ellen, 169n23
Durham, Rev. Jeremiah (*Incidents in
the Life of a Slave Girl*), 99–100

Edith ("Amy"), 34–36, 159n63
Ellen (*Incidents in the Life of a Slave
Girl*), 101–2
Embodiment. *See* Bodies; Corporeal
identity; Embodiment, poetics of
Embodiment, poetics of, 10, 54–55;
and disembodiment, 56–57, 75;
as extravagant, 78–79; and incorporeality, 79–80; political import
of, 51, 74–75, 160n3. *See also* Corporeal identity; Whitman, Walt
Erotic. *See* Sexuality
Escape, 152n27, 155n36; in Dickinson's vocabulary, 172n10; and
domesticity, 11, 87; and fugitive
image, 75–78, 86; and pseudonymous authorship, 86–87; and
sentimental fiction, 155n36; and
sexuality, 127–28, 168n19. *See
also* Liberty

Family: breakup of, 152n27, 157n56;
conflation with slavery, 11, 43–
45, 90, 157n56, 158n60. *See also*
Domesticity
Female body. *See* Female gender
roles; Female slaves; Feminism;
Sexual exploitation; Sexual exploitation of female slaves

Female gender roles: and antislavery stories, 24, 35; and black feminism, 169n23; and domesticity, 111–12, 113, 118–19; and feminist-abolitionist intersection, 17–18, 20–22, 94, 150n18; as moral status, 46, 94, 159n63; and political roles, 23–24, 130; and sexual exploitation, 22, 34–35, 40, 93, 94, 98–99, 150n18, 156n48; and slave narrative, 165n10. *See also* Domesticity

Female slaves: and breastfeeding, 90–91; and domesticity, 87–88, 165n11; and female gender roles, 20–21; power of, 91, 166n15. *See also* Feminist-abolitionist intersection; Sexual exploitation of female slaves; Slave body; Slavery

Feminism: and American Anti-Slavery Society schism, 4, 144n5; and divisions from abolitionism, 5; and domesticity, 42; dominant-culture appropriation of, 147n14; and incorporeality, 3; modern, 12–13; and racial differences, 12–13, 20; and sexual exploitation, 22–23. *See also* Female gender roles; Feminist-abolitionist intersection

Feminist-abolitionist intersection, 15–16; and amalgamation, 33–34, 36; and appropriation, 17, 19, 34; and bodies as texts, 15, 19–20, 26; and domesticity, 41–42; and female gender roles, 17–18, 20–22, 94, 150n18; and identification of slavery and marriage, 14–15, 40–41, 150n18; political origins of, 16–17, 149n4; and sexual exploitation of female slaves, 21–23, 41–42, 152n27; and sexual exploitation of white women, 22–23, 36, 156n49; slavery as image of women's oppression, 18–20, 150n15. *See also* Abolitionism; Antislavery stories; Feminism

"A Few Words about American Slave Children," (Coleman & Thompson), 43–44

Fiedler, Leslie, 58
Fifteenth Amendment, 4–5
Fisher, Philip, 157n56
Flint, Dr. (*Incidents in the Life of a Slave Girl*), 91–92, 95–96, 97, 100, 101, 166n16
Flint, Mrs. (*Incidents in the Life of a Slave Girl*), 94–97, 166–67n16
Follen, Eliza Lee, 31–32
Foreman, P. Gabrielle, 102–3
Foster, Thomas, 117
Foucault, Michel, 7
Fourteenth Amendment, 4–5
Franklin, Ralph, 172n11
Franklin Evans (Whitman), 10, 57–63, 64; amalgamation in, 59–60; difference in, 59–60, 161n9; self-effacement in, 60–61; sexuality in, 61–63, 161n10; violence in, 59, 63, 162n11
Fugitive, 75–78, 86
Fuller, Margaret, 20–21

Garrison, William Lloyd, 21, 23, 169n26. *See also The Liberator*
Gates, Henry Louis, Jr., 84, 164n5
Genre: of antislavery literature, 25, 153n32; and difference, 64, 134; and disembodiment, 138–39; instability of, 71, 87, 162n15, 165n10; intersections of, 9–10, 12–13, 147n14; and mediation, 63–64; and merger, 64; and political content, 72–73, 74; sensation fiction, 154n36; slave narrative, 87, 135–36, 165n10. *See also* Lyric poetry; Sentimental fiction
Gilbert, Sandra, 171n9
"The God of the Bible against Slavery" (Beecher), 158n60
Gordon, Linda, 169n23
Gordon, Nina (*Dred*), 27–28, 157n50
Green, Frances, 29–30, 39–41, 153n33
Grimké, Angelina, 19, 22, 23, 149n4, 150n18; and decomposition metaphor, 2–3, 8
Grimké, Sarah, 19, 22, 149n4, 150n18

Grossman, Allen, 160n3, 161n4
Gubar, Susan, 171n9

Higginson, Thomas Wentworth, 170n2
Home. *See* Domesticity
Homosexuality, 160n3, 174n3
Horniblow, Margaret, 165n13
"How many times these low feet staggered" (Dickinson), 118–19
Humphrey, Jane, 129

"I am afraid to own a Body" (Dickinson), 107–8
Identity: compulsory nature of, 108, 117, 171n6; duality of, 81–82, 107–8, 116–17, 120; house image of, 113; and ownership, 53–54, 108; poetic, 50–51, 52–54, 76, 81–82, 137–38, 163n19. *See also* Corporeal identity; Personhood; Personhood, annihilation of
"I dwell in Possibility" (Dickinson), 112–13
"I felt my life with both my hands" (Dickinson), 119–20
"If you were coming in the Fall" (Dickinson), 173n18
"The Inalienable Love" (Dall), 156n48
Incidents in the Life of a Slave Girl (Jacobs), 10–11, 83–84, 86–104, 171n6; authenticity of, 164n9; and authorial body, 135, 137; domesticity in, 11, 87–91, 111, 112, 165nn10,11,13, 166nn15,16; generic instability of, 87, 165n10; narrative concealment of sexual exploitation in, 91–92; and political content, 106–7, 138–39; pseudonymous authorship of, 86–87, 165n9; representation as sexual in, 93–97; responsive audience in, 97–101; sexuality of audience in, 102–4
Incorporeality, 3, 4, 5; limitations of, 105–6; and poetics of embodiment, 79–80; and political representation, 1, 3, 6, 139, 140–41, 143n3, 143n4; and white male

privilege, 3, 143n4. *See also* Corporeal identity; Disembodiment
Indians. *See* Native Americans
Interracial bodies, 30, 32–33; and blood, 57; and sexual exploitation, 33, 34, 156nn47,49; and white women's sexuality, 36, 38–39. *See also* Amalgamation
"I Sing the Body Electric" (Whitman), 54–55, 56, 68, 75
"I tie my Hat—I crease my Shawl" (Dickinson), 114–15, 172n11

Jacobs, Harriet: and Harriet Beecher Stowe, 85–86, 164n6; reluctance of, 83, 85. See also *Incidents in the Life of a Slave Girl*
Jameson, Fredric, 163n18
"Jan and Zaida" (Child), 157n50
Jefferson, Thomas, 3, 143n4

Karcher, Carolyn, 152n27
Keller, Karl, 171n4
Kelley, Abby, 4, 144n5
Key to Uncle Tom's Cabin (Stowe), 85

Language. *See* Representation; Writing
Leaves of Grass (Whitman), 10, 80–81; amalgamation in, 54, 81; body and soul in, 50–51, 81; genre of, 64; invisibility of poet in, 60; separation in, 71–72; slavery in, 50, 51, 55–56, 71–72, 163n17; title drawing of, 55–56
Lesbianism, 174n3
Letters and Diaries (Towne), 146n10
"Let Us play Yesterday" (Dickinson), 125–26
The Liberator, 21, 152n27. *See also* Garrison, William Lloyd
Liberty: and corporeal identity, 110, 123–24; and disembodiment, 105, 117–18, 128, 140–41; and domesticity, 11, 87, 111–13, 172n10; instability of, 125–26; and sexuality, 41, 127–28, 140, 168n19; and tears, 30. *See also* Escape
The Liberty Bell, 24, 25, 152n27, 153n29

Liberty Chimes, 48
Literacy, 93, 168n20
Little Eva (*Uncle Tom's Cabin*), 174n2
Louis (*Franklin Evans*), 60–61, 162n11
Luke (*Incidents in the Life of a Slave Girl*), 167–68n19
Lyric poetry, 10, 11–12, 64, 147n14. See also Dickinson, Emily; Genre; Whitman, Walt

McNeil, Helen, 171n9
Margaret (*Franklin Evans*), 59–60, 61–62, 63, 161n9, 162n11
"Mark and Hasty" (Thompson), 153n33, 159n63
Marriage, 14–15, 22–23, 40–41, 150n18. See also Domesticity; Family; Female gender roles; Sexual exploitation
Martin, Emily, 7–8
Martin, Wendy, 171n9
"Mary French and Susan Easton" (Child), 26, 30, 136–37, 153n33, 155n44
Maternity, 89–91, 100–102. See also Domesticity; Family
Matthiessen, F. O., 162n15
Mattison, H., 168n21
Mediation, 50–52, 58–59; and amalgamation, 59–60; and auctioneer image, 54–55; and difference, 59–60, 161n9; and genre, 63–64; and merger, 59, 60–61, 66; and political content, 74, 163n18; and self-effacement, 60–61, 65; and sexuality, 61–63, 67; and violence, 70–71
"A Melancholy Boy" (Follen), 31–32
Merger, poetics of, 10; and amalgamation, 52, 68; and blood image, 57; and darkness image, 67–68; and genre, 64; and mediation, 59, 60–61, 66; and sexuality, 52, 63, 65–68; and slavery, 72, 77; and violence, 59, 63, 73, 78, 162n11. See also Whitman, Walt
Miller, D. A., 154n36
Miscegenation. See Amalgamation; Interracial bodies

Mott, Lucretia, 149n4
Mudge, Jean, 172n10
Murray, Harriet W., 6

Narrative fiction, 64, 69–71. See also Antislavery stories; individual works
Native Americans, 144n6, 157n51
Natural Symbols: Explorations in Cosmology (Douglas), 143n2
New Historicism, 13, 148n16
Niemtzow, Annette, 164n9, 165n10
Norton, Anne, 143n4

Oasis, 152n27
Octoroons. See Interracial bodies
Our Nig: or, Sketches from the Life of a Free Black (Wilson), 157n53
Ownership: and corporeal identity, 52, 53; and disembodiment, 119–20; and identity, 53–54, 108; and marriage, 15, 23; of one's body, 19, 23, 33, 41, 126. See also Slave body; Slavery

Pain, 8
Particularity. See Difference
Pateman, Carole, 143n3
Patriarchy. See White male privilege
Penn School, 6, 146n10
Personhood: and female gender roles, 17–18; and representation, 12, 15, 85–86; of slaves, 1, 135, 157n56; and soul, 46–47, 159nn63,65; and writing, 136, 165n9. See also Constitution; Corporeal identity; Identity; Incorporeality; Personhood, annihilation of
Personhood, annihilation of: and cattle metaphor, 21, 151n23; and corporeal identity, 33; and difference, 15, 143n3; and feminist-abolitionist intersection, 15, 19–20; and horror of slavery, 108; and interracial bodies, 33; and representation, 85–86; and sexual exploitation, 97, 168–69n22. See also Disembodiment; Personhood
Phrenology, 28–29

Piquet, Louisa, 135, 168n21
"A Pit—but Heaven over it" (Dickinson), 172n11
Political identity: and antislavery stories, 24, 151n26, 152n27; and corporeal identity, 4–5, 51–52, 107; Dickinson's detachment from, 11–12, 106–7, 129–31, 169n2, 171n4; and difference, 4–5; and female gender roles, 23–24, 130; and genre, 72–73, 74; internalization of, 11–12, 106–7, 130–31; in lyric poetry, 12, 147n14; and mediation, 74, 163n18; and personal experience, 106–7, 138–39; and poetics of embodiment, 51, 74–75, 160n3; and representation, 1, 3, 5–6, 139, 140–41, 143n3, 143n4; and rhetorical structures, 13; and sexuality, 82; in Whitman's works, 51, 72–73, 74–75, 81, 106, 107, 160n3. *See also* Abolitionism; Feminism
Post, Amy, 83, 85, 97, 163n1, 164n7
Prince, Mary, 135
"A Prison gets to be a Friend" (Dickinson), 109–10
Purity. *See* Female gender roles

Quadroons. *See* Interracial bodies
Quincy, Edmund, 152n27

Racial prejudice: and antislavery stories, 29–31, 155n44; and blackwhite moral symbolism, 155n45; and decomposition metaphor, 2; and fantasy of colorlessness, 155n43; and interracial bodies, 33; and obliteration of blackness, 31–32, 155nn43,44,45
Rape. *See* Sexual exploitation
Ray, Laco ("The Slave-Wife"), 29–30, 39–40, 41, 159n63
"Remembrance has a Rear and Front" (Dickinson), 113–14
Representation: and antislavery stories, 24–25, 32, 46; and corporeal identity, 12, 46, 122–23, 128–29, 137–38, 147n12; and dominance, 43, 147n13; double meaning of, 9;

and identity, 137–38; and personhood, 12, 15, 85–86; and poetics of embodiment, 79–80; political, 1, 3, 5–6, 139, 140–41, 143nn3,4; and presentability, 85, 86, 164n5; and sexual exploitation, 35, 93–97, 100, 102, 156n48, 168n21; and slave body, 135–36; and suffrage, 5–6; and violence, 8–9, 147nn12,13. *See also* Discourse; Incorporeality
Reproductive function. *See* Female gender roles; Maternity
"Resergemus" (Whitman), 161n4
Rich, Adrienne, 171n9
Rousseau, Jean-Jacques, 143n4

"The St. Domingo Orphans" (Child), 152n27
Sands, Mr. (*Incidents in the Life of a Slave Girl*), 91, 92, 93, 98–99
Scarry, Elaine, 8
Self-effacement, 60–61, 65
Sensation fiction, 154n36
Sentimental fiction, 10; and bodies as texts, 27–29; bodily nature of, 26–27, 134–35, 154n36, 155n37; conventions governing, 25, 153n32; and slave narrative, 87, 165n10; and stereotypes, 27, 155n39. *See also* Antislavery stories
The Sexual Contract (Pateman), 143n3
Sexual exploitation: and abolitionism, 92, 168n21; and annihilation of personhood, 97, 168n22; and female gender roles, 22, 34–35, 40, 93, 94, 98–99, 150n18, 156n48; and interracial bodies, 156n47; of male slaves, 167n19; and representation, 35, 100, 156n48; of white women, 22–23, 36, 38–39, 156n49. *See also* Sexual exploitation of female slaves; Sexuality
Sexual exploitation of female slaves, 32, 152n27; and amalgamation, 34–35; and female gender roles, 22, 34–35, 150n18, 156n48; and feminist-abolitionist intersection,

Sexual exploitation of female slaves
(*continued*)
    21–23, 41–42, 152n27; and interra-
    cial bodies, 33, 34, 156n47; narra-
    tive concealment of, 91–92, 96–97;
    and representation, 93–97, 102,
    168n21; and white women's sexu-
    ality, 22–23, 34, 35–36, 39
Sexuality: and abolitionism, 169n26;
    discourse of, 95, 97, 99; and dis-
    embodiment, 121, 124–25; and
    domesticity, 114, 173n12; and lib-
    erty, 41, 127–28, 140, 168n19; and
    maternity, 101–2; and mediation,
    61–63, 67; and merger, 52, 63,
    65–68; and political content, 82;
    slavery described in terms of,
    83–84; and topsy-turvy doll, 133–
    34; and violence, 61–62, 63, 70–
    71, 162n14; white women's, 22–
    23, 34, 35–36; and writing, 94,
    102–4. *See also* Amalgamation;
    Sexual exploitation; Sexual exploi-
    tation of female slaves
Shelby, Mrs. (*Uncle Tom's Cabin*), 46
Slave body: and constraints on
    writing, 84; and corporeal iden-
    tity, 145n7; feminist appropria-
    tion of, 18–19; and fugitive im-
    age, 75–78; and merger, 10, 77;
    and obliteration of blackness, 31–
    32, 48, 155nn43,44,45; person-
    hood of, 1, 135, 157n56; and po-
    etics of embodiment, 10, 55, 75;
    and representation, 135–36; sui-
    cide of, 48–49, 105, 159n66; as
    text, 15, 18, 149n11; as useful
    flesh, 7. *See also* Bodies; Escape;
    Interracial bodies; Slavery;
    specific topics
Slave narrative, 87, 135–36, 165n10.
    See also *Incidents in the Life of a
    Slave Girl* (Jacobs)
Slavery: and annihilation of person-
    hood, 108; apologies for, 15, 45,
    46, 92, 148n3, 149n11, 159n63;
    and breakup of family, 152n27,
    157n56; and family structure, 11,
    43–45, 90, 157n56, 165n13; and
    Lucifer image, 72, 162n16; and

    marriage, 14–15, 150n18; and
    three-fifths rule, 1; Whitman on,
    50–51, 55–56, 71–72, 75–78,
    162n16, 163nn17,18.
The Slave's Friend, 155n39
"The Slave-Wife" (Green), 29–30,
    39–41, 153n33, 159n63
"The Sleepers" (Whitman), 64–71;
    generic instability in, 71, 162n15;
    night and day in, 73–74; separa-
    tion in, 71–73; sexuality in, 65–
    68, 70–71, 162n14
Smith, Valerie, 165n10
"Song of Myself" (Whitman), 51,
    55–56, 62, 75, 76–78, 82
Soul: and amalgamation, 81; and
    corporeal identity, 46–48, 50–51,
    81, 107, 108, 159n63; and disem-
    bodiment, 121; and dual identity,
    81–82, 107, 108, 116–17; and es-
    cape, 127–28; and mediation, 50–
    51; and personhood, 46–47,
    159nn63,65; and sexuality, 62
"The Soul has Bandaged moments"
    (Dickinson), 126–28, 173n18
Spillers, Hortense, 146n12, 165n11,
    168n22
Stanton, Elizabeth Cady, 19, 22,
    149n4
Stereotypes, 27, 155n39
Stone, Lucy, 23, 36, 149n4
Stowe, Harriet Beecher, 27–29, 85–
    86, 157n50, 164n6. See also *Uncle
    Tom's Cabin*
Suffrage, 5, 12. *See also* Representa-
    tion, political
Sunday school primers, 42–46
Swisshelm, Jane, 169n26

Tears, 26–27, 30, 154n36, 155n37
Telling. *See* Representation
Tennenhouse, Leonard, 147n13
Thompson, Matilda, 42–44, 157n56
"A Thought upon Emancipa-
    tion," 48
Tompkins, Jane, 155n37, 157n56
Tom (*Uncle Tom's Cabin*), 47, 159n63
Topsy-turvy doll, 133–34, 139,
    174nn2,3
Topsy (*Uncle Tom's Cabin*), 174n2

Towne, Laura M., 6, 7, 146n10
True womanhood, cult of. *See* Female gender roles
Truth, Sojourner, 151n20
Turner, Nat, 92, 167n18
Turner, Victor, 143n2

Uncle Tom's Cabin (Stowe), 25–26, 154n34, 155n37, 158n56; personhood and soul in, 46, 47–48, 159n65; and topsy-turvy doll, 174n2

Vendler, Helen, 160n3
Violence: and abolitionism, 167n18; allure of, 25, 167n18; and corporeal identity, 123; and difference, 70–71, 77; and discourse, 141; and merger, 59, 63, 73, 78, 162n11; and representation, 8–9, 147n12, 147n13; and sexuality, 61–62, 63, 70–71, 162n14

Walters, Ronald G., 144n5
White male privilege, 3, 37, 143n4
Whitman, Walt, 50–82; and authorial body, 136–37; on diversity, 65, 162n13; and genre, 63–64; on liberation, 161n4; poetic identity

in, 50–51, 52–54, 76, 81–82, 163n19; political content in, 51, 72–73, 74–75, 81, 106, 107, 160n3; sexuality in, 160n3; on slavery, 50–51, 55–56, 71–72, 75–78, 162n16, 163nn17,18; "you" in, 67. *See also* Embodiment, poetics of; Mediation; Merger, poetics of
William (*Incidents in the Life of a Slave Girl*), 91–92
Wilson, Harriet E., 157n53
Woman's Rights Convention (1856), 19
Women and Sisters: The Antislavery Feminists in American Culture (Yellin), 147n14
World's Anti-Slavery Convention (1840), 149n4
"Wounded in the House of Friends" (Whitman), 161n4
Writing: anxiety about, 93; and bodily incorporation, 168n20; and personhood, 136, 165n9; as politically productive, 13; pseudonymous, 86–87, 165n9; and sexuality, 94, 102–4; as violation, 10–11, 84. *See also* Genre; Representation

Yellin, Jean Fagan, 147n14

Zanger, Jules, 156n47

Compositor:	BookMasters, Inc.
Text:	10/12 Palatino
Display:	Palatino
Printer and Binder:	BookCrafters, Inc.